Congress and the Decline of Public Trust

TRANSFORMING AMERICAN POLITICS

Lawrence C. Dodd, Series Editor

Dramatic changes in political institutions and behavior over the past three decades have underscored the dynamic nature of American politics, confronting political scientists with a new and pressing intellectual agenda. The pioneering work of early postwar scholars, while laying a firm empirical foundation for contemporary scholarship, failed to consider how American politics might change or recognize the forces that would make fundamental change inevitable. In reassessing the static interpretations fostered by these classic studies, political scientists are now examining the underlying dynamics that generate transformational change.

Transforming American Politics brings together texts and monographs that address four closely related aspects of change. A first concern is documenting and explaining recent changes in American politics—in institutions, processes, behavior, and policymaking. A second is reinterpreting classic studies and theories to provide a more accurate perspective on postwar politics. The series looks at historical change to identify recurring patterns of political transformation within and across the distinctive eras of American politics. Last and perhaps most important, the series presents new theories and interpretations that explain the dynamic processes at work and thus clarify the direction of contemporary politics. All of the books focus on the central theme of transformation—transformation in both the conduct of American politics and in the way we study and understand its many aspects.

BOOKS IN THIS SERIES

Congress and the Decline of Public Trust

edited by

Joseph Cooper

JOHNS HOPKINS UNIVERSITY

foreword by

Senator Bill Bradley

SPONSORED BY THE

DIRKSEN CONGRESSIONAL CENTER PROJECT

ON PUBLIC TRUST

Westview Press

A Member of the Perseus Books Group

Transforming American Politics

Copyright © 1999 by Westview Press, A Member of the Perseus Books Group

Published in 1999 in the United States of America by Westview Press, 5500 Central Avenue, Boulder, Colorado 80301-2877, and in the United Kingdom by Westview Press, 12 Hid's Copse Road, Cumnor Hill, Oxford OX2 9JJ

Find us on the World Wide Web at www.westviewpress.com

Library of Congress Cataloging-in-Publication Data
Congress and the decline of public trust / edited by Joseph Cooper:
with a foreword by Bill Bradley.
    p.   cm. — (Transforming American Politics)
  Includes bibliographical references and index.
  ISBN 0-8133-6837-5 (hc). — ISBN 0-8133-6838-3 (pbk.)
    1. United States. Congress—Public opinion.   2. Representative
government and representation—United States—Public opinion.
3. Public opinion—United States.   4. Trust—United States.
I. Cooper, Joseph. 1933–   .   II. Series.
JK1041.C6   1999
328.73—DC21   99-21970
                                                              CIP

The paper used in this publication meets the requirements of the American National Standard for Permanence of Paper for Printed Library Materials Z39.48-1984.

10   9   8   7   6   5   4   3   2   1

Contents

Tables and Figures

Tables

Figures

Foreword:
Trust and Democracy

Causes and Consequences of Mistrust
of Government

SENATOR BILL BRADLEY

During the years I spent in the U.S. Senate, when young people visiting Washington on a school trip asked me what to do with their time, I usually encouraged them to visit the Lincoln and Jefferson Memorials, particularly the Jefferson Memorial, at night, taking enough time to read the inscriptions on the walls, to really read and absorb them. I made this pilgrimage of democracy myself, occasionally alone, though more often with out-of-town guests on warm Washington nights.

From a new book on the Declaration of Independence by Pauline Maier, we now know how the words came to be as they are. In May 1941, the Jefferson Memorial Commission sent President Roosevelt a draft for the inscription, an excerpt from the Declaration of Independence beginning with the second paragraph, "We hold these truths to be self-evident . . . ," through the sentence in which Jefferson affirms that when government fails to meet its ends, "it is the right of the people to alter or abolish it."

FDR, however, preferred to jump ahead to end the inscription with the words that end the entire Declaration, altered slightly: "For the support of this declaration, with a firm reliance on the protection of divine providence, we mutually pledge our lives, our fortunes, and our sacred honour." He was the president, of course, and from the many sometimes contradictory words in the Declaration, it was the phrase he preferred to be carved in stone.

FDR's decision highlights a long-standing tension about the place of trust in this democracy. Do we treat government as a temporary expedient, to be "altered or abolished" when it fails to work as expected? Or do we pledge ourselves to it, wish for "divine protection," and throw in our lives and our honor?

It was a question taken up in the Federalist Papers, in the Civil War, in the Progressive Era, and I believe it is one we should be thinking about more openly today.

In recent years, we seem to have forgotten the reality that our government is not, as it was for Jefferson in 1776, an exploitive power across the ocean, but instead, it is simply ourselves.

I have always believed that the message of America is that if you work hard you can get ahead economically, if you get involved you can change things politically, and if you reason patiently enough you can extend equality to all races and both genders. Today many Americans doubt these basic American precepts. In the information economy, four computer workstations replace three hundred people in a credit department no matter how hard they work. In our political dialogue, money drowns out the voices of the people. In our social interactions, few risk candor to create racial harmony.

Our political process is at a standstill. Democrats and Republicans both march along the well-worn paths of symbolic politics, waving flags labeled "welfare," "crime," and "taxes" to divide Americans and win elections.

Underlying the paralysis of government is a collapse of trust. Democracy is paralyzed not just because politicians are needlessly partisan. The process is broken at a deeper level, and it won't be fixed by replacing one set of elected officials with another, any more than it was fixed in 1992 or 1994. Citizens believe that politicians are controlled: by special interests that give them money, by parties that crush their independence, by ambition for higher office that makes them hedge their position rather than call it like they really see it, and by pollsters who convince them that only the focus-group phrases can guarantee them victory. Citizens affected by the choices we have to make about spending and regulation simply don't trust that the choices are made fairly or independently, or in some cases even democratically. They doubt that the facts will determine the result, much less the honest convictions of the politicians. Voters distrust government so deeply and so consistently that they are not willing to accept the results of virtually any decision made by this political process.

In 1990 I tried to tell people in New Jersey that the Tax Reform Act of 1986 reduced their federal taxes by $1 billion a year, and they didn't believe me because their state and local tax increases offset the reduction. By the time I left the Senate, constituents were routinely calling to ask how I voted on a particular bill, and when my office told them that the vote hadn't even occurred yet, they didn't believe it because a radio talk show host had said otherwise. For nearly a decade, beginning roughly with the repeal of the catastrophic care legislation in 1989, through the erosion of environmental laws, the failure of health care reform, and the backlash against the budget in 1995, every major step taken by government has been jeopardized by this mistrust, by a deep and widespread conviction that politicians are acting in their own individual interests rather than as honest representatives of the democratic will. And while there are plenty of hardworking, honest politicians who strive to understand the issues of their time, and then act on principle, the public impression of politicians generally is negative—in part because we refuse to reform a system that produces little change in people's real-life circumstances.

It is possible, though unlikely, that the budget agreement of 1997 marks a change in this climate of mistrust. For the first time in years, Democrats and Republicans were able to find the points on which they agreed, and yet the agreement itself is of little consequence. Big issues were not decided, and the political climate is no less polarized. Government estimators simply came in with new projections of economic growth that suddenly allowed both parties to claim victory. It seems unlikely that this will form a precedent for further action, and indeed, there seems little else on which such common ground will be found in this Congress. (Witness the debacle on campaign finance reform.) Further, the budget agreement itself embodied all the forces that have caused the kind of mistrust that cripples democracy, from the role of money in politics (look at the special favors in the tax legislation) to the influence of the media, which are more interested in personal intrigue and celebrity than in giving citizens the information they need to participate effectively.

Does This Politics Deserve Our Trust?

Mistrust is a corrosive force in American democracy, but it is also an appropriate response to certain circumstances.

The first such circumstance is money. To be in politics today, even for the noblest ends, means that a part of your professional life must be devoted to raising money. Fine public servants are stuck in a bad system; in fact, money drives politics in America in a way that it never has before, even in its darkest moments. We have reached a point where nothing but money seems to matter. Political parties have lost their original purpose, which was to bring together people with broadly similar views from the precinct level to the national level; instead, they have become primarily conduits for cash. National membership organizations measure their clout not by how many members they have, but by how much money they can put into the political process. Anyone interested in running for any office, on approaching party leaders or consultants, will be asked, "How much can you raise?" or better yet, "How much do you have and will you spend?" before questions like "Do you have support in the community?" or "Do you have experience that would help you serve in this office?" Many good people can't run for office, and those who do find themselves doing little other than raising money and spending more time with those who can finance their campaigns than with those they would represent.

It is not just that there is too much money in politics. All the campaigns for president, the House, and the Senate in 1996 put together spent about $17 for every American who voted. This amount would hardly be excessive if it provided useful information, if it was distributed fairly, and if it came without strings attached. Indeed, many citizens would gladly pay $17 for useful, balanced information that would help them decide who should represent them.

But look at the reality of what money in politics pays for, how it is distributed, and the effect it has on elected officials. It is spent in roughly equal amounts for three things: (1) raising more money, (2) consultants and polls, and (3) thirty-second television advertisements. Sometimes the ads are vicious wars that portray opposing candidates not just as undeserving of public office, but as unworthy to walk on the face of the earth. There is some reason to think that negative ads may even be designed to turn voters off, to reduce turnout to the advantage of a candidate who might benefit from lower turnout. Even when the advertisements are not negative or designed to foster mistrust, thirty seconds is rarely enough time to provide useful information for voters or foster the sense of confidence and trust that one should have in a representative.

The way political money is distributed is also guaranteed to make voters doubt a basic premise of democracy, which is that their vote matters. Money does not need to be equal for an election to be competitive, but candidates do need to have enough to get a message across about who they are and what they stand for. More than 40 percent of members of the House of Representatives, however, outspent their opponents by more than ten to one. And no candidate for the House who spent less than 20 percent of what his opponent spent won. Money goes to incumbents; it goes to certain challengers opposing incumbents who have been targeted for defeat by particular interests; and it goes to candidates who have a lot of money of their own or have wealthy friends. If an election has only one candidate who meets one of these criteria, it is not likely to be a competitive election, and in a sense, your vote won't matter. In a nation that prides itself on the principle of one person–one vote, money gives some people much more clout than one vote.

Finally, money fosters mistrust of the political process because it comes with strings attached that, either in perception or reality (and we never quite know which it is), distort representatives' votes and their priorities. Campaign finance reformers often become obsessed with distinctions between different sources of money: political action committees (PACs), political party soft money, or individual contributions. They lose sight of the fact that some money, whatever channel it comes through, comes with strings attached.

It is also clear that many contributors make contributions based not on their political conviction, but on the influence they believe they will gain. How else to explain the numerous companies that give soft money to both political parties? How else do we explain the shift in PAC contributions to the Republicans after the GOP takeover of Congress in 1994, then back to the Democrats after the Republican juggernaut collapsed? What else explains contributors who give to one candidate in a race in May, when that candidate is ahead, then to his opponent in September after the tide has shifted? Opponents of campaign reform, like the Supreme Court in the 1976 decision *Buckley v. Valeo,* tend to speak of political contributions as if they were the same as political speech and deserve the same protection, but the realities of patterns of giving suggest that they have far less to do with expressing political opinions than with investing in influence.

As a member of the Senate Finance Committee, I often noted obscure tax favors that just happened to appear in legislation before our committee. Occasionally I wondered whether there was a connection between these gifts and campaign contributions. When I identified such specific instances, my former colleagues protested, often convincingly, that in every case, they voted and set priorities based on their conscience, the needs of their state, and what they thought were the interests of their constituents, not money. And I believe it is very, very rare—perhaps never—that a member of Congress consciously thinks, "I know the right vote on this amendment is no, and it's probably no good for the folks in my district, but the guy who's pushing it raised $100,000 for me last time, so I'll vote for it."

And yet the unavoidable reality is that Congress is far more attentive to the corporation demanding relief from the alternative minimum tax than to the family looking for help to pay for escalating health care costs. It is more responsive to investors seeking a reduction in the tax rate on capital gains than to working parents who would like a reduction in their own tax rate. It may be that these are not favors in return for contributions, but simply a side effect of the amount of time spent raising money, so that representatives know only one side of any story because they spend so much time with contributors. A company well known for flying members of Congress around on its airplanes, for example, persuaded its friends to tie up the Senate for almost a week in 1996 fighting for an obscure change that would help the company keep labor unions out. Were the senators returning a favor? Or was it just that they spent so many hours in planes with the company's executives that they came to think the company's problems were their own?

The problem is that we'll never know. We don't know whether politicians genuinely believe that the alternative minimum tax is an unreasonable burden, or whether they simply intend to repay contributors. We can't know whether money or conscience governs the priorities they set. If we could figure out exactly how money distorts the political process, it could be self-correcting. The conservative argument that the only campaign finance reform needed is enhanced disclosure would be correct, in that voters could identify contributors, identify political favors, and vote against candidates who put contributors' interests above those of constituents.

But it doesn't work that way. We can't figure out what's a favor and what isn't, and as a result, the only reasonable response is mistrust. Campaign finance reform can potentially restore some of the trust that is needed for democracy to work, but only if the reform is clear, simple, and complete enough that voters can really see how it would change the nature of politics. If reform means just one more set of complicated rules that party fund-raising experts will find clever ways to evade, it will only deepen the sense that government can't even solve its own problems.

Nothing about the role of money in politics would anger people as much as it does, however, if government seemed to be able to respond to the economic circumstances of nonwealthy Americans. Through the deep recession of the early 1990s, the government was unable even to restructure unemployment benefits in a way that helped people survive stretches of a year or more without a job. After the recession ended, and a period of corporate downsizing accelerated, government was once again unable even to acknowledge that the forces that would make us better off in the long run endangered many Americans in the short run. Now that the economy is healthier, we are reaping some, though not all, of the benefits of this abrupt corporate restructuring, but the fact remains that when times are tough, government is no longer anywhere to be found. And when times are good, government seems more eager to reduce taxes for investors than to think about investing in long-term economic security for families whose income will come from work, not capital gains.

Even with a healthy economy, there are profound problems. Millions of Americans work part-time who want to work full-time. Even more are without health insurance than a few years ago. The economic situation of urban America remains tragic, although with crime rates lower and people slightly less fearful in their suburban gated communities, it is a tragedy we now comfortably ignore. Until government begins to show some ability to respond to the economic anxieties about both the present and the future that are on the minds of most American families, it is not unreasonable for them to mistrust that government.

Media and Responsibility

To the extent that the news media are a part of a democratic system of government—and in both Jefferson's theory and our reality, it is—the press too has failed to provide the kind of confidence that Americans need to be constructive, participating citizens. As with money-driven political campaigns, television is the common denominator, the one media outlet that reaches the broad majority of citizens. Yet local television news, governed by the motto "If it bleeds, it leads; if it thinks, it stinks," all but ignores the significance of local representatives and the deliberations that lead to legislation that affects human lives. Every few months, the media report with disdain some poll showing that most Americans can't name their member of Congress, with no hint of self-consciousness that the press itself takes an interest in those members only when they become embroiled in scandal, celebrity, or personal intrigue. A few politicians, like former House Speaker Newt Gingrich, have taken temporary advantage of the media's fascination with eccentric celebrity, personal conflict, and Machiavellian intrigue (and discovered painfully how temporary it is), but the majority of members toil in obscurity, knowing that neither their accomplishments nor their shortcomings will attract the camera's eye.

Nor, when it comes to elections, do the media add the kind of information that voters need to counter the misinformation of paid television advertising. The press remains mesmerized by the horse race itself, by who's ahead, who's behind, and just how vicious a conflict might become. An "ordinary" campaign, between two or more people with distinguished careers of competent service, respect for one another, and differing but non-extreme political views, is likely to receive so little coverage that voters cannot but doubt that such elections and such politicians exist. Indeed, the media even magnify the effect of negative ads. Under the high-minded pretext of examining the tone of the campaign itself, they often rebroadcast a negative ad several times free of charge. And don't think that political consultants don't know that the more outrageous they get, the more they can use the media to magnify their message.

Part of what I hear from citizens who are looking for a new way to relate to government is a call for information that is direct and accurate, unmediated by the media. This comes not just from those who are convinced that the media have a liberal bias or a conservative bias, but from those who believe that the media, except for the occasional sitcom, simply fail, like government, to acknowledge and connect to the realities of life of the nonwealthy American. A few years ago, this plea manifested itself in a sudden outpouring of people who wanted to read for themselves copies of complex legislation such as the North American Free Trade Agreement (NAFTA). More recently, Internet sites have emerged to provide this unmediated access to information. Although these new channels of information will open up government to a few of the most actively engaged citizens, there are few people who will read a two-thousand-word trade agreement and understand what it means for their community. There is no substitute for media that interpret information, but do so in a way that is constructive and useful.

To be fair to the media, theirs is a vast, diverse enterprise (although concentration of ownership makes it smaller and less diverse every day) with more than a few bright spots of careful and relevant reporting amid the depressing sameness. Further, the media in recent years have developed a self-consciousness about their own shortcomings and responsibilities, leading to experiments like the much-criticized "public journalism" initiative. One wonders, though, why the idea of systematically providing citizens with the information that is most useful to them in doing the work of democracy should be considered an experiment.

Mistrust as a Political Commodity

Although the political system bears responsibility for much of the public's mistrust of it, it is fair to say that the mistrust is far out of proportion to the actual failings of the system. Mistrust has become in itself a political commodity, a means of gaining short-term advantage in a system that is increasingly managed by operators interested only in short-term advantage.

The emergence of mistrust as a political commodity goes hand in glove with the increasing domination of political discourse by interest groups that not only are contributors to political candidates but increasingly act almost like political parties themselves, dominating the information that flows between government and citizens, controlling perception, and taking over the grass roots of politics through direct mail, talk radio, and phone and fax networks.

For example, over the period 1993–1996, there was a serious, bipartisan effort to consolidate the several hundred job training programs funded by the federal government into a few simpler programs, including one or two block grants to states. (Although block grants are an unwise strategy to avoid federal responsibility for cohesive programs such as welfare, they can be a good way to reduce the confusion in an area where there are many small programs.) The most conservative House members had been working comfortably together with Ted Kennedy and the U.S. Department of Labor on this important legislation that would make job training far more accessible for young people as well as for experienced workers who were the victims of downsizing.

Then the phone calls started coming in. Phyllis Schlafly's Eagle Forum had put out the word through its network that Congress was about to consider legislation under which bureaucrats, Soviet-style, would tell each child what his or her occupation was to be. The charge was completely made up; it had nothing at all to do with anything that was in the legislation, as several of the most conservative supporters of the job training legislation had made clear. But the phone calls from outraged parents determined to protect their children's American right to choose to make a living any way they saw fit were enough to scare Congress away. After the crime bill and the 1994 budget crisis, members knew that if it was their word against an interest group's, they might as well be talking to their dog. Instead of fighting misinformation, the thousands of hours of careful, cooperative work on the job training consolidation bill were scrapped, along with the bill itself.

What was going on here? My hunch is that the Eagle Forum had little interest in the job training bill itself. It can hardly matter to them whether there are 240 ineffective training programs or just three that do basically the same thing more efficiently. But facing aggressive competition from other conservative interest groups, Eagle Forum found an angle that was guaranteed to produce not just outrage but also members and money. And they got away with it because they knew that the mistrust of government was so deep that many people would quite readily believe that their representatives in this free democracy might suddenly adopt an oppressive system of occupational planning. Mistrust in this way can breed deeper mistrust, and mistrust can even leave citizens more vulnerable to deception.

Just as a few politicians are steered too often by money, the citizens they are trying to represent are steered too often by the clutter of interest groups, making it all the more difficult for elected officials to see and follow the path of the true public interest. Each of us has a multitude of identities, opinions, interests, and connections to others. But interest groups try to take our voices and turn them into single-minded protests on behalf of our most narrow identity: gun owner, senior, pro-choice, small businessperson, environmentalist, and smoker.

Each of these groups and many others clamor to speak for us in Washington, Sacramento, or Trenton, but for most of us, no group can represent us in our fullness as citizens, with all our interests and opinions.

That we can do only for ourselves, in the setting of a lively and varied civic sector that provides opportunities for education, discussion, and fierce debate not provided by national membership groups. As citizens withdraw from these varied, local forums, they have not withdrawn from participation altogether but shifted their engagement into mass-mail–driven organizations that can operate only in a certain way. They seek to convince us *not* that some of our interests and opinions are in conflict, nor that some of our ideals require compromise, but simply that we are not getting what we want from government because government itself is corrupt, dishonest, out of control, controlled by corporate interests, controlled by those dependent on "the welfare state," dominated by liberals, or dominated by conservatives. They don't help us to think of ourselves as citizens who are part of a democratic dialogue, or to think of government as something of which we're a part and have the power to change. Most certainly they don't encourage us to think of ourselves as citizens who think of the general interest. Rather, these organizations depict government as some sort of black art, in which they alone have mastered the spells and incantations that make it dance.

In the end, our democracy is losing its most essential ingredient: the willingness of citizens to accept the results of the process itself, especially if they are not complete winners. Driven by groups whose professional survival depends on an endless fight, citizens are discouraged from accepting that they might be in the minority on a particular question, or that they need to compromise their position with others whose interests are different. They are told again and again that corruption drives the process, or that choices that appear to be made democratically are in fact the authoritarian will of an outside force called "government."

Mistrust eats away at every pillar of democracy. It eats away at elections, which are distorted by money and negative ads. It eats away at representative democracy, because citizens cannot accept that their position was simply in the minority and are convinced—sometimes rightly, sometimes not—that they are the victims of nefarious activity. It eats away not only at the larger idea of an open system of government that can make fair decisions for all of us, but it even undermines the core notion of our democracy—that legitimacy rests with individuals who as citizens promote what is good for all of us as much as what is good for themselves personally.

If things continue as they are, Americans' doubts about their own government will eventually leave that government completely marginal to just about every aspect of life. Already government seems barely relevant to most of the issues that concern us. We have quite complacently given up the idea that government can protect us from the ravages of the economic cycle or that it might systematically protect very poor mothers and their children from the extremes of poverty. The less we are capable of trusting government, the more we leave our most personal choices about family, education, and community to the market, because the market, unlike democracy, does not require our trust to exist—it simply exists. The consequence of that unconscious and unplanned act would be to squander one of the most important insights of Western history—that government, if it acts responsibly and with the consent of the people, can help parents help their children, create an environment in which people live up to their potential, and enable people to work together to take their communities and their nation to a higher level.

Signs of Hope

Fortunately, things cannot continue as they are. Already there are hopeful signs that the era of mistrust may be just that: a long era, of a decade or more, for historians eventually to decipher. People across the country are waking up to the role of money in politics and educating themselves about the solutions, so that instead of hoping that Congress will somehow negotiate a compromise, they are working it out for themselves. Interest groups are facing stricter scrutiny. The media are continuing their long self-examination, and meanwhile, new channels for constructive political communication and honest deliberation are emerging every day, on the Internet and even on cable television. The year 1997 also saw a movement for campaign finance reform take root. More than fifty thousand petitioners gathered more than one million signatures demanding congressional action on campaign reform. The people are poised to take back their government from special interests.

If the era of mistrust comes to an end, it will be because it is followed by an era of reform, comparable in its scope, daring, and imagination to the Progressive Era. It will require a rethinking of some of the basic premises of American democracy. What is the role of political parties? What is the right balance between freedom of political expression and the corruption and narrow choices of money-driven political campaigns? How should representative institutions be structured to give everyone a voice? How can technology give citizens access to unmediated, useful information and open deliberation about solutions? What are the obligations of the media—especially the broadcast media, whose profits depend on the public's generous loan of the airwaves—to democratic participation?

Questions like these, rather than the narrow questions about which political party bureaucrat skirted the campaign rules most aggressively, have the potential to help us finally understand why we mistrust government so deeply, give the political process a way to earn back some of the trust that it has lost, and give citizens the means to put their trust in government again. The purpose is not necessarily to restore activist government, but to restore the sense that government is the creation of the people, not an outside force acting upon their lives.

Senator Bill Bradley

Acknowledgments

The editor would like to acknowledge with thanks the assistance of the following persons. The Board of the Dirksen Congressional Center provided generous and warm support from the time it first approved a project on public trust through the publication of this volume. Frank Mackaman, executive director of the Dirksen Congressional Center, served as a source of continuing good counsel and shared the burdens of managing the project with grace and effectiveness. He played a key role in conceptualizing the themes of this volume and in the work required to bring it to completion. The editor also benefited greatly from the willingness of Charles Jones, Roger Davidson, Susan Hammond, and Sheilah Mann to serve on the Dirksen Center subcommittee that planned the volume and to respond with cheerful patience and helpful answers to a multitude of questions regarding the organization of the chapters and possible authors. Johanna Zacharias read the manuscript before it was submitted for publication as only an experienced and skilled editor can. She was generous with her time, unbending in her standards, and the source of many valuable suggestions, most notably to add a data appendix. Larry Dodd played a major role in the inclusion of this volume in the series he edits and suggested a number of detailed changes in content and format that added substantially to the clarity and depth of the analysis. Leo Wiegman's good offices as executive editor substantially facilitated the progress of this volume and provided both helpful oversight and strong support. Once accepted for publication, the manuscript has been in the capable hands of Kristin Milavec, the senior project editor, and I have appreciated her calm competence and diligence in shepherding a multi-authored manuscript through the vagaries of the publication process.

Joseph Cooper

Congress and the Decline of Public Trust

1

The Puzzle of Distrust

JOSEPH COOPER

There is no issue in American politics that is more difficult to unravel, or more significant for the future of representative government in the United States, than the issue of public trust. In recent decades cynicism and suspicion regarding the processes of democratic government and the officials elected to operate them have been deep and pervasive in the United States. Most ordinary citizens do not trust public officials to act responsibly and effectively in the service of the public interest. They do not believe that public officials care about or respond to their views, and many doubt their fundamental honesty. Bill Bradley's analysis in the Foreword of the low state of trust in government and politicians in the United States eloquently captures prevailing public attitudes and is amply supported by a variety of recent surveys, articles, and books. Similarly, John Hibbing and Elizabeth Theiss-Morse's characterization of Congress as a "public enemy" in a recent work (1995) provides an apt metaphor for the public's low regard for Congress and is also amply supported by a number of surveys and other scholarly works. Figure 1.1 presents results on two frequently asked survey questions to illustrate the sharp and persistent drop since the late 1960s in the trust that ordinary citizens have in the representativeness, integrity, and effectiveness of government. Figure 1.2 presents results on two popular and repeated survey questions that pertain more specifically to the premier political institutions of the national government. It clearly indicates that the decline of trust in government has been accompanied by declining trust in the leadership of the Congress and the presidency.

Issues and Goals

The depth and persistence of low levels of trust in government and in key political institutions provide substantial grounds for concern over the fate of representative government in the United States. Even markets, which rely simply on the clash of self-interest as their primary ordering principle, cannot work effectively without trust in the enforceability of contracts and the value of money.

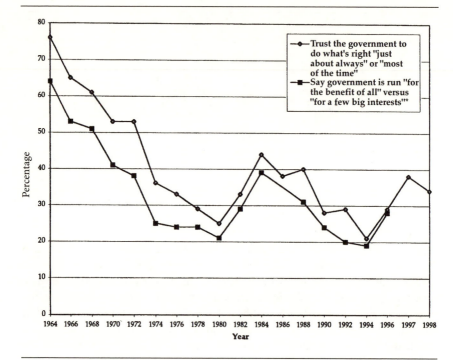

FIGURE 1.1   Trust in Government

*Question not asked in 1986.
SOURCE FOR 1964–1996 DATA: American National Election Studies; source for 1997 and 1998 data:
Pew Research Center for the People and the Press.

Representative government, which must not only rely on the clash of self-interest but also seek to regulate and even transcend it, has far more stringent requirements. Trust in the fundamental purposes and design of the political system, in the representativeness and integrity of its decisionmaking structures and processes, and in the ability of government to produce policies that satisfy citizen needs is essential, in all these regards, to the maintenance of a viable democratic order.

Nonetheless, current evidence regarding low levels of public trust needs to be placed in historical and comparative perspective. Distrust of politics and politicians in the United States is nothing new. It rather has been a continuing feature of American politics from the eighteenth century to the present (Huntington, 1981). We may note, for example, that in the pre–Civil War period one article in the *North American Review* complained that Congress was "the most helpless, disorderly, and inefficient legislative body that can be found in the civilized world," and another observed that in Washington politicians were publicly bought and sold "like fancy railroad stock or copper mine shares" (White, 1954, pp. 26–27). In the post–Civil War period Henry Adams (1931) wrote that "the

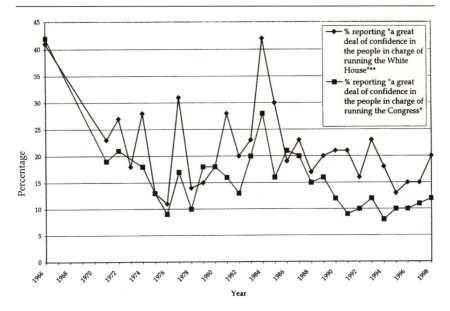

FIGURE 1.2   Trust in the Congress and the Presidency

NOTE: No poll taken in unmarked years. In 1966, 1971, 1972, and 1975, the first question refers to confidence in "the people in charge of running the executive branch of government." Comparable results were achieved in years when both wordings were used, although scores for "the White House" were usually slightly higher than for "the executive branch of government."
SOURCE: Harris

grossest satires on the American Senator and politician never failed to excite the laughter and applause of every audience. Rich and poor joined in throwing contempt on their representatives" (p. 272). In the same period Mark Twain called congressmen the only "native American criminal class" (Kimball and Patterson, 1997, p. 702). In the early decades of the twentieth century Woodrow Wilson argued that the government of the United States was "a foster child of special interests" (Green, Fallows, and Zwick, 1972, p. 29). In the years between the two world wars Will Rogers described Congress as the best that money can buy, and a lead article in the *American Mercury* was titled "Why All Politicians Are Crooks" (Green et al., 1972; Wilson, 1951). As a final example, less than two years after the end of World War II, George Gallup wrote that "the public sickens and turns its head away from the very thought of politics" and "would rather see their children work as street sweepers than besmirch themselves in politics" (Wilson, 1951, p. 242). Nor does history provide the only testimony to the fact that distrust in American democracy is a complex problem, not a simple one. A recent Pew Research Center survey (1998a) that compares distrust in the United States and stable Western European democracies reveals some striking similarities, strongly suggesting that stable democratic orders invariably blend elements of trust and distrust.

The character and consequences of public trust in American democracy thus pose a puzzle that we are a long way from solving (Nye and Zelikow, 1997). If trust is required in the policymaking capacity, institutional processes, and fundamental design of the American political system, the persistence of distrust throughout American history raises the question of the degrees of trust that are required in all these regards. This question, in turn, raises two further questions: What are the relationships between the different types or components of trust? And what determinants govern these relationships, both inside the political system and between the political system and the broader society? These are extremely difficult issues to analyze and assess. Nonetheless, they are questions that must be addressed. Despite the fact that distrust is no stranger to American government, current levels of distrust in politics and politicians in the United States are difficult to discount. The American political system is clearly in no imminent danger of demise, but the rampant cynicism and suspicion that have characterized American politics since Vietnam and Watergate provide dramatic evidence of factors and conditions that may well threaten the long-term viability of American democracy. It is thus no accident that the problem of distrust has attracted widespread attention among pollsters, scholars, and the press (Hibbing and Theiss-Morse, 1995).

Pollsters have been asking questions that bear on public trust for more than half a century. Over time, and particularly since the 1970s, the scope and depth of these surveys, the number of polling organizations involved, and the continuity of inquiry have increased greatly as survey research has become professionalized and institutionalized and as the stark characteristics of distrust in politics and politicians have been revealed (Bowman and Ladd, 1994; Lipset and Schneider, 1987). The chapters of this volume often draw on the large body of data that have been gathered; a summary of the most salient features of these data is presented in the Appendix. Similarly, while congressional scholars since the 1960s have been concerned with explaining why public confidence in Congress is low, treatments of distrust in governmental decisionmaking generally, in major political institutions, and in other sectors of society have mushroomed in the 1980s and 1990s (Durr, Gilmour, and Wolbrecht, 1997). As can be seen from the references cited in the chapters of this volume, a host of books and articles have been published by a broad mix of academics, working journalists, pollsters, and political commentators. The chapters in this book are informed and instructed by this work, as well as by polling data.

The goal of this volume is to advance our understanding of the character, causes, and dangers of distrust in modern American politics and to consider the merits of possible remedies. In pursuing this goal, we focus our analysis at the national level, with emphasis on distrust in Congress because of the pivotal role that Congress plays in the success and viability of representative government in the United States. As the long history of popular criticism of Congress suggests, trust in Congress serves as a critical component and determinant of public trust, both because of the formal responsibilities of Congress under the Constitution and because of the breadth and depth of its electoral ties to the complex multiplicity of individuals and groups that make up the American public. This was true in the nineteenth century, and it is even more true today, given the vast expansion in the scope of the federal government. Although the character of the expectations its constitutional position generates has changed with the rise of the modern presidency, Congress's power over and responsibility for the success of representative government at the national level continue to be so substantial that they render trust in politics and politicians at all levels of government particularly sensitive to judgments of the representativeness, integrity, and effectiveness of its processes and members.

The formal position of Congress in our constitutional order as lawmaker and overseer of the executive branch, the great leverage over public policy it retains, and the public perception of its role and responsibilities make the dynamics of public distrust far more understandable. Whatever the realities of American politics, the public's predispositions to see Congress as the most powerful branch, to attribute inaction to its penchant for careerism and partisanship, and to judge it more harshly than the president for legislative stalemate become far less anomalous than they first appear (Hibbing and Theiss-Morse, 1995; Durr et al., 1997). Nonetheless, distrust in Congress is only part of the puzzle and cannot be understood in isolation. It is impacted by and related to distrust in political institutions and politicians generally, to distrust in institutions and leaders in other sectors of society, to declining levels of personal trust, and in the end to the changing values and interests of American society (Uslaner, 1993). Indeed, the complex character of these relationships is itself perhaps the most defining feature of the puzzle. The various chapters of this volume thus treat the problem of distrust in Congress as part of a more general problem. As a result, although most of them focus directly on distrust in Congress, they vary greatly in terms of the features of distrust they emphasize and the scope and character of the causal factors they address.

My purpose in this chapter is to provide a context for understanding the thrust, fit, and significance of the work of each of the authors in this volume. To do so both the shared assumptions that unite these authors and the rationales for the different stances they take in analyzing distrust must be understood. I will therefore begin by expanding my sketch of the puzzle so that I can tie these assumptions and rationales to the major issues that constitute the puzzle. Once that is accomplished, the work of the authors can be briefly summarized in a manner that delineates their relationships to one another and identifies their contributions to understanding and alleviating distrust.

Distrust in the 1990s

To unravel the puzzle of public distrust both in government and in Congress, we must deal with several central issues. What are the causes of distrust? How dan-

gerous is the current state of distrust for the future of American democracy? If
distrust is sufficiently dangerous to arouse concern, what can be done to alleviate
it? Answers to these questions are complicated not only by the complexity of the
relationships between causal determinants within the political system and between the political system and the broader society, but also by the variegated
character of public trust itself. From the polling data alone we can sense that trust
is not a unidimensional entity, but rather a layered one, consisting of different
forms or types of trust at different levels of governance. As suggested earlier, belief in the basic legitimacy of the political system, in the representativeness and
integrity of governmental decisionmaking units and officials, and in the ability of
government to devise and implement policy programs that satisfy citizen demands are all components of public trust. They can and should be seen as different dimensions or levels of trust that exist simultaneously but vary greatly over
time, both individually and relative to one another. Thus, the contours of public
trust in recent decades need to be broadly identified before causes can be analyzed, dangers assessed, and remedies evaluated.

These contours appear to be quite different from those that led to the breakdown of the political system in the 1850s.* Whereas distrust in that era focused
far more on the legitimacy of the purposes and design of the political system than
on the integrity of politicians and their responsiveness to the electorate, distrust
at present appears to have very different features or characteristics. But it too is
far from consistent across the various levels or dimensions of trust.

On the one hand, as I have suggested, trust or confidence at what we may call
the governmental level is low. Public cynicism regarding the manner in which
government works and the factors that motivate politicians seems almost palpa-
ble in its strength and intensity (Hunter and Bowman, 1996; Orren, 1997).
Elected officials are widely dismissed as self-serving politicians who are far more
concerned with promoting their careers and gaining partisan advantage than with
acting responsibly to promote the general welfare (Craig, 1996). Though many
believe that public opinion, when united and intense, can check these tendencies,
they also recognize that as a practical matter such occasions are rare. As a result,
the public views politics as a process, dominated by special interests that trade
campaign funds and electoral support for access and influence at the expense of
the broader public and the public interest (Hibbing and Theiss-Morse, 1995).
Similarly, it views politicians as persons whose honesty and adherence to principle are in most cases corrupted by their career ambitions and the requirements
for success in politics (Bowman and Ladd, 1994). There is more confidence in the
integrity of non-elected officials, especially the federal bureaucracy, but limited
confidence in their effectiveness and efficiency. Government generally, and especially the federal government, is thus not viewed, as it was from the late 1930s
through the late 1960s, as a ready and reliable instrument of public purpose, but

---

*I owe this point to Eric Schickler of the University of California at Berkeley.

rather as a flawed mechanism of questionable integrity and effectiveness (Craig, 1996; Blendon et al., 1997).

On the other hand, prevailing attitudes at other levels or dimensions of trust can and do differ significantly from those that prevail with respect to trust in the character of governmental decisionmaking and decisionmakers. Though it is true that the public sees politics as controlled by special interests, politicians as dishonest and unprincipled, and government generally, especially the federal government, as ineffective and wasteful, this is only part of the truth, not the whole truth. Public attitudes are also marked by a number of anomalies or contradictions. Despite the fact that most Americans believe that the processes of representative government are corrupted by money and dominated by special interests, belief in the legitimacy of the political system and emotional attachment to it remain high (Hunter and Bowman, 1996). Thus, belief in and attachment to the constitutional roles of the three branches of the national government remain strong, whatever the character of opinion toward their actual performance or the honesty of the individuals who constitute and lead them (Hibbing and Theiss-Morse, 1995). As a result, though it may be true that the public tends to judge Congress harshly for simply doing its job, a job that necessarily involves conflict and controversy, it remains true that the necessity for and role of a legislature are accepted, not challenged. Indeed, the fact that the Congress invariably scores lower than the president on a number of indicators of trust can be read, in part, as testimony to the strength of public attachment to the principles of representative government implicit in the Constitution. As suggested earlier, these principles lead citizens to take a very pristine view of Congress's constitutional responsibilities and to judge the Congress more stringently than the president when results are perceived to be inadequate.

Similarly, although the poll data show quite clearly that since the early 1970s most Americans have consistently believed that government cannot be trusted to do "what's right" all or even most of the time, and that their trust in the people who lead Congress and the White House has decreased, public approval of the job performance of the president and Congress, as well as of the state of the nation and the direction in which it is moving, is quite volatile and has varied widely over the past quarter-century (American National Election Studies, 1996; Gallup, 1998). In short, as the data presented in the Appendix show, trust at the policy level as well as trust at the system level can diverge significantly from trust at the governmental level.

To illustrate the point, in the spring of 1998 (when this chapter was written) both presidential and congressional job performance scores were high, despite the scandal that broke in January 1998 involving President Clinton. Presidential job approval scores in the first four months of 1998 were in the mid to upper 60s. These scores compare well with the upper range of scores attained by other presidents in recent decades, and they are also the highest scores Clinton had attained since entering office in 1993 (Stanley and Niemi, 1995; *Washington Post*, 1998).

Congressional approval scores over time have been consistently and substantially lower than presidential approval scores. But in the first four months of 1998 they climbed into the mid 50s before declining to the high 40s, a height and a range they have attained only rarely in recent decades (Stanley and Niemi, 1995; *Washington Post*, 1998). General measures of approval of the state of the nation or the direction in which it is headed, which can also be read as indicators of satisfaction with and confidence in the broad course of public policy, reflect comparable patterns of instability and contradiction. They do tend to approximate and vary with measures of institutional job performance, especially presidential job performance. Thus, most Americans in the spring of 1998 both approved of the job the president was doing and believed that the nation was headed in the "right direction" (Gallup, 1998; *Washington Post*, 1998). However, as is true of the job performance scores, broader measures of policy satisfaction or confidence have been far more volatile and less consistently negative than measures of belief in whether the government can be trusted to do "what's right" or is run for the "benefit of all the people" rather than "special interests" (American National Election Studies, 1996). Thus, in the spring of 1998 more than 60 percent of the public gave negative responses to trust in government questions at the same time that 55 percent affirmed that the nation was headed in the "right direction" and was not "seriously off on the wrong track" (Pew Research Center, 1998a; *Washington Post*, 1998).

Finally, despite the fact that most Americans have lost faith in the ability of government generally, and the federal government especially, to operate in an effective and efficient manner, there is little support for any large reduction in the role of the federal government. Whatever their concerns over the effectiveness of government or its power, since the New Deal most Americans expect the federal government to assume broad responsibility for guarding the general welfare both domestically and internationally (Bennett and Bennett, 1996; Mayer, 1992; Pew Research Center, 1998a). As a result, problems perceived as serious almost invariably trigger intense demands for federal action, and often in a manner involving large numbers of citizens. Current conflicts over curbing teen smoking and HMO restrictions on patients provide good illustrations.

Explaining Distrust

The uneven contours of public trust in modern American politics define the content of the puzzle to be solved. However, efforts to explain these contours and the anomalies they involve operate under a number of severe constraints. As suggested earlier, perhaps the most important relate to the variety of determinants that appear relevant and the complexity of their interrelationships. Such complexity has posed a formidable barrier to understanding. It has placed comprehensive analysis of the intricate patterns of determinants, both within the political system and between the political system and the broader society, beyond our reach. To correct the situation, what would be required is a general theory of the political system that is more than a set of abstract propositions with highly opaque connections to concrete questions, but no such theory exists. As a result, whereas present efforts at causal explanations rarely ignore broader societal determinants, analysts vary greatly in the ones they choose, the priority they accord them, and the manner in which they bring them to bear in framing explanations of results in the political system (Nye and Zelikow, 1997).

It should not be surprising, then, that the authors in this volume pursue no uniform approach to causal analysis. Instead, their choices and treatments of the key causal factors vary. Some emphasize the impact of broader societal factors or forces on the processes of representative government, the role of the general decline of trust across societal institutions and professions that has occurred in recent decades, the influence of the modern media in subverting trust, especially with respect to Congress, and the failure of civic education to foster understanding of the practice of American democracy as well as its formal structure and ideals. Such analysis derives the causes of distrust largely from the character of these broader societal factors or forces. It treats the role of political structures and processes as mediating factors that transmit the effects of broader forces, but it recognizes their importance in the political system and can include errors of cognition in dealing with political information that are rooted in human thought processes.

Others emphasize the structures and processes of representative government as they respond to rapid social, economic, and technological change—the ways in which the demanding character of representative institutions in the United States promotes stalemate and inaction when issue divisions increase; the manner in which candidate-centered campaigns, the role of money, the power of interest groups, and ideological politics reinforce one another in undermining trust; the role played by misperception of the existence of a simple and uniform will of the people in leading citizens to disdain political conflict and compromise; and the impact of the very openness of Congress in breeding distrust. Such analysis places the causes of distrust primarily in the character of the representative process in the United States under modern conditions of government, but it typically also recognizes the role of broader societal forces or factors.

In describing these differences in approach, the word *emphasize* is used quite advisedly. No author in this volume draws hard-and-fast lines between the broader society and the political system, either implicitly or explicitly. Each in his or her own way interweaves these factors. That is as it should be. Given the current state of our understanding, the drawing of boundaries and the identification of patterns of interaction must be discretionary and determined by the explanatory lens an author favors. Thus, in this volume as elsewhere, the only reasonable test of success in explaining distrust is and must be the perceptiveness and persuasiveness of the analysis.

Nonetheless, our understanding of the difficulties of causal analysis will not be complete if limited only to problems of identifying and ordering the determinants. As important as these problems may be, the difficulties of causal analysis derive from more than the complexity of the relationships that exist among a host of societal and political determinants. Two other important sources of constraint must also be cited—the variegated character of public trust and the fact that trust is a cause as well as an effect.

In the first regard, we have argued that trust is layered and complex rather than unidimensional and uniform, that different forms or types of trust exist at different levels of governance. What must be recognized now is that the different forms or types of trust that we have identified impact one another. Indeed, it is our lack of precise understanding of the ways in which trust at each level is both dependent on and independent of trust at other levels that is the primary source of the anomalies that now confuse us. The causal analysis of distrust thus must be sensitive not only to the different types and amounts of trust that exist but also to the interrelationships between them. If not, explanation that pertains to one dimension or level of trust alone may be mistaken for explanation of the state of trust generally, and little progress will be made in putting all the pieces of the puzzle of distrust together.

The importance currently attributed to performance in popular accounts of public trust provides a good example. Though it is easy to assume that sheer performance, especially economic performance, is the primary determinant of trust, that approach is far less powerful than it may appear (Lawrence, 1997). It cannot explain why high levels of faith in the legitimacy of the political system have persisted through good economic times and bad over the course of American history. It cannot explain why high levels of distrust in the representativeness and integrity of political processes and officials have persisted in good economic times and in bad since the late 1960s. Though it can explain the correlation between job approval ratings and approval of the state of the nation and/or the direction in which it is headed, it cannot explain the presence or consistency of the differences in presidential and congressional job approval ratings that have characterized these scores for decades. Nor can it explain the similarities or the differences in patterns of distrust that now prevail in the United States as compared with Western European nations. In short, it cannot account for many of the anomalies that confuse our understanding.

In the second regard, the problem is that trust is both a consequence of a viable political system and a factor that contributes to its viability. There is wide agreement now, even among those who emphasize the determining role of self-interest in politics, that trust is a critical ingredient in the solution of collective action problems, that is, in generating results that realize the benefits of social cooperation (Ostrom, 1998). To see trust as merely a consequence of societal or political determinants is thus to take an overly rigid and static view. Causal explanation must be sensitive to the fact that trust is both cause and effect. It must recognize that the relationship between trust and the success of political institutions is a dynamic or interactive one over time (Uslaner, 1993).

These constraints on causal analysis are as difficult to deal with as the complexity of the determinants. Moreover, while the latter constraint is well recognized, the difficulties for analysis posed by the variegated character of trust and its causal impacts are often ignored. It would be disingenuous to claim that the authors in this volume resolve the difficulties posed by these constraints any more than they resolve the difficulties that derive from the complexity of the determinants. However, once again, the authors cope with these problems in a manner that serves to advance analysis. Whatever the balance they strike in interweaving societal and institutional factors, they focus their efforts in explaining distrust on distrust at the governmental level, on distrust in the representativeness and integrity of governmental decisionmaking processes and officials. Moreover, because Congress is the linchpin of representative government in the United States, they focus their analysis of distrust at the governmental level on distrust in Congress.

Such an approach has definite advantages. Though most of the chapters that follow do not formally identify different levels of trust, a focus on trust at the governmental level implicitly recognizes the existence of different levels of trust and concentrates attention in explaining distrust at the level that is pivotal for the existence of trust or distrust at all levels. At the same time it concentrates attention in explaining distrust on the key decisionmaking process at this level—the legislative process in Congress. Similarly, though most of the chapters that follow do not explicitly distinguish between the role of trust as cause and effect, a focus on trust at the governmental level highlights the importance of trust at this level, and particularly so as it pertains to Congress. In so doing, it leads analysts to treat trust as a cause as well as an effect, based on the critical role that trust at the governmental level plays in shielding the legitimacy of the political system from dissatisfaction at the policy level and the critical role that trust in Congress plays as a component of trust at the governmental level (Hibbing and Theiss-Morse, 1995). Indeed, if this were not the case, it would not be possible to use causal analysis of the determinants of distrust to support analysis of the dangers that distrust, especially in Congress, poses for the continued viability of representative government in the United States. Yet this is a common concern in the chapters that follow.

Assessing Dangers

All this brings us to the final set of issues we need to explore to place the individual chapters in perspective—the dangers of and remedies for distrust. Assessing the dangers of the current state of public trust raises a set of questions that are just as difficult to resolve as those connected with the causal analysis of trust. I have touched on the reasons assessment is difficult, and they can easily be identified. First, the evidence is mixed. Now, as in the past, the contours of trust are neither uniform nor entirely stable. Indeed, at the present moment ratings of the job performance of the president and Congress are high relative to past levels, as are approval of the state of the nation and belief that it is moving in the right direction. The problem, as the authors of this volume generally assume, pertains largely to trust at the governmental level. It is trust in the tie between governmental decisionmaking processes and decisionmakers and government in the public interest that has consistently been low in recent decades, and especially so with respect to Congress.

Second, low regard for politics, as now practiced in the United States, has not produced any fundamental challenge to the traditional institutions and processes of representative government. Public disdain for politics and politicians appears not to be accompanied by any deep and lasting sense of outrage. It seems rather to be accompanied by heightened public apathy, laced with intermittent flare-ups of public anger and wavering efforts to change existing institutional arrangements in a very targeted set of areas—legislative tenure, campaign funding, and budgetary spending. The primary result of distrust thus appears not to be intense and widespread public support for basic institutional change in any direction, but rather lowered expectations on the part of the public with respect to the realism of the traditional values and beliefs of representative government and the wisdom of depending on government to solve problems that threaten or distress the lives of ordinary citizens. Third, and perhaps most important of all, it is undeniable that distrust at the policy and governmental levels has been a continuing presence in American politics. Moreover, the reasons these types or forms of distrust have always been present in American democracy are not arbitrary or irrational, but are tied to fundamental features of both representative government and American culture (Huntington, 1981; Morone, 1990). Nor are the effects of distrust wholly negative (Craig, 1993). At the policy level, distrust serves as a catalyst for change, and at the governmental level it bolsters incentives for accountability.

The question to be asked is thus a relative, not an absolute, one. In the 1990s, as in the past, the basic issue is whether the forms and amounts of distrust that exist are so destructive in their consequences that they threaten the future of representative government in the United States. This is not a determination that can be made with certainty or precision. Though we suspect that there is something significantly different about the current state of distrust and the threat it poses, we have neither the historical benchmarks to confirm this fact nor the analytical tools and evidence to establish firmly the nature of the relationships between various forms or types of trust and the successful operation of representative institutions in the United States or elsewhere. We thus are seriously handicapped in assessing the evidence contained in the poll data on trust and possible remedies. Nonetheless, as noted, the authors in this volume not only assume but in many cases argue that the current state of distrust is in fact dangerous. In addition, several recommend broad strategies for reform based on their analysis of causes and dangers.

Though it cannot be definitive, there is a strong case to be made for concern and reform, a case that rests both on the present contours of trust and on the lowered character of expectations. The fact that trust at the policy level, as measured by job approval ratings or by general approval of the broad course of governmental policy, is now high provides a slender reed on which to rely. Approval ratings are highly volatile and not necessarily subject to the actions or manipulation of actors in the political system. Public policy can influence whether economic times are good, or whether the security of the United States is threatened, but it cannot control or ensure these outcomes. Hence, at the policy level politicians receive more credit or blame than they deserve, and over time this predilection is as much a source of weakness as strength. Equally, if not more important, measures of approval or satisfaction at the policy level provide imperfect measures of trust. The fact, then, that ratings of institutional job performance and the broad course of policy are now high, while measures of belief in the representativeness and effectiveness of government remain low, is quite suggestive. It is a strong signal that confidence in the ability of government to meet citizen needs remains fragile, and it helps to explain both the volatility in approval ratings and the fact that in recent decades high levels of approval at the policy level have not bolstered trust at the governmental level. In short, the fact that trust at the policy level varies and is now relatively high in terms of some key measures is far less reassuring than it may appear.

A similar point applies to the predominance of lowered expectations. The fact that the primary consequence of distrust appears to be lowered expectations, not action to change existing institutional arrangements in any far-reaching way, provides little basis for equanimity. That declining trust lowers expectations speaks to the basic role of trust in underpinning and sustaining cooperative action in a representative democracy (Fenno, 1978; Putnam, 1993). As a result, the consequences of lowered expectations are not benign. Quite the opposite—they are highly corrosive of the continued viability of representative government in the United States.

A number of destructive forces are set in motion by lowered expectations. Perhaps the most basic relate to the manner in which lowered expectations undermine the standards or norms of individual behavior and collective decision-making in representative government that are vital to its success (Uslaner, 1993). For voters to believe that all politicians are dishonest and act in a self-serving manner encourages such behavior on the part of politicians and establishes patterns of reinforcement for such behavior. Not to play the game in as crafty and self-serving a manner as one's opponents simply becomes a source of disadvantage. Similarly, for voters to believe that everything is politics and is done for political advantage inclines politicians to forgo choices that temper narrow self-interest with deliberate regard for the values and interests that are broadly shared. To the degree that one believes that others will follow only the narrowest definition of their self-interest, it becomes an act of foolishness or charity to act otherwise.

The consequences of lowered expectations in all these regards are quite detrimental. The overall result is to define deviancy downward and, in so doing, to impair the prospects for responding to the nation's problems through the processes of representative government in ways that can combine substantive merit and political viability. It may well be true, to quote Mr. Dooley, that "politics ain't beanbag." But what is also true is that without norms and standards to discipline self-interest and establish conditions of trust, the processes of politics replicate the conditions of a prisoner's dilemma game in which expectations dictate adherence to narrow self-interest and decisionmaking cannot resolve or even alleviate the problems it is supposed to address (Axelrod, 1997; Ostrom, 1990).

A second negative consequence of lowered expectations is to impair the linkages between citizens, elected officials, and administrative officials that are critical to the success of representative government. Increased cynicism about the role of elections, the role of Congress, and the role of government has a destructive impact on the viability of representative government. Cynicism regarding the efficacy of elections lowers citizen participation and has a number of detrimental effects (Abramson, Aldrich, and Rohde, 1998). For citizens to withdraw from politics because they feel remote and ineffective is to enhance the role of those who do vote, and these are normally the wealthier members of society (Verba, Schlozman, and Brady, 1995). It is also to enhance the role of those who actively participate in political campaigns, and these are normally the most ideologically committed on both the left and the right (Dionne, 1991; Wright, 1986). As a result, the chances increase that the apathy of disadvantaged members of society will turn into alienation. The needs of the disadvantaged, both black and white, are less likely to be served, even though they bear much of the brunt of change in the economy and society. In addition, the prospects for finding solutions to the nation's problems through the processes of representative government diminish, though for reasons different from those cited earlier. Highly disproportionate participation by the ideologically committed both impairs the ability of parties to present candidates and programs that constructively combine substantive merit and political viability and undermines the ability of individual politicians to stand up to the demands of single-issue interest groups.

Similarly, cynicism about the role and contributions of Congress impairs trust in a manner that is very threatening to the future of representative government in the United States. Congress is far from perfect, but it remains the linchpin of the demanding balance between consent and action that the Constitution establishes. This role, however, to be preserved, must be recognized and valued. If it is denied by viewing Congress, not as an agent of the general welfare, but as a captive of special interests and the career interests of its members, the ability to preserve it withers. In short, when cynicism abounds, declining confidence in congressional performance fosters continuing reductions in congressional power and the gradual transformation of the decentralized form of deliberative democracy intended by the Framers into a centralized form of plebiscitary democracy, based on presidential and bureaucratic power (Cooper, 1975; Dodd, 1993).

Finally, cynicism about the ability of government to implement programs effectively and efficiently serves to undermine the linkages so vital to representative government in yet another regard. When combined, as has been the case in recent decades, with continuing commitment to the notion that government bears broad responsibility for the general welfare and strong opposition to the elimination of most existing programs, the result is to confuse the task of policy choice and the grounds on which elected officials are to be held accountable (Bennett and Bennett, 1996). It may well be argued that such attitudes simply reflect our inability to cope with the profound patterns of change that mark the end of the twentieth century (Dodd, 1997). Nonetheless, the result is to complicate the difficult task of devising formulas for identifying the proper forms and boundaries of government involvement in society and to encourage elected officials to seek to escape responsibility by dissimulation.

A third negative consequence of lowered expectations is to restrict the capacity for political leadership and program innovation. Because it is easy and quite human for elected and non-elected officials to see the ways in which public distrust reflects both ignorance of the facts and misunderstanding of the constraints on decisionmaking, the increased distrust voters have for politicians and bureaucrats generates increased distrust among politicians and bureaucrats for the public (Simendinger, 1998; Pew Research Center, 1998b). In addition, because much of the public now equates effective leadership with the presence of good times and no longer assigns much weight to the connection traditionally made between personal character and effective leadership, there is a widespread inclination to see politicians primarily as political technicians (Maisel, 1998; Wattenberg, 1991).

Once again the results in both respects are destructive. For most Americans to see and judge politicians primarily as technicians is not only to tie public trust or confidence too tightly to volatile and uncontrollable forces, but also to downgrade the role of leadership in confronting issues and shaping opinion. Given the harsh incompatibilities that often separate conflicting interests on major policy issues, the role of leaders must be proactive and creative, not simply in the use of bargaining advantages but also in framing issues so as to increase the salience of shared values and interests. This view of the role of leaders is quite traditional. It is reflected in Madison's claim in Federalist #10 that the role of legislators is "to refine and enlarge the public view," as well as in Theodore Roosevelt's belief that the presidency should be regarded as a "bully pulpit." But it is far from outmoded. Proactive leadership, based on a broad conception of the public interest, continues to be critical to the success of representative democracy, and it continues to rest on trust in the integrity of leaders (Bessette, 1994; McFarland, 1969). Similarly, mounting mutual suspicion between officials and the public is detrimental to the viability of a democratic order. To the degree that officials do not believe they will be reasonably held accountable, they will be inclined to minimize risks rather than pursue policies in the public interest. Hence, elected officials may look far more to polls and appearances than to meeting substantive needs, and non-elected officials may also prize safety rather than achievement in decisionmaking. These tendencies, combined with the ambivalence the public feels regarding new government programs, work to stifle the very innovation needed to meet the challenges of rapid societal change, and they promote either stalemate or deeply flawed policy decisions that are doomed to ineffectiveness (Dodd, 1994, 1997).

Identifying Remedies

We may conclude that there is ample reason for concern over the present state of public trust in the United States. Though the ideals and processes of representative government necessarily generate a sizable gap between expectations and performance in every era, the viability of this system of government requires continuing efforts at and success in narrowing these gaps. What is striking about recent decades is the persistence as well as the range and depth of the gap. These features stem from the high degree to which declines in trust and expectations have reinforced one another in a context in which it is more difficult than ever to find effective solutions to the nation's problems through the processes of representative government. More important, they suggest that in recent decades traditional patterns of cycling with respect to distrust have been disrupted, that the ebb-and-flow pattern that has characterized distrust in every era of our history has been frozen at a stage in which distrust is very high.

To conclude that traditional patterns of cycling with respect to distrust have been disrupted is not to see representative government in the United States as close to collapse, to ignore the wealth and resources that are at its disposal, or to disregard the dynamism that continues to be inherent in free institutions, both political and economic. It is to argue that the character and conduct of American politics from Nixon through Clinton have grown far more discordant and self-destructive, and that the reasons are closely tied to rampant cynicism and lowered expectations regarding the representativeness and integrity of governmental decisionmaking processes and decisionmakers, particularly in Congress (Uslaner, 1993). The size and persistence of the forms of distrust that now prevail should therefore be seen as very strong signals of a high degree of stress in the arches and buttresses that sustain the structure of representative government. Despite its strengths, the fact that representative government in the United States has endured for two centuries is no guarantee that it will endure for a third century. As the Framers well understood, representative government is not a gift that can be taken for granted, but rather a prize that must be won in every generation.

The maintenance and renewal of trust are critical components of such an endeavor. However, the task of remedying problems in the contours of trust is not simply a matter of will. The design of proposals for change that will have truly beneficial effects is severely constrained by the character and strength of the forces that shape or determine these contours. Thus, even if one concludes that the consequences of present levels of distrust are threatening, what also must be conceded is that neither distrust nor its consequences exist for arbitrary or random reasons. Rather, they result from the complex interweaving of a host of cultural, societal, political, and institutional factors. It is equally true that normative considerations impose constraints on the design of remedies that are just as determinative of their benefits as the empirical constraints. Though often ignored or misunderstood, the needs of the republican form of democracy established by the Constitution are far more subtle than those of purer forms of democracy. They cannot be served by changes that ignore the balances between consent and action and responsiveness and deliberation that the Constitution seeks to establish.

The authors in this volume who discuss or propose remedies thus share a number of premises. The first is that, for all the reasons already noted, it is distrust at the governmental level, and particularly distrust in Congress, that should be the focus of remedial effort. Second, all agree that emphasis should be placed on change whose scope is not confined by institutional boundaries and whose effects can directly bolster trust at the governmental level, not on change that is confined by institutional boundaries and seeks to bolster trust indirectly by improving the capacity for performance—committee reform, limiting the filibuster, enlarging the power of party leaders, and so on. Third, this volume's authors presume that the proper strategy for success is not to weaken the professionalism or the power of Congress, but to correct errors of commission or omission that undermine expectations and trust. As a consequence, they identify campaign spending, civic education, and the role of the media as the prime areas for reform. They give little or no attention to the traditional forms of structural engineering that have characterized approaches to congressional reform throughout the twentieth century. Nor do they have much regard for proposals that see "citizen legislators" or increased democracy as the best approach to building trust.

In sum, then, the authors in this volume understand that efforts to improve trust are constrained by forces that are difficult, if not impossible, to control, and that it is no simple task to design reforms whose benefits will be correctly anticipated and not overwhelmed by unanticipated costs. But they also believe that the existence of determinants does not mean determinism. The very complexity of the interactions that produce results makes the conditions of interaction critical and renders cause-and-effect relationships contingent. This is true in the hard sciences and even truer in politics, a sphere of action in which purposive and adaptive human agents are involved. Moreover, the fact that trust itself is a cause as well as an effect means that the benefits of change are not linear. All this is not to argue that the design of reforms that will truly be beneficial is easy, or that even well-designed reforms can correct the current imbalance between trust and distrust so quickly or successfully that all problems will be resolved. Still, if we are not the masters of the empirical forces that constrain our purposes, neither are we their captives. That is perhaps the primary article of faith that motivates the reform discussions and proposals contained in this volume.

Approaches and Topics

Our discussion of the issues involved in the analysis of distrust in modern America politics and of the approaches taken by this volume's authors provides the elements of background or context necessary to place all the chapters, including the Foreword, in perspective. What we may conclude from our discussion is that the differences that mark the authors' approaches to explaining and assessing distrust are less important than their commonalities. This is true both because of the variety and complexity of the factors that can be seen as valid determinants of distrust and because of the unifying effect of the assumptions the authors share with respect to the role of trust at the governmental level, the importance of trust in Congress as a component of trust at this level, and the dangers of the current state of distrust for the future of representative government in the United States. As a result, as we shall soon see in greater detail, though approaches to causal analysis vary and conclusions on dangers and remedies clash in some important respects, on the whole the authors in this volume provide a mosaic of related and reinforcing pieces of analysis, not a whirlpool of conflicting treatments and claims.

In the Foreword, Senator Bill Bradley identifies many of the themes that define this volume, and he does so in a manner that is inspired both by his understanding of the fundamental purposes of representative government in America and by his own experience in politics. He analyzes the problem of distrust on the basis of a vision of the nature and promise of representative government that is rooted in the intent and words of the Constitution. In short, he sees representative government, in normative terms, as a mechanism based on consent for identifying and promoting the general welfare. Yet he finds the political process in modern America to be at a standstill and believes that the reasons are deeper than the mundane and familiar ones usually cited, such as blind partisanship, ambitious politicians, truculent and powerful interest groups, or overreliance on pollsters. Instead, he asserts that the process is broken at a deeper level and that a collapse of trust underlies the paralysis of government. He argues that citizens believe that government is controlled by special interests, do not believe that facts determine results, and doubt that politicians make decision on the basis of their honest convictions. He concludes that citizens simply do not believe that our present political system makes policy choices fairly, independently, or even democratically.

These conclusions are informed by his own experience in the Senate, as are his views on the causes and consequences of public distrust. In terms of causes, Bradley focuses on the role of money and the role of media. He details the varied and often subtle ways in which the present system of campaign finance undermines trust and argues that, given the difficulty of distinguishing what is a favor from what is not, the only reasonable response on the part of ordinary citizens is distrust. In addition, he argues that the media fail to provide citizens with the information they need to counter the misinformation of paid television advertising. In terms of consequences, he argues that distrust is now so severe that it is eroding the pillars of democracy in the United States—that distrust has become a political commodity exploited for short-term advantage by self-serving politicians and interest groups; that distrust has obscured the necessity for and benefits of compromise and led citizens to see their inability to get their own way as conspiracy; that distrust has undermined the critical core notion that legitimacy rests with individuals who seek to promote the common interest, not simply their self-interest; and that distrust, by encouraging cynicism and blocking governmental response to problems that distress and concern citizens, has made government increasingly marginal to their lives. He argues that the overall result is to betray the role and purpose of representative institutions, and he calls for various forms of action to build trust, not necessarily to restore activist government but to restore the sense of what a republic is and should be—a creation and instrument of the people to advance their common interests, a commonwealth in the full meaning of the term.

David Shribman in the second chapter provides a wide-ranging analysis of the causes of the decline of public confidence in Congress. He begins by documenting the decline of trust in Congress since the 1960s and argues that it must be seen in the context of a steady decline in respect for American institutions generally and in government as a whole. His point is that Congress is not an island, but subject to the same forces that have generated distrust in all sectors of society and produced an especially sharp sense of alienation from the officials who are supposed to provide direction in solving the problems of the country, that is, from the governing elite. He also argues that Congress is particularly unsuited to resist these forces. Congress, he believes, is a victim of its own openness. Admitting that this has always been true, he argues that the negative consequences have been exacerbated by the character of modern politics, and especially by the power and style of the modern media.

Shribman's analysis highlights the greater degree to which all the nooks and crannies of the legislative process are now open to public scrutiny and the rampant individualism of a candidate-centered politics. But these points are part of a general argument that emphasizes the manner in which a more professionalized style of politics has combined with more powerful, organized, and active interest groups to feed the cynicism of the public and convince it that politicians are dishonest and government is run by special interests. In all these developments he accords the modern media a critical role, not only as a causal factor in the emergence of modern politics, but also as an engine of distrust. The reasons are varied, but they all relate to the emergence and impact of important changes in the manner in which Congress is covered and presented to the public by the media. He argues that traditional reporting and analysis of the news have been eroded, most notably by increased reliance on "sound bites" and a growing emphasis on "drama," both of which accentuate the impression that Congress is conflict- and scandal-ridden. He believes that public distrust has severely undermined Congress's traditional regard for deliberation and compromise and, in so doing, impaired the ability of representative government to succeed. The irony, he concludes, is that the intent of the Framers to make Congress subject to external forces has succeeded all too well.

John Hibbing has done seminal work on the question of public trust in Congress. In the third chapter he refines and extends the trenchant analysis of the causes of distrust he has presented in prior publications. Hibbing begins by discussing the complexities of public trust in American political institutions, and particularly in Congress. He argues that what the public dislikes is Congress as a collection of members, not Congress as an institution or their own particular member. According to Hibbing, the public reacts favorably to the constitutional role of Congress as lawmaker in the public interest and to the role of individual members as representatives of their districts and their states. What the public reacts unfavorably to are the realities of the legislative process as it perceives them—to Congress as a gaggle of squabbling politicians who are both the captives of special interests and overly concerned with their careers and the perks of office. Other facets of congressional distrust Hibbing analyzes are the tendency for the more educated to be the more distrustful (confirming his findings on the anomalies of distrust in Congress), the relationships between distrust in other societal institutions and distrust in Congress, and trends over time. Here he finds that trust in Congress does not track with policy satisfaction or economic performance, that it is influenced by trust in the presidency, and that, while trust in Congress has usually been low, it has clearly declined in recent decades.

In explaining the reasons for distrust in Congress and its increase in recent decades, Hibbing discounts the importance of factors others believe to be of substantial significance. He argues, for example, that neither improved media coverage nor an absence of scandal would significantly improve the situation. Rather, he sees the primary cause of distrust in Congress to be that Americans do not understand or like democracy. His argument, amply supported by interview data, is that the American people do not like conflict in any area of life and reject it as a facet of politics as well. They thus fail to appreciate the role and necessity of conflict in representative government. Instead, they have an overly simplistic view of the public interest as the manifestation of some clear and homogeneous popular will, and they regard conflict and compromise as testimony to the presence and triumph of special interests. The persistence of distrust in Congress can thus be readily explained. So can its increase in recent decades, given the increased number of grounds for policy conflict that the pace of social, economic, and technological change has generated. In short, Hibbing believes that the American people's own policy divisions, combined with their ambivalence about representative democracy, provide the primary explanation of the current state of distrust in

Congress. Though he recognizes that distrust in politics and politicians has had and continues to have positive consequences for representative government, he nonetheless feels that current levels of distrust are dangerous and in need of correction. Given his analysis, the most appropriate and promising strategy is a very basic and long-term one—civic education. What is required, in Hibbing's view, is that we fundamentally improve the ways in which we educate America's youth about Congress, that we do a far better job of instructing them about the relationships that exist between defining features of democratic practice, such as conflict and compromise, and the achievement of democratic ideals.

In the fourth chapter, Roger Davidson directs his attention to the manner in which the characteristics of decisionmaking in Congress serve to arouse and validate public distrust. He argues that the ways in which Congress organizes itself and conducts its business are an important source of the ambivalence many citizens feel toward it. He notes that Congress is a complex organization. It involves two chambers and hundreds of work groups—committees, subcommittees, task forces, party committees, informal caucuses, and support agencies. It also conducts its business through a set of complex procedures. The multiplicity of work groups thus combines with a host of intricate procedures regarding the referral of bills, the setting of floor agendas, the handling of bills on the floor, and the use of conferences to make the legislative process so involved and tortuous that it is difficult to explain to outsiders.

However, the fact that Congress's organization and procedures make it difficult to understand is not the only reason its institutional characteristics generate distrust. Equally if not more important, Davidson argues, are the degree of partisanship that prevails in Congress and its openness to public scrutiny. Congress is composed of committed partisans, organized on a partisan basis, and directed by party leaders. Moreover, levels of partisanship have heightened in the last decade not only in voting but also in language and tactics. Yet the American people disdain the controversy necessarily involved in partisan decisionmaking. In addition, Congress is a far more open and accessible institution than either the presidency or the Supreme Court. This openness makes the delays and conflicts inherent in its processes, as well as the vices of its worst members, easy for journalists to identify and even exploit. But it does little to lessen the difficulty of explaining the course of legislation to the public or to provide incentives for responsible journalism. Davidson concludes that public unhappiness with Congress goes beyond policy dissatisfaction or scandal. He argues that Congress can and should change so as to make its deliberations more understandable to the average citizen and to lessen its dependence on journalists in presenting itself to the American people.

In the fifth chapter, Diana Mutz and Greg Flemming bring a perspective to bear on distrust that substantially enriches our understanding. They focus their analysis on how people acquire and process information about politics and the consequences for distrust. This approach enables them to analyze and resolve a paradox that has long puzzled students of Congress. This paradox was first formulated by Richard Fenno in the 1970s: Americans consistently rate the Congress significantly lower than the individual members who constitute it. Mutz and Flemming argue quite perceptively and persuasively that this disjunction stems both from certain cognitive errors or perceptual biases inherent in human beings and from the sources of information. They point out that human thinking involves negative and positive perceptual biases that produce different results in judgments of what is personal and familiar as opposed to what is remote and collective. Thus, a disjunction in judgments of the individual and the collective is not a phenomenon special to Congress. It applies generally in social life, and the authors provide data and a host of examples to demonstrate the fact. For example, people judge their own doctors as better than all doctors, the problems of their particular communities as less severe than those of other communities, and their personal economic prospects as better than the nation's.

The authors give equal attention to the role of information sources and the ways in which they combine with cognitive errors. In so doing, they enhance and extend their cognitive approach to explaining the disjunction in the case of Congress. They argue that, as a result of the nationalization of the news, information about Congress is homogenized and, given the penchant of the national media for drama, very apt to have a negative slant. In contrast, local media, except in large metropolitan markets, are likely to be quite positive in their reporting. Given the fact that the national media are now the dominant source of information about Congress, but that most information about individual members comes from local media, the effects of perceptual biases and sources of information are reinforcing. In closing, Mutz and Flemming bring their cognitive perspective to bear on the prospects for lessening distrust through civic education. They caution that results are likely to be limited. Arguing that learning will have to be experiential, not abstract and academic, they are skeptical that experiential learning in local communities can fully cope with the feelings of remoteness and unresponsiveness inevitably engendered by national politics in an extremely large and highly pluralistic society.

Mary Hepburn and Charles Bullock share the assumptions of other authors in this volume regarding the critical importance of Congress in achieving representative government in the United States and the pivotal role of distrust in Congress as a component of distrust in government generally. In the sixth chapter, they direct their attention to a strategy for alleviating distrust that is not only favored by several authors in this volume but also a topic of widespread discussion among political scientists, educators, and concerned citizens across the nation—improving civic education, with particular emphasis on Congress. They find that students in high school and college display the same attitudes of distrust toward government and politicians that their elders do and are equally, if not more, inattentive to politics. They also find that students at all levels are poorly informed about our system of government. Instruction at the high school level does give students a sense of the basic institutions of American government, but a very limited one. More important, it gives them little or no sense of the processes of representation and democratic decisionmaking, no feel for the dynamics of representative government. Nor does instruction at the college level remedy these defects for the great majority of students. The authors argue that these results, particularly in high schools, are tied to the dominance of belief in a rigid fact-value distinction, which has had the effect of leading educators to strive so hard not to be cheerleaders that they either abet or do not counter the cynicism about politics that has prevailed in American society since Vietnam and Watergate.

Hepburn and Bullock identify formidable barriers to refashioning civic education so that it can fulfill its vital role in a democratic order. They cite the highly decentralized character of school systems and colleges, competition for time with a host of other subject areas, the lifeless character of textbooks, poor teacher preparation, inadequate instructional guidelines and supplementary materials, and the inevitability of political resistance to changes in content and requirements. Hence, they do not see civic education as a quick and easy panacea for distrust. Nonetheless, they regard improving it to be of great importance in countering distrust. What is required, in their view, is to alter instruction so as to convey an understanding of politics and conflict as well as structure and duties and, in so doing, to give as much attention to the strengths of congressional decisionmaking in serving the needs of a representative democracy as to its weaknesses. To this end, they identify changes in orientation to the subject, instructional guidelines, supplementary materials, and teacher preparation that can and should be made. Finally, they conclude that rescuing what they see as a failing system of education for democratic citizenship will require a collaborative effort among college specialists, high school teachers and administrators, and professional organizations that far exceeds past efforts.

In the final and concluding chapter, I present an overview of the problem of distrust in Congress that seeks to integrate and extend the arguments and insights in the preceding chapters. Analysis in this overview takes its cue from the fact that distrust in Congress has been present in all periods of our history, but in varying, not constant, amounts. The underlying assumption is that, if we can understand the factors that cause distrust in Congress to be endemic and the factors that cause it to vary, we will have a basis for explaining why it has been so high and persistent in recent decades, for analyzing its impacts on the conduct of politics in the 1990s, and for assessing the dangers it poses and possible remedies.

I attribute the continuing presence of distrust in Congress to the combined effects of the demanding, ambiguous, and contradictory character of basic democratic values and beliefs and the formidable barriers to action that the institutional framework of government and the diversity of interests impose. Distrust is thus rooted in very basic parameters of American culture and politics. In every period performance falls far short of expectations, and the dissatisfactions that result are easily transformed into cynicism regarding the representativeness, wisdom, and integrity of political decisionmaking processes and decisionmakers. In accounting for the fact that distrust has nonetheless ebbed and flowed in all periods of our history, I argue that the patterns of dissatisfaction and distrust that inevitably arise have been countered by the emergence and triumph of unifying public philosophies that rationalize the role of the government as an instrument of the public interest and reorient opinion so as to energize the ability of the government to respond to the major policy problems of the period. These public philosophies thus serve as mechanisms for building and renewing consensus and trust, though their strength decays as change transforms one era into another with a new set of problems to solve.

To explain why distrust in Congress has been so high and persistent in recent decades, I emphasize the manner in which change in the character and conduct of American politics has strengthened the factors that cause distrust to be endemic and weakened the factors that cause it to cycle. The result has been the rise of a form of politics that plays to democracy's weaknesses far more than to its strengths and disrupts the traditional dynamism of American politics by freezing the processes of cycling on which it depends. Given the role that declines in trust and expectations have played in producing these results, high and persistent levels of distrust in Congress should not be dismissed. They provide ample grounds for serious concern. I therefore conclude by identifying standards and reviewing strategies for alleviating distrust based on the key role that expectations play in sustaining trust and the possibilities for reducing the gap between democratic ideals and democratic practice.

REFERENCES

Abramson, Paul R., John H. Aldrich, and David W. Rohde. 1998. *Change and Continuity in the 1996 Elections.* Washington, DC: Congressional Quarterly Press.

Adams, Henry. 1931. *The Education of Henry Adams.* New York: Modern Library.

American National Election Studies. 1996. *National Elections Studies Guide to Public Opinion and Electoral Behavior.* Center for Political Studies, University of Michigan. Available at www.umich.edu:80/~nes/nesguide.

Axelrod, Robert. 1997. *The Complexity of Cooperation: Agent-Based Models of Competition and Collaboration.* Princeton, NJ: Princeton University Press.

Bennett, Linda L. M., and Stephen E. Bennett. 1996. "Looking at Leviathan: Dimensions of Opinion About Big Government." In *Broken Contract? Changing Relationships Between Americans and Their Government.* Boulder, CO: Westview Press.

Bessette, Joseph H. 1994. *The Mild Voice of Reason: Deliberative Democracy and American National Government.* Chicago: University of Chicago Press.

Blendon, Robert J., et al. 1997. "Changing Attitudes in America." In *Why People Don't Trust Government*, ed. Joseph S. Nye, Philip D. Zelikow, and David C. King (pp. 205–216). Cambridge, MA: Harvard University Press.

Bowman, Karlyn, and Everett C. Ladd. 1994. "Public Opinion Toward Congress: A Historical Look." In *Congress, the Press, and the Public*, ed. Thomas E. Mann and

Norman J. Ornstein (pp. 45–58). Washington, DC: American Enterprise Institute/Brookings Institution.

Cooper, Joseph. 1975. "Strengthening the Congress: An Organizational Analysis." *Harvard Journal on Legislation* 12: 307–368.

Craig, Stephen C. 1993. *The Malevolent Leaders: Popular Discontent in America.* Boulder, CO: Westview Press.

_____. 1996. "Change in the American Electorate" and "The Angry Voter and Popular Discontent in the 1990s." In *Broken Contract? Changing Relationships Between Americans and Their Government,* ed. Stephen C. Craig (pp. 1–20 and pp. 46–66). Boulder, CO: Westview Press.

Dionne, E. J. 1991. *Why Americans Hate Politics.* New York: Simon & Schuster.

Dodd, Lawrence C. 1993. "Congress and the Politics of Renewal: Redressing the Crisis of Legitimation." In *Congress Reconsidered,* ed. Lawrence C. Dodd and Bruce I. Oppenheimer (pp. 417–446). Washington, DC: Congressional Quarterly Press.

_____. 1994. "Political Learning and Political Change: Understanding Development Across Time." In *The Dynamics of American Politics: Approaches and Interpretations,* ed. Lawrence C. Dodd and Calvin Jillson (pp. 331–364). Boulder, CO: Westview Press.

_____. 1997. "Re-envisioning Congress: Theoretical Perspectives on Congressional Change." Paper delivered at the annual meeting of the American Political Science Association, Washington, DC (August 28–31).

Durr, Robert H., John B. Gilmour, and Christina Wolbrecht. 1997. "Explaining Congressional Approval." *American Journal of Political Science* 41: 175–208.

Fenno, Richard F. 1978. *Home Style: House Members in Their Districts.* Boston: Little, Brown.

Gallup Organization. 1998. Gallup Poll. Available at www.gallup.com/poll/index.

Green, Mark J., James M. Fallows, and David R. Zwick. 1972. *Who Runs Congress? The President, Big Business, or You?* New York: Bantam/Grossman Books.

Hibbing, John R., and Elizabeth Theiss-Morse. 1995. *Congress as Public Enemy: Public Attitudes Toward American Political Institutions.* Cambridge, UK: Cambridge University Press.

Hunter, James D., and Carl Bowman. 1996. "Summary Report" and "Summary Tables." In *The State of Disunion: 1996 Survey of American Political Culture* (vols. 1 and 2). Charlottesville, VA: Post-Modernity Project.

Huntington, Samuel P. 1981. *American Politics and the Promise of Democracy.* Cambridge, MA: Harvard University Press.

Kimball, David, and Samuel Patterson. 1997. "Living Up to Expectations: Public Attitudes Toward Congress." *Journal of Politics* 59: 701–729.

Lawrence, Robert. 1997. "Is It Really the Economy, Stupid?" In *Why People Don't Trust Government,* ed. Joseph S. Nye, Philip D. Zelikow, and David C. King (pp. 111–132). Cambridge, MA: Harvard University Press.

Lipset, Seymour M., and William Schneider. 1987. *The Confidence Gap: Business, Labor, and Government in the Public Mind.* Baltimore: Johns Hopkins University Press.

McFarland, Andrew S. 1969. *Power and Leadership in Pluralist Systems.* Palo Alto, CA: Stanford University Press.

Maisel, L. Sandy. 1998. "Political Parties on the Eve of the Millennium." In *The Parties Respond: Changes in American Parties and Campaigns,* ed. L. Sandy Maisel (pp. 356–371). Boulder, CO: Westview Press.

Mayer, William G. 1992. *The Changing American Mind: How and Why American Public Opinion Changed Between 1960 and 1988.* Ann Arbor: University of Michigan Press.

Morone, James A. 1990. *The Democratic Wish: Popular Participation and the Limits of American Government.* New York: Basic Books.

Nye, Joseph S., and Philip D. Zelikow. 1997. "Conclusions: Reflections, Conjectures, and Puzzles." In *Why People Don't Trust Government,* ed. Joseph S. Nye, Philip D. Zelikow, and David C. King (pp. 253–281). Cambridge, MA: Harvard University Press.

Orren, Gary. 1997. "Fall from Grace: The Public's Loss of Faith in Government." In *Why People Don't Trust Government,* ed. Joseph S. Nye, Philip B. Zelikow, and David C. King (pp. 77–107). Cambridge, MA: Harvard University Press.

Ostrom, Elinor. 1990. *Governing the Commons: The Evolution of Institutions for Collective Action.* New York: Cambridge University Press.

_____. 1998. "A Behavioral Approach to the Rational Choice Theory of Collective Action." *American Political Science Review* 92: 1–23.

Pew Research Center for the People and the Press. 1998a. "Overview, Survey, and Selected Tables." In *Deconstructing Distrust: How Americans View Government* (March 10).

_____. 1998b. "Overview and Survey." In *Public Appetites for Government Misjudged: Washington Leaders Wary of Public Opinion* (April 17). Available at www.people-press.org.

Putnam, Robert D. 1993. *Making Democracy Work: Civic Traditions in Modern Italy.* Princeton, NJ: Princeton University Press.

Simendinger, Alexis. 1998. "Of the People, for the People." *National Journal* (April 18): 850–856.

Stanley, Harold W., and Richard Niemi. 1995. *Vital Statistics on American Politics.* Washington, DC: Congressional Quarterly Press.

Uslaner, Eric M. 1993. *The Decline of Comity in Congress.* Ann Arbor: University of Michigan Press.

Verba, Sidney, Kay L. Schlozman, and Henry E. Brady. 1995. *Voice and Equality: Civic Voluntarism in American Politics.* Cambridge, MA: Harvard University Press.

Washington Post. 1998. Poll Vault. Available at www.washingtonpost.com/wp-srv/politics/polls/polls.htm.

Wattenberg, Martin P. 1991. *The Rise of Candidate-Centered Politics.* Cambridge, MA: Harvard University Press.

White, Leonard D. 1954. *The Jacksonians: A Study in Administrative History, 1829–1861.* New York: Free Press.

Wilson, H. H. 1951. *Congress: Corruption and Compromise.* New York: Rinehart & Co.

Wright, Gerald C. 1986. "Elections and the Potential for Policy Change: The House of Representatives." In *Congress and Policy Change,* ed. Gerald C. Wright, Leroy N. Rieselbach, and Lawrence C. Dodd (pp. 94–119). New York: Agathon Press.

2

Insiders with a Crisis from Outside

Congress and the Public Trust

DAVID M. SHRIBMAN

In the early 1930s—when there was a political crisis worthy of the name and when, according to Arnold Toynbee, "men and women all over the world were seriously contemplating and frankly discussing the possibility that the Western system of society might break down and cease to work"[1]—social commentators trained their attention and their gibes on government. Government didn't work, they argued, and in truth, there seemed to be a lot of evidence for that view. Millions were out of work, all the assumptions that animated society and the economy were open to question, and lawmakers seemed especially ineffective in the crisis. Listen to the testimony of H. L. Mencken: "Next to kidnappers, politicians seem to be the most unpopular men in this great republic. Nobody ever really trusts them. Whatever they do is commonly ascribed to ignoble motives. The country is always glad to see them humiliated, as when Congress is forced to dance as the White House whistles."[2]

These days the White House seldom whistles and Congress seldom dances; the reverse is more often the truth. No matter. Politicians are indeed most unpopular, and hardly anyone really trusts them. It is a public conviction that whatever they do can be ascribed to ignoble motives. And Congress, conceived as the federal government's most intimate tie to the governed, is held to special ridicule, fodder for late-night television and cabaret comedians. Scores of lawmakers announce their intention not to seek reelection, citing their own impatience with the institution—and leaving unsaid their impatience with the public contempt that they endure in office. Many of the freshmen legislators who went to Washington in the 1994 election that ended four decades of Democratic rule in the House regarded their own institution as suspect, often using the word *they* instead of *us* when speaking of the work of Congress or, more often, of the inability of Congress to move with swiftness and decisiveness.

As Mencken and other wise-guy commentators, including Finley Peter Dunne and Will Rogers, have proven, Congress often makes for an easy target, and in the fairly recent past (low) public attitudes toward Congress have been fairly stable. Indeed, two decades ago, when those in the legislative branch spoke easily of a "reform Congress"—and when the legislative branch could compare itself favorably with the executive, suffering as it was from the damage of the resignation of Richard M. Nixon from the presidency—polls showed that only 14 percent of the public regarded the honesty and ethics of members of Congress as "high" or "very high." That is precisely the slice of the public that gave Congress the "high" or "very high" rating in 1996. And when compared with other occupations, the public looks askance at Congress, especially the House. Druggists place first in public respect, with 69 percent of the public considering them to have "high" or "very high" ethics, according to one prominent public poll. Members of the clergy, college teachers, doctors, and dentists also win ratings of above 50 percent. Funeral directors, bankers, building contractors, local officeholders, and real-estate agents get higher ratings than members of the House.[3]

This essay examines the decline in public confidence and respect for the Congress, with an emphasis on its external causes and the outside factors that reinforce that decline. But it also argues that the decline in the public's view of Congress is part of a decline in the standing of all institutions, and especially all government institutions. Public opinion surveys have shown that alarmingly slender portions of the population have a great deal of confidence in government—at a time when, more ominous still for government, members of the public remain skeptical that government even has much of a role in their lives.

This essay also argues that a number of problems related to Congress, but still outside of the actual work of Capitol Hill, have undermined the position of the institution in the public eye. These include, but are not limited to, repeated findings showing that the public believes politics is more influenced by special interests than it has been before, and separate findings showing that the public believes politicians don't care about "people like me." The combination of these factors would be incendiary even if this situation were not being conducted amid a campaign finance scandal that seems to reinforce every bad impression the public has of Washington and of Washington's local face, the Congress. And it comes at a very difficult political time, when, despite the diminished role of Washington, people still expect government to provide relief for the pain in their lives (or, as the baby boomers view medicare and social security, for the periods of economic stress in their lives) but cannot reach any agreement about how to underwrite these obligations.

Though public skepticism about Congress has been part of the psychic landscape of American political life for two decades, a longer look at public attitudes illuminates a precipitous fall in the public's regard for an institution that calls itself, without irony, "the people's house." Three decades ago, in 1966, 42 percent of the public said it had "a great deal of confidence" in Congress. By 1971 that figure had dropped to 19 percent, on its way to 11 percent in 1997.[4] The cause of that fall isn't difficult to divine. Congress played a passive role in the buildup in Southeast Asia in the 1960s, much of the time not pressing its prerogative to challenge the war-making powers of the presidency. A series of scandals, culminating in Abscam, House bank overdrafts, and flagrant abuse of the House dining facilities and post office, reinforced the view that Congress was, as Mark Twain put it more than a century ago, America's only native criminal class.

More recent events are not likely to enhance Americans' view of the institution. The capital press corps' fascination with the way President Clinton and his presidential campaign raised money for the 1996 election inevitably spilled over to Congress, which is as much a captive of the money game in Washington as the White House. It has long been well known on Capitol Hill, and it is now becoming increasingly well known outside Washington, that members of Congress spend much of their time worrying about money—their own, not the country's. In earlier times the watchword of Washington might have been: "Tax and tax, spend and spend, elect and elect." Today the watchword might more accurately be: "Raise and raise, spend and spend, elect and elect."

With increasing public awareness of the Capitol Hill obsession with money, each new damaging report about Congress and money has contributed to negative feeling about the institution itself. There has been, moreover, much to validate and reinforce the fresh public suspicions about the money obsession on Capitol Hill. Early figures, for example, showed that congressional incumbents were raising more money for the 1998 elections, and faster, than ever before. Senators seeking reelection in 1998 had raised, on average, nearly $1.4 million by the end of 1996, far more than they had at similar points in the six-year election cycle before.[5] Three incumbent senators whose elections were two years away, Alfonse M. D'Amato (R-NY), Lauch Faircloth (R-NC), and Carol Moseley-Braun (D-IL), had spent more than $2 million each by the end of 1996. (All three were defeated in 1998.) At the end of December 1996, twenty-two months before his next election, D'Amato had nearly $7 million of cash on hand.[6] Though Congress moved to examine its own fund-raising house, the senatorial sheriff in the effort, Fred Thompson of Tennessee, is no naif in the money woods; he's a prodigious fund-raiser himself. Nor are congressional campaign committees exempt from scrutiny: The two national committees and their Senate and House campaign committees evoked questions by raising more than $8 million from American subsidiaries of foreign countries.[7]

The convergence of the White House money scandals and the queasiness about congressional fund-raising practices reinforces the hypothesis at the heart of this essay, the notion that no characterization of Congress can be made in isolation. Indeed, Congress, representing as it does all parts of the country, reflects broad public attitudes as much as it creates them. That was one of the Founders' intentions, and in a time of declining respect for institutions, that characteristic redounds to the disadvantage of Congress. Congress is no island, existing by itself.

TABLE 2.1   Percentage of Public with a Great Deal of Confidence in Institutions

	1997	1987	1977	1966
Military	37	35	27	61
Medicine	29	36	43	73
Supreme Court	28	30	29	50
Educational institutions	27	36	37	61
Organized religion	20	16	29	41
Major companies	18	21	20	55
Executive branch	12	19	23	41
Press	11	19	18	29
Congress	11	20	17	42
Organized labor	9	11	14	22

SOURCE: Harris Poll.

It is buffeted by the same winds that buffet the rest of the nation, and by its very nature—comprising 535 members, each the master of his own office and, for House members at least, of his own constituent district—Congress is peculiarly unsuited to buck those winds.

And so the decline of public respect for Congress must be viewed in the context of the decline of public respect for all institutions. For thirty years the Harris Poll has been tracking confidence in public institutions, and its index of public confidence hit a low in 1997. The Harris confidence index, using a rating of 100 in 1966—when the questions first were asked—reached 42 in 1997, down from 47 a year earlier. But what is most instructive is the steady decline of public respect for all institutions: The index averaged 57 in the 1970s, 51 in the 1980s, and, so far, 45 in the 1990s. As Table 2.1 shows, every institution suffered drops in the past thirty years: The percentage of Americans saying they had a great deal of confidence in the military dropped from 61 percent in 1966 to 37 percent in 1997; from 73 percent to 29 percent for the medical field; and from 61 percent to 27 percent for major educational institutions. In that context, the drop in confidence in Congress (from 42 percent to 11 percent), while alarming, is not incongruous.[8]

The last third of the century (represented in Table 2.1) was a period of remarkable upheaval and uncertainty, a time when the buoys of national life no longer seemed reliable or fixed. The period, especially the 1960s, was marked by an unusual set of challenges to national institutions, many of them mounted by the very elites who, in earlier times, had been the most dependable and eloquent defenders of those institutions. No sphere of national life escaped scrutiny, and no sphere escaped damage, as Table 2.1 shows. To a large degree, in fact, American politics in the period after the 1960s consisted primarily of efforts to react, regroup, and recover from the damage of the attacks from various elites. The reaction to those attacks spawned, for example, the religious right, which mounted a counterattack that was particularly effective in politics in the early 1990s; a

TABLE 2.2   Trust-in-Government Index

1964	52
1966	61
1968	45
1970	39
1972	38
1974	29
1976	30
1978	29
1980	27
1982	31
1984	38
1986	47
1988	34
1990	29
1994	26
1996	32

SOURCE: American National Election Studies, University of Michigan.

Republican resurgence in 1994, ending four decades of Democratic rule in the House, as blatant a slap imaginable at the way things had been done; and a new aggressiveness from organized labor, with its muscle displayed in Walter Mondale's capture of the Democratic presidential nomination in 1984 and in the Democratic congressional offensive in 1996 (and the historic Democratic pickup of four House seats in 1998, when, according to historical trends, Republicans should have made substantial gains). Even so, the reactions did not live up to a rule of physics, for they were not equal to the challenges that spawned them.

The decline in the public's trust in Congress, though consistent with a decline in the public's trust in all institutions, is also a subset of the public's declining trust in government as a whole. The American National Election Studies trust-in-government index shows a remarkable decline in the public's overall trust in government. As Table 2.2 shows, there have been small increases in public trust over the years—note a small peak in 1986, when the White House and Congress were working on an overhaul of the tax system—but overall the trend is down: The startling fact is that between 1964 and 1994 public trust had declined by half.[9]

The American National Election Studies figures illuminate another troubling finding: Public confidence was lower in 1994, when the nation was at peace and the economy was reasonably robust, than it was in 1974, when the country was still facing a cold war threat from the Soviet Union and President Nixon was fighting the Watergate battles that would lead to his resignation. Though 1994 included public hearings on the Whitewater land deal and the defeat of President Clinton's effort to overhaul the health care system, the low confidence ratings at a time of relative tranquillity suggest that the current crisis represents the public's deep sense of disquiet rather than its response to any individual episode, or even to any group of current developments. The "malaise" that was at the heart of Jimmy Carter's frustration (though the word never was expressed in what has come to be called the Carter "malaise speech") has settled in and deepened, infecting each organ of the body politic. With such a virus, Congress could not expect to be exempted.

That is especially true considering the virulence of public opinion. The 1996 survey of American political culture undertaken by the Post-Modernity Project at the University of Virginia found that only 32 percent of Americans have "a great deal" or "quite a lot" of confidence in the federal government; one American in five expressed no confidence that "when the government decides to solve a problem, the problem will actually be solved."[10] The evidence for that conviction, of course, was manifold: press reports routinely trace government ineptitude and overspending, congressional travel excesses, pork-barrel expenditures, bureaucratic snafus, and the trials of frustrated citizens. Television news, moreover, has developed a new genre, sometimes aired during the evening news hours but increasingly aired in prime time—reports that concentrate on unearthing examples of government waste, fraud, and abuse. Indeed, the phrase "waste, fraud, and abuse" has become so much a part of the lexicon that the four words seem inextricably linked to each other—and linked to the government.

All this comes at a time when members of the public feel alienated from their government, believing that they do not (and what is worse, cannot) have much impact on its course. In 1952 about one American in three believed that people don't have a say in what the government does. By 1996 that view was shared by more than half of all Americans. In 1952 about one-third of Americans believed that public officials didn't care what people think; now nearly two-thirds of Americans feel that way. The figure tellingly reached 50 percent in 1974, when Nixon resigned; by 1996 the figure rested at 62 percent. The 66 percent figure in 1994 was the highest ever recorded for the question.[11]

There is no meaningful or accurate measure of whether the federal government is more remote, more prone to obfuscation, more resistant to public inquiries, or more attuned to its own needs (longevity) than to the needs of the public (service). Even so, there is no question that criticism of Washington has been a durable part of the political environment in recent years. The challenge has come both from the left (in the Vietnam and student protest days of the late 1960s) and from the right (during the first flowering of the Reagan revolution in the mid-1970s, the election of Ronald Reagan in 1980, and the appearance of the self-styled revolutionaries of the Gingrich wing of the GOP in 1994). Since 1976 three men have reached the White House by running as "outsiders," and the message from the victories of Jimmy Carter, Ronald Reagan, and Bill Clinton is clearly that Washington is not capable of fixing itself. As recently as 1996 a Republican presidential contender, former Governor Lamar Alexander of Tennessee, himself a onetime secretary of Education, nonetheless campaigned on a platform of stripping power from Washington. His slogan, aimed at Congress, was pointed and re-vealing: "Cut their pay and send them home."

At the heart of this sentiment is the belief that the people who run the gov-ernment are different in character, motivation, outlook, and morals from the peo-ple whom they govern. The public views the government (and the entire Washington crowd, including the press) as a governing elite that is out of touch with the rest of the nation. As James Davison Hunter and Daniel C. Johnson put it:

> The majority also views the governing elite as irreligious, out of touch with reality, out of the mainstream and devoid of character. Interestingly, public cynicism about our nation's leadership cuts even more sharply. Eight out of ten Americans agree that "our country is run by a close network of special interests, public officials, and the media." By the same margin, Americans agree that the government itself "is pretty much run by a few big interests looking out for themselves." Twenty years ago, just 60 percent of the population agreed with this statement. By 1992, the number rose to 75 percent. Suspicion and cynicism seem to have increased sharply in the last two decades.[12]

One of the appeals of the anti-Washington jeremiads is the view, expressed in recent years by both President Clinton and Ross Perot, that Washington is the province of special interests, not the national interest. It is true that throughout American history critics of U.S. politics and culture have argued that special in-terests have had disproportionate influence on government. Early examples in-clude tobacco and cotton farmers in the South, manufacturing interests in the Middle Atlantic and New England states, and the rail and mining companies of the West. In this century alone, agribusiness has shaped farm policy, organized labor has shaped laws involving workers, and big companies, ranging from the steel companies to airplane manufacturers to auto companies, have played out-sized roles in the nation's capital, fighting for contracts and fighting regulation. But beginning in the mid-1970s, when Reagan began his outsider challenge to Washington, the notion that special interests have the government in its thrall—with traditional Republicans beholden to big business, Republican insurgents to small business, and Democrats to organized labor, especially teachers and gov-ernment workers—has won wide acceptance. In 1964 two Americans out of three believed that the government was run for the benefit of all. By 1994 only one American in five believed that, with 76 percent believing that government was being run for the benefit of a few big interests; though there was an uptick after 1994, the figure (27 percent) remained alarmingly low in 1996.[13] As Table 2.3 in-dicates, there has been a steady erosion of the view that the government is run for the benefit of all; a separate survey indicates that half of all Americans believe that ordinary people "don't have any say about what the government does."[14]

This feeling of political impotence is accompanied by twin dangers: growing ignorance and growing alienation. The interplay between the three is impossible

TABLE 2.3   Public View of Who Benefits from Government

	Benefit of a Few Big Interests	Benefit of All
1964	29	64
1966	33	53
1968	40	51
1970	50	41
1972	53	38
1974	66	25
1976	66	24
1978	67	24
1980	70	21
1982	61	29
1984	55	39
1986	*	*
1988	64	31
1990	71	24
1992	75	20
1994	76	19
1996	70	27

* Figures not available.

SOURCE: American National Election Studies, University of Michigan.

to calibrate, but it is not unreasonable to venture the conjecture that alienation from politics and ignorance of politics are related. In any case, both are strong, and from Congress's point of view, both are dangerous. One poll showed that the percentage of Americans who could correctly identify the host of *The Tonight Show* (64 percent), the judge in the O. J. Simpson criminal trial (64 percent), and even the star of the movie *Striptease* (59 percent) was greater than the number who could correctly identify the speaker of the House (52 percent). Indeed, that figure is even more alarming given the fact that Newt Gingrich was perhaps the most prominent House speaker in years.[15]

The public verdict on the work of government is no more encouraging, though like other aspects of Americans' views on government, the disapproval has deep historical roots. Six decades ago, two Americans out of three believed that "politics" helped determine whether their area of the country won federal relief from the Great Depression. In 1943 nearly half of all Americans believed it was almost impossible for people to stay honest if they went into politics. And the percentage of Americans who believed that the people running government were "a little crooked" more than doubled between 1958 and 1994, though the rate declined after 1994.[16]

But the erosion in public confidence has grown deeper with time. In 1958, 43 percent of Americans believed that the government wasted a lot of the money they paid in taxes. In 1980 the figure had reached 78 percent.[17] Now, nine Americans in ten believe that "people in government waste a lot of the money we pay in taxes." Eight of ten believe that "our leaders are more concerned with managing their images than with solving our nation's problems." And eight of ten believe that "political events these days seem more like theatre or entertainment than like something to be taken seriously."[18] So it should be no surprise to learn that the percentage of Americans who actually care about the outcome of congressional elections is sliding as well; in an atmosphere in which politics is devalued, there is no individual incentive to follow it or to take it seriously—in short, no incentive to value a devalued commodity. In 1970, 65 percent of the public said that it cared "very much" or "pretty much" how the elections to the House came out. In 1994 the figure was 59 percent.[19]

The result: A sense of pessimism about the direction of the country has spawned, or is accompanied by, a pointed sense of public alienation from the people who are supposed to provide direction to the country. As Hunter and Johnson put it:

> With regard to the current political leadership and, more broadly, America's governing elite, people's opinions turn toward cynicism. Two-thirds of the American public believe that while the American system of government is good, "the people running it are incompetent." Additionally, there is a widespread sense that politicians have an imperious disregard for the concerns of ordinary citizens. . . . If unconcerned with ordinary citizens, politicians, according to public opinion, are supremely concerned with themselves and their own personal interests.[20]

It is clear that public disapproval of Congress is intimately connected with the more general disapproval of government and of leading national institutions, but that alone doesn't explain its low esteem among the public. One of the major external factors for the decline in public confidence that Congress has suffered can be traced directly to some internal characteristics of the institution. Political scientists and commentators have long distinguished between the public's view of their individual member of Congress (often highly regarded) and their view of the institution itself (often low).

The public gets much of its view of the broader institution from news reports—an external factor that contributes to the body's lack of public trust. But the interplay between the way Congress works and the way the press works plays into, creates, and then reinforces negative views of the institution.

Congress is in part a victim of its own openness. Unlike other national institutions—and here organized religion, organized labor, the courts, and the White House immediately come to mind—Congress is an institution with open doors and open windows. The legislative branch, to be sure, has its totems and its taboos, its hoary traditions and its colorful folklore. But unlike any other major institution in American life, almost everything it does is done in public, in front of the hungry eyes of the Capitol press corps, themselves arguably more aggres-

sive than the reporters who cover other institutions and indisputably more accustomed to personal contact with the principals on their beats than are reporters
who cover other national institutions. (That is why Hill reporters, who wander
freely among members of Congress on the second floor of the Capitol, encoun-
tering them on their way to and from votes, in dining areas and in special rooms
set aside for interviews, often say that their beat is the best in Washington. The
openness of Congress translates into "access" for news correspondents, and access
is the coin of the realm in reporting.)

Though Hill reporters have long had access to members of the House and
Senate, the broader institutional openness of Congress is a fairly recent development. For most of its first two centuries of existence, Congress operated in a mys-
terious way, with heavy influence from party leaders. But the advent of an ever
more aggressive press corps, the growth of the influence of television, and several
spurts of congressional reform brought Congress out into the open. No longer,
for example, does seniority rule without question, and no longer is party discipline immutable. Committee meetings are open, and televised more often than
ever. (In the past only blockbuster committee hearings, such as the Army-
McCarthy and Watergate hearings, received television coverage. The growth of
all-news networks and C-SPAN has vastly expanded the menu of congressional
broadcasting available to the public.)

But even within those congressional committee meetings, great changes have
occurred. Chairmen no longer rule with an iron hand, or even with certainty.
Closed meetings or party caucuses are rarer, and when they occur, they provoke
an outcry not only from members of the Capitol press but from watchdog groups.
The very existence of watchdog groups, in fact, is a recognition of the ability—
and the right—of the "dogs" to watch. The result is the development of an institution that is remarkably open to inspection.

Most of the work of the president is done far from the eye of reporters and
photographers, and chairmen and chief executive officers of big companies do
their most important work in private offices or in closed meetings of boards of
directors, but the important work of Congress is done in the open. Indeed, the
only aspects of the daily life of Congress that are closed to the roaming eyes of reporters are national security briefings (which are rare), the congressional lavato-
ries, the congressional gymnasium, the Tuesday party luncheons in the Senate,
and the cloakrooms. Most of the important work is done in the open, with one
new development: The advent of C-SPAN has brought the workings of the floor,
not only the big-investigation committee chamber, into every living room in the
nation, demystifying the institution, to be sure, but also exposing millions of
viewers to the balky, sometimes awkward, often messy world of a legislative body.
From the moment the cameras rolled in the House in March 1979, and in the
Senate in July 1986, the Congress was a changed body. But the changes were not
only internal. They were external as well. With the tumbling of the walls came the
tumbling of the public's esteem.

The ever greater exposure to the gritty work of the national legislature, combined with increasing reports about the mounting influence of special-interest groups, feeds the latent cynicism of the public. The business of legislating has never been sterile; indeed, that's its appeal to many of its practitioners and to nearly all of its observers, professional and amateur. But only now is the process in all its glory and all its preposterousness accessible to every voter in every hamlet across the country. As John R. Hibbing and Elizabeth Theiss-Morse write:

> So together, modern professionalized politicians and modern professionalized interest-group representation form a deadly mix in the public mind contributing greatly to dissatisfaction with the political system. But we fear that the problem runs deeper than dissatisfaction with perquisites and special interests. A surprising number of people, it seems, dislike being exposed to processes endemic to democratic government. People profess a devotion to democracy in the abstract but have little or no appreciation for what a practicing democracy invariably brings with it. The focus-group evidence supporting this contention was overwhelming (although unfortunately our survey questions were not suitable for providing confirmation). People do not wish to see uncertainty, conflicting options, long debate, competing interests, confusion, bargaining, and compromised, imperfect solutions. They want government to do its job quietly and efficiently, sans conflict and sans fuss. In short, we submit, they often seek a patently unrealistic form of democracy.[21]

This exposure to the quotidian aspects of legislative life comes at a time when the essence of legislative life—the compromise—is severely damaged as an art form. Although Americans are accustomed to celebrating the lives of uncompromising leaders, the fact is that most of its greatest leaders were masters of the art of the compromise. Abraham Lincoln and Franklin Roosevelt, often regarded as the greatest American presidents, were great compromisers. Lincoln threaded a middle way in the slavery dispute, putting off until 1863 (two years after the emancipation of the serfs in Russia) the emancipation of the slaves, and even then his proclamation covered slaves in states over which he held no power. Roosevelt, too, compromised constantly in his drive to fight the Great Depression and World War II; indeed, one can easily view the New Deal itself as a bundle of compromises. In both these examples and in various episodes in American history, compromise has won the day and saved the day; the Great Compromise made the Constitution possible and the Missouri Compromise put off the Civil War, at least for a time. When contemporaries called Henry Clay "the Great Compromiser," they were using a term of endearment and respect, not one of opprobrium.

But since the 1960s, the notion of compromise has been degraded in the American mind. The rebels of the left in the 1960s regarded compromise with contempt; at the heart of their creed was resistance to compromise. So, too, the rebels of the right went to Washington in 1994 sworn against compromise; much of the Gingrich rebels' distrust of Bob Dole, for example, was rooted in their disapproval of his ability to see, and then to win, a compromise. The more the

Congress was identified with compromise, the more its integrity was compromised.

Moreover, the two great movements that have affected the Congress in the last quarter of a century—reform and television—removed the discipline from the system. Television has permitted lawmakers to mug for the cameras, to perform for the folks at home, to grandstand. Much of it has been unseemly. But reform and the removal of party discipline permitted individual members of Congress to blossom into individuals, many of them quirky and colorful, even eccentric. Though congressional ethics are probably higher today than they were in the past, before limits on campaign contributions and laws requiring disclosure were passed; though the Congress is surely less unrepresentative than it has been in the past, with more women and members of minorities in the two houses; and though the Congress is far more professional than it ever has been, with highly trained aides and higher standards of conduct, the public still is confronted with a legislature that, on its surface, seems less disciplined and dignified. The presence of all that freedom and all those reporters has changed things:

> Against the disheveled backdrop of the open system, turmoil and trouble are readily found. The dissension is often real because the mechanisms designed to bring Congress to order are far less available than they were a generation ago. When disagreement appears in the news, however, it is inevitably portrayed as problematic rather than derivative of a complex, unkempt system. When friction results, the media dutifully report it as a sign that things are malfunctioning. Viewers and readers learn of the political infighting and institutional disharmony of a body we are to assume should behave more suitably—even though by design it is decentralized and prone to protracted disagreement.[22]

The changing nature of the news media is another external factor contributing to the diminishment of public trust in the Congress. As newspapers struggle to find a role for themselves in a world dominated by the electronic media of television, radio, and the Internet, they have led a dramatic change in how the mainstream press portrays the Congress. As recently as twenty years ago, beat reporters for the major national newspapers and for the three major television networks covered the Congress in a time-honored, traditional way, differing only slightly from the way their colleagues covered the mayor's office or the state house, mainly chronicling the events on the floor, in committee, and in subcommittee. These reporters wrote profiles and mood pieces, to be sure, but their primary focus was on the daily event. For the most part they wrote "straight" news accounts.

But by 1980 great shifts were under way in the mainstream media, and these shifts spilled over into congressional coverage. No longer was it enough to cover merely the floor action or the "news." Congressional reporters increasingly wrote about personalities, about the folklore of the Congress, about lobby battles, and they increasingly wrote in colorful language that emphasized conflict. The popularity of the style section of the *Washington Post*, read by nearly all congressional correspondents, played a big role in this trend; by the beginning of the 1980s, the feature approach to congressional coverage was taking hold in many mainstream newspapers. Many of these features were in-depth examinations of Congress, its foibles, and the often colorful characters who give life to Congress—lobbyists, press secretaries, longtime aides, and, of course, members of the House and Senate themselves.

This new sort of news coverage in some ways imitated television, with its emphasis on personality and its use of the clever remark, sometimes from the reporter, sometimes from the subject of the piece. The linear equivalent of the "sound bite," these remarks, often no more than quips, were completely at odds with the character of the Congress and the idiom of the Congress, both of which stress the deliberate. Congressional action is slow, not swift. Congressional speech is long, not short. Congressional discourse is formal, not informal. But the new journalism rewarded the quick, brief, and informal remark, putting the practitioners of Congress at odds with the practices of Congress.

In their effort to present "drama," many of those who prepared the feature accounts often gave emphasis to disagreements. To buttress the dramatic, they frequently cited the complaints of outsiders impatient with congressional delay or inaction. As "paper-of-record" coverage declined—most reporters no longer are under instructions not to leave Capitol Hill if either house is in session—feature coverage grew, and it was often written critically.

The modern way of covering Congress courts the danger of skewing the public's view of the Congress. Most of the work of the body is unglamorous and thus unsuited to the conflict and scandal orientation of some of the coverage. Routine bills, the difficult detail work of the thirteen appropriations bills, the fine print of tax legislation, the grueling process of shepherding unremarkable legislation through Congress—that is the usual work of Capitol Hill, and it's almost always done without fireworks, without passion, without colorful exchanges between angry lawmakers, and, alas, without coverage.

Although the coverage the Congress does receive has a sharper edge, its frequency is declining. One study found that network coverage of congressional news has gone from 124 stories a month (1972 to 1978) to 42 stories a month (1986 to 1992).[23] The result was that public attitudes toward Congress increasingly came from the feature coverage, which was inherently more critical, or from the cable outlets such as CNN and C-SPAN, which are widely available but, ironically, in many ways inaccessible. C-SPAN in particular leaves many viewers mystified. Cloture motions, quorum calls, votes on rules, sessions in the Committee of the Whole are difficult concepts to grasp (or even to explain). For that reason, unannotated coverage of a legislative session often has an unintended effect: It brings the action into a viewer's living room, but at the same time it makes the action seem farther away, not closer.

Quite apart from this problem, the nature of congressional coverage is different from the nature of White House coverage, mainly because congressional pieces generally talk about the process of reaching a result—committee meetings, votes, conference reports, compromises—while the White House pieces generally describe decisions already made, almost always out of the glare of the cameras. As Doris A. Graber puts it, "Stories about the executive branch that describe *what* is actually done are far more memorable than reports about *how* the laborious process of hammering out legislation works."[24] But that is only half the point. White House decisions often come out sounding crisp and finished. Congressional decisions often come out sounding muddled and decidedly unfinished. The distinction is important: Congressional coverage is about work in progress, whereas White House coverage is about work that is completed. Indeed, the public aspects of congressional action—markups, subcommittee votes, committee action, floor votes, conference committees, negotiations, final floor action—are, because of the nature of the congressional system, simply steps along the way, and often untidy ones. Even when Congress is done with its work, it often isn't really finished. The president still has the option of vetoing the legislation, and then the work of the Congress begins anew. The result is a messy process that looks all the more disorderly as the press reports on it. "Fundamentally, this will and must remain an institution where there is political dissent, debate and disagreement," Speaker Thomas D. Foley told the Joint Committee on Reorganization of Congress in January 1993. "Democracy in its purest forms is often not pretty."[25]

As if the challenges from mainstream technology—principally the electronic media—were not enough, Congress also now faces challenges from emerging technology. There is increased talk, both in the academic world and in the political arena, of new initiatives in electronic and participatory democracy. In his 1992 presidential campaign, Ross Perot floated the idea of electronic, democratic votes, much like plebiscites, on important issues. The technology now exists to permit Americans to participate directly in national decisionmaking, and a small academic cottage industry has evolved to examine how some of the electronic advances might be grafted onto the political system. This discussion both grows out of and contributes to the idea, already present in the culture, that Congress may not be as relevant in the age of Lott, Hastert, and Gephardt as it was, say, in the age of Webster, Calhoun, and Clay.

But the relevance of Congress remains a relevant topic. The Roper Institute's examination of the nation's main challenges is illustrative in this regard. The pollsters asked a survey sample to evaluate how strong the country's decline or improvement was in a number of areas, and it is instructive to use that data to examine the public's views of the challenges the country is facing. In the public's view, the strongest declines have been in the areas of crime and public safety (74 percent say there has been a strong or moderate decline); the quality of television and entertainment (71 percent); the nation's moral and ethical standards (70 percent); the criminal justice system (67 percent); and family life (64 percent). Of the five areas where the public believes the decline is greatest, at best two (crime and the justice system) are within the purview of Congress, and then only marginally.[26] Most of the important challenges are in areas over which Congress has no jurisdiction and about which Congress can do little. Again, it is external influences—changing American priorities at the end of the twentieth century—not internal factors, that are undermining the importance of Congress to the public.

Congress may be a flawed institution; it may conduct its business in a rhythm that has gone out of favor and fashion; it may be riddled with procedural problems and eccentricities; it may be an eighteenth-century institution struggling to adapt to the challenges of the twenty-first century; it may be composed of rogues and ruffians, of the shallow and the shadowy. All of those things could, with slight adjustments, just as easily have been said in 1949, or 1899, or 1849, as today. What is different today is as much outside the chambers as within them, the external factors that reflect and contribute to and, in many cases, multiply the internal factors undermining the public's trust in one of its greatest national institutions. The Framers conceived of a legislature that was peopled by, shaped by, and influenced by the world outside its walls. In that they succeeded, perhaps too well.

Notes

1. Quoted in William E. Leuchtenburg, *The FDR Years* (New York: Columbia University Press, 1995), p. 6.

2. H. L. Mencken, "Why Nobody Loves a Politician," *New York Times,* September 13, 1980, p. 21.

3. Gallup Organization poll, "Honesty and Ethics," December 9–11, 1996.

4. Harris poll, "Confidence in Institutions" (annual poll since 1966).

5. Jonathan D. Salant, "Incumbents Filling '98 Coffers Earlier Than Ever," *Congressional Quarterly,* February 22, 1997, p. 491.

6. Ibid., p. 496.

7. Don Van Natta Jr., "U.S. Subsidiaries of Foreign Companies Gave Heavily to GOP," *New York Times,* February 21, 1997, p. A25.

8. Harris poll.

9. American National Election Studies, University of Michigan, 1964–1996. (ANES has constructed two seperate Trust-In-Government Indexes. The Index reproduced in Table 2.2 relies on the same four questions relied upon in the Index reproduced in Table A.8 in the Appendix. But it applies a different metric to standardize the scores on these questions and the results are averaged to produce a single, annual overall score.—Editor's Note)

10. James Davison Hunter and Carl Bowman, *The State of Disunion* (Charlottesville, VA: Post-Modernity Project, 1997), p. 4.

11. American National Election Studies, University of Michigan.

12. James Davison Hunter and Daniel C. Johnson, "A State of Disunion," *The Public Perspective* (February/March 1997): 37.

13. American National Election Studies, University of Michigan.

14. Hunter and Bowman, *The State of Disunion,* p. 4.

15. Gallup Organization poll for CNN/*USA Today,* July 1996.

16. Karlyn Bowman, "Do You Want to Be President?" *The Public Perspective* (February/March 1997): 39; National Election Studies, University of Michigan.

17. Seymour Martin Lipset and William Schneider, *The Confidence Gap: Business, Labor, and the Government in the Public Mind* (New York: Free Press, 1983), p. 17.

18. Hunter and Bowman, *The State of Disunion,* p. 36.

19. American National Election Studies, University of Michigan.

20. Hunter and Johnson, "A State of Disunion," p. 36.

21. John R. Hibbing and Elizabeth Theiss-Morse, *Congress as Public Enemy* (Cambridge: Cambridge University Press, 1995), p. 147.

22. Matthew Robert Kerbel, *Remote and Controlled: Media Politics in a Cynical Age* (Boulder, CO: Westview Press, 1995), p. 117.

23. S. Robert Lichter and Daniel R. Amundson, "Less News Is Worse News," in *Congress, the Press and the Public,* ed. Thomas E. Mann and Norman J. Ornstein (Washington, DC: American Enterprise Institute/Brookings Institution, 1994), p. 134.

24. Doris A. Graber, *Mass Media and American Politics* (Washington, DC: Congressional Quarterly, 1989), p. 257.

25. Ronald D. Elving, "Brighter Lights, Wider Windows," in Mann and Ornstein, *Congress, the Press and the Public,* p. 187.

26. Roper Institute, *Survey of American Political Culture* (1996).

3

Appreciating Congress

John R. Hibbing

What did the American public think of its Congress in the 1990s? Not much. In 1996, when the Harris Organization asked a random sample of Americans how they felt about twelve institutions in our society, the U.S. Congress finished dead last, with only 10 percent of the people admitting to having a great deal of confidence in it. A year later this figure was basically unchanged at 11 percent. Gallup's procedures are different from Harris's, but the general tenor of its results is not. In late May of 1996, that organization asked people about their confidence in fourteen institutions of society and took special note of the number of individuals expressing either "a great deal or quite a lot of confidence." Congress ended up second to last, barely nudging out the criminal justice system, 20 percent to 19 percent. Relatedly, only a small portion of the people—34 percent in mid-1996—could even say they approved of the job Congress was doing. To be sure, approval of Congress improved briefly starting in the summer of 1997, in the wake of the balanced budget accord reached between Congress and the president. But the open controversy in Congress over the issue of the possible impeachment of President Clinton promptly brought those approval ratings back to their typically low levels. The general conclusion at the close of the century has to be that Congress is not the subject of much public confidence and approval.

It was not supposed to be this way. The founders viewed Congress as the people's branch, the first branch. Their major worry was that the public would disapprove of a newly created chief executive who, owing to the bad experience with the Articles of Confederation, was being ceded more power than was preferred. Thus, concern subsequent to the drafting of the Constitution centered on potential adverse public reaction to the president, not Congress. After all, a reasonably potent legislature had long been seen as the champion of the people against the potentially capricious actions of an executive (see Locke, 1947, p. 190). Most residents of the new country were not fond of the only meaningful national executive they had encountered—George III. So when they cried out, "No taxation without representation," they were hoping to secure legislative, not executive, representation. Their own legislature is what they wanted. Their own executive is what they had to take, since it seemed that government could not function without one. Moreover, such illustrious individuals as Nathaniel Gorham and George Washington thought that the fewer people in the constituency of an elected official, the fewer objections people would have (Madison, 1987, p. 655). This inverse relationship between population of constituency and public approval would make it difficult, they reasoned, for the president, with the entire country for a constituency, to be as popular as congressional representatives, with individual constituencies of originally only thirty thousand.

Then there is the Supreme Court—an institution with only the most tenuous connections to democratic processes, and one that the people view as distant and Delphic. Most people know little of the Court except that it occasionally wields tremendous power and tends to make controversial and unpopular decisions that may protect minority sentiment against that of a resentful majority. Such an institution is unlikely to be the subject of public approbation. Scholars of the Court frequently refer to it as a vulnerable institution, since it cannot claim to be "of" the people and clings to a power source, judicial review, that may or may not be present in the Constitution (see Caldeira and Gibson, 1992, p. 635). How could an institution that brazenly defends the rights of Nazis, flag burners, and fat-cat campaign contributors expect to be popular among the real people of America?

Congress, not the presidency or the Supreme Court, was to be the institution that had a close and special relationship with the people, but as we have seen, by the 1990s this was far from the case. Congress's surprising estrangement from the American people is the topic of this chapter (and volume). The issue is of the utmost importance not just because the disrepute of the people's body is startling, but also because the situation may create potentially dire consequences for the functioning of Congress. Given the constitutional location of Congress in our government, if Congress were to have difficulty functioning, the entire system could be jeopardized.

This is not the place for a detailed discussion of the potential consequences produced by public disapproval of a central governmental institution, but brief comments are in order. Often the impression is given that public dissatisfaction with Congress "threatens to undermine its legitimacy and diminish its authority in national policymaking" (Mann and Ornstein, 1992, p. 2). But other scholars have pointed out that suspicion of government and its institutions is not necessarily all bad. Paul Sniderman (1981) demonstrates that people who trust government are the same people who are willing to compromise civil liberties. The overarching concern of this essay with the nature and causes of public disapproval of Congress should not be taken to imply that disapproval is invariably bad. A healthy skepticism can be useful. Still, the prevailing mood in the 1990s has been one more likely to instill in observers the fear that disapproval is too intense to allow the government to do its job than the fear that disapproval is insufficiently intense to protect the people from a reckless government.

The first section of my chapter offers a detailed description of the nature of public attitudes toward Congress; this review is necessary because most previous writings on the topic give short shrift to description of the public mood itself. The second section addresses possible causes of the negative attitudes toward Congress, with particular emphasis on the cause that Elizabeth Theiss-Morse and I have written about before (Hibbing and Theiss-Morse, 1995). Fuller treatments of the wide range of contributing causes can be found in the chapters by David Shribman and by Roger Davidson (this volume).

The Nature of Public Attitudes Toward Congress

For whatever reason, hyperbole runs rampant when the topic is the public's views of Congress. Accordingly, my goal in this section is to present as dispassionately as possible the facts and context necessary for readers to reach accurate conclusions on the extent to which the public has turned against Congress. The situation is more complex than it would seem. As negative as the public has been toward Congress, the picture is not unremittingly bleak. Public opinion may not seem quite so bad when four facts are considered: Certain components of Congress are actually viewed favorably by people; certain people hold a sympathetic view of Congress; most societal institutions, not just Congress, are seen in a generally unflattering light by Americans these days; and finally, negative attitudes toward Congress are anything but a novel phenomenon.

Components of Congress That Are Viewed Favorably

Although it may be convenient for survey researchers to ask people about their feelings toward a generic "Congress," the truth of the matter is that Congress has many different components and people react quite differently to these various components. Determining the parts that are viewed more (or less) favorably can help us to come to grips with the nature of the public's attitudes toward Congress and government and to speculate about possible methods of improving those attitudes.

The conventional wisdom, thanks largely to Richard Fenno (1975), is that people view their own member of Congress favorably but view Congress as a whole unfavorably. This is true—as far as it goes. People *do* like their own members (though not as much as they did a decade or two ago), but they also like Congress if by that we mean its buildings, traditions, constitutional role, and institutional structures. In fact, according to a national survey conducted in 1992 (see Hibbing and Theiss-Morse, 1995), people favor this "institutional" component of Congress more than they favor their own member (see figure 3.1).

The aspects of Congress that people dislike are the leadership and the membership generally. Both of these referents involve members of Congress other than the survey respondent's own representative, and people usually react negatively to

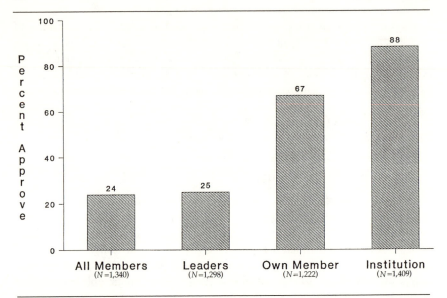

FIGURE 3.1   Evaluations of Congressional Referents

NOTE: "Percent approve" includes people who approve or strongly approve.
SOURCE: Perceptions of Congress Survey, 1992 (see Hibbing and Theiss-Morse, 1995: 163–171,
for details).

such referents. A majority of respondents believe most members of Congress
(other than their own) are not worthy, and even though many people are fond of
the institution of Congress in the abstract, constitutional sense, they are not fond
of the living, breathing, fallible members whom they see attending fund-raisers,
arguing on the House or Senate floor, and, rarely but memorably, cavorting on
Caribbean beaches. Tellingly, when people are asked about Congress in a general
way, they respond as though the question were about the generic membership.
For most people, Congress is this membership, not the institution surrounding
the membership and not an individual who constitutes an insignificant portion
of the entire membership. As a result, inquiries about Congress become identical
with inquiries about the congressional membership. Though this equation is bad
news for Congress, the discovery that people are supportive of the concept of a
legislative institution is at least something on which broader support for Congress
might be built.

If the concept "Congress" is broken down even further, to specific features and
practices, other revelations are possible. The strongest negative public sentiments
seem to be reserved for elements of the enterprise that bespeak its professionalization or institutionalization: Staffers, salary, long-term members, perquisites,
and congressional infrastructure, all are despised by the public. The American
people agree on very little, but they do agree that deprofessionalizing Congress

into a less pretentious, more casual, and pastoral body would be all to the good. Seventy-one percent of the public, as of a few years ago, believed that the salary of members of Congress should be cut, and 80 percent wanted the number of terms to be statutorily limited. What makes these findings even more amazing is that when the public was asked how much they thought members of Congress were paid and how long a typical member had served, they tended to *underesti-mate*. Presumably, if the public knew how much members really made and how long, on average, they had really served, there would have been even more support for salary cuts and term limits (Hibbing and Theiss-Morse, 1995, pp. 72–75). Survey research has demonstrated quite convincingly that the American people habitually give negative evaluations to things they believe to be swollen and bureaucratic. And the public certainly believes that Congress, with its elaborate infrastructure, fits that description.

Second only to congressional professionalization as a source of public unhappiness is the way Congress is perceived to represent interests. Specifically, the public is convinced that Congress represents only "special" interests, not the interests of ordinary people. By nearly a two-to-one margin, the public disagrees with the statement that "Congress does a good job representing the interests of Americans, whether black or white, rich or poor." Is Congress too far removed from ordinary people? Seventy-eight percent of a random national sample said yes, and only 15 percent said no. Is Congress too heavily influenced by interest groups when making decisions? A whopping 86 percent said yes and only 8 percent said no (Hibbing and Theiss-Morse, 1995, p. 64). This is a level of public consensus that is rarely seen in surveys, and never seen when honest questions are asked about tough policy issues. The people obviously have a strong feeling that they are not being appropriately represented in the U.S. Congress.

The American people like what Congress is supposed to be, and the concept of a legislature representing the interests of the people is attractive to them. They react favorably to the historical traditions and institutional purpose of Congress. They also react favorably to the particular members representing their own district and state. But this is about as far as it goes. When people see Congress as a contentious gaggle of political beings—which is how Congress is usually viewed—reactions to the modern Congress are quite hostile. When people are given the opportunity to comment on the manner in which Congress has burgeoned and developed and the manner in which Congress represents the interests of ordinary people, denunciations follow with alacrity.

People Who View Congress Sympathetically

Just as some parts of Congress are not disliked, some people are not disillusioned with Congress as a whole. Who are these unusual individuals? Answers must be obtained cautiously, since many forces are operating. Through various statistical procedures, it is possible to "control" for other relevant factors in order to determine the variables that are truly and not spuriously related to approval of Congress. Some of the relationships revealed by these multivariate procedures are totally unsurprising. People who identified with the same party and general ideological positions as the majority in Congress were more likely to approve of the performance of Congress (although even then, 60 to 70 percent of those identifying with the *majority* party in Congress still disapproved of Congress), as were people who felt personally efficacious. But other relationships are more puzzling. Although many observers might have anticipated that high-income white males with substantial education and a tendency toward political involvement would be the most approving of Congress, this is not the case. Other things being equal, women, the poor, racial minorities, the uneducated, and the uninvolved were actually somewhat *more* approving of Congress than their counterparts (though some of these relationships are not particularly strong, and indications are that some of them are not consistent over time).

Perhaps the most surprising relationships are those between education and congressional approval, and between political involvement and congressional approval. It would be natural to anticipate that the more active and educated among us would be more likely to have some sympathies for what Congress is up against, but this is hardly the case. Consistent with the empirical results (Davidson, Kovenock, and O'Leary, 1968, p. 51; Patterson, Ripley, and Quinlan, 1992, p. 450; Young and Patterson, 1994), though not the theoretical expectations reported in previous research (see Dennis, 1973, p. 22; Patterson, Hedlund, and Boynton, 1975, p. 56; Prothro and Grigg, 1960, p. 22), the more educated and politically involved a person is, the less likely that person is to approve of Congress. Because educated and politically involved individuals have higher expectations and are more aware of the occasional missteps made by members of Congress, they are a tougher audience.

One relationship is notable for its absence. It is often believed that dissatisfaction with Congress is due merely to the fact that people are unhappy with particular policies or particular conditions existing in the country and that they are better satisfied with government when policies and conditions are pleasing. This is simply not true. When "satisfaction with Congress's handling of the country's most important problem" (as identified by the respondents themselves) is added to the mix, it shows no significant relationship with dissatisfaction. Moreover, those who tend to be the most satisfied with their own piece of the pie are the most dissatisfied with the performance of Congress. On the whole, the very people with the most to be dissatisfied about give Congress the highest (albeit still low) ratings. And finally, mean approval of Congress over time does not track with the overall condition of the country—economic or otherwise (see Durr, Gilmour, and Wolbrecht, 1997). The mid-1997 increase in approval mentioned earlier came nearly five years after marked improvements in economic conditions.

Thus, though the educated and involved stratum is undeniably an important one in terms of the health of the overall political system, it is important to note that there *are* some individuals who approve of Congress. For example, back in 1992 when the Democrats still held the congressional majority, among Democrats with a sense of efficacy but not much income, nearly 60 percent approved of Congress. The problem, from the standpoint of Congress, is that not very many people in the survey fell into this category (52 out of 1,433, to be exact), and therefore the overall level of approval tends to be, as we have seen, quite low. Still, just as some parts of Congress are liked, certain types of people do tend to like Congress.

Other Institutions That People Dislike

While in no way controverting the conclusion that most people lack confidence in Congress, it is important to note that the public has little confidence in much of anything. The key finding of Lipset and Schneider's important work (1987) was that public confidence in almost all societal institutions declined precipitously in the late 1960s and early 1970s. Seen in this light, it may be an error to attempt to find some feature unique to Congress that has caused the public to go into a lather. Instead, it may be more appropriate to attempt to learn why the public is so negative toward nearly all institutions. This constitutes an important shift in investigative strategy.

According to Harris results of a few years ago, not one of the fourteen societal institutions about which people were asked was the recipient of "a great deal" of confidence from more than 37 percent of respondents. Harris's cumulative index for the battery of institutions in 1997 was lower than it has ever been—forty-two compared to a base of one hundred in 1966. Only the military was considered worthy of a great deal of confidence from more than three of ten Americans, and it may very well be that subsequent surveys will indicate lowered public confidence in our nation's armed forces, owing to scandals and well-publicized incidents of adulterous activity in the military.

Congress is certainly less supported than most other institutions, but we should bear in mind that very few institutions these days receive much confidence from the people. While some recent writings have attempted to explain why Americans hate Congress (Broder and Morin, 1994), other writings have attempted to explain why we hate the media (Fallows, 1996), why we hate politics (Dionne, 1991), and even why we are not as nice to and involved with other people as we used to be (Putnam, 1993). To some extent, Congress's trouble with the public is only slightly greater than that of many other societal institutions—from organized labor to organized religion, from big business to big universities.

Not only do public attitudes toward Congress need to be seen in the context of public attitudes toward other societal institutions, but we also need to recognize that public attitudes toward Congress are influenced by attitudes toward these other institutions—or at least this is the case for the political institution that works most closely with Congress: the president.[1] In the best early work on the public and Congress, Davidson, Kovenock, and O'Leary (1968) describe how public evaluations of Congress are best seen as residing in "the shadow of the President" (p. 59). They note that a popular president often makes for a popular Congress, particularly if the Congress is not seen as obstructing the agenda of the president, and they produce evidence indicating that "members of the President's party judge Congress more favorably even when it is controlled by the opposition" (p. 64). How people feel about the executive branch and about government in general will affect their feelings toward Congress. Here again, the late 1997 improvement in approval of Congress is a perfect example: It was undoubtedly assisted by the strong popularity at that time of President Clinton. Since many people have a fuzzy and undifferentiated view of government (see Delli Carpini and Keeter, 1996), their tendency to render these more encompassing judgments is not all that surprising, even when the president and Congress are controlled by different parties (see Durr et al., 1997). Public attitudes toward Congress must be viewed in context.

Public Disapprobation of Congress: Not a New Phenomenon

Of course, prior to the popularization of modern survey techniques in the 1940s, we cannot be certain of the precise level of public trust in Congress. But it can safely be said that Congress has always been the butt of jokes, leading Davidson, Kovenock, and O'Leary (1968) to remark on the "colorful literature of congressional denigration" and to state that "belittling Congress is a venerable national pastime" (p. 38).

In March 1816, the members of Congress decided to give themselves an annual salary of $1,500 (for details, see *Congressional Ethics*, 1977, p. 30). Prior to this time, they had received only "per diem" compensation of $6 per day. The public was outraged, newspapers were full of indignant commentary, and less than 41 percent of the Fourteenth Congress (1815–1816) reappeared in the Fifteenth (1817–1818)—the highest level of turnover since the beginning of the Republic (Polsby, 1968, p. 146). Nine members simply resigned on the spot when public anger became clear; one of the election casualties in November 1816 was none other than Daniel Webster, who would later become famous for his Senate orations. Though an extreme case, the events of 1816 indicate that a dynamic similar to that of the present day has long been present. The public has never subscribed to an "our legislature through thick and thin" attitude and instead has been wary of Congress from the outset.

Congressional job approval questions have been asked for more than fifty years, and except for temporary blips here and there, these questions show a public that generally disapproves of how Congress performs its job. For example, in 1947 only 21 percent rated Congress's performance as "good" rather than "fair" or "poor"; in 1958 the comparable figure was 30 percent. Brief episodes of relative popularity are detectable in the mid-1950s, the mid-1960s, the mid-1980s, and the late 1990s. But these aberrations are just that. For the most part, low public approval is much more the norm than high public approval. Some alarmists seem to forget that congressional popularity did not fall off the table in the 1990s but rather moved down from already low levels.

Still, even though Congress has never been tops in popularity (for more on this point, see Parker, 1981), it must be acknowledged that recent decades have witnessed a marked decrease in its public esteem. In 1937 Roper found that a healthy 44 percent of the people believed that "Congress is about as good a representative body as it is possible for a large nation to have" (see Bowman and Ladd, 1994, p. 49). Even as late as the 1960s, confidence in Congress was running quite high: Six times as many people expressed a great deal of confidence in Congress as expressed "hardly any" confidence. Specifically, in 1966 nearly 41 percent claimed to have a great deal of confidence in Congress (Hibbing and Theiss-Morse, 1995, p. 32), and less than 7 percent said they had hardly any confidence. However, around the late 1960s trust in Congress went into a tailspin. When Roper repeated its 1937 question in 1990, it found that only 17 percent believed "Congress was about as good a representative body as a large nation could have"–a twenty-seven-point drop. And when Harris repeated its 1966 question on confidence in Congress just five years later in 1971, it recorded a twenty-three-point drop to 18 percent. By 1973 more people had "hardly any" confidence in Congress than had "a great deal" of confidence, a far cry from the 1966 results, obtained just seven years earlier. Somewhere between 1937 and 1990, and probably between 1966 and 1971, Congress lost a good deal of the public's confidence.

It may be that public opinion of Congress worsened even more in the 1990s. Although the percentage of people lacking confidence in Congress has increased only marginally since the early 1970s, there seems to be an intensity to recent dissatisfaction that may not have been present a couple of decades ago. Traditionally, survey research has not measured emotions and intensity particularly well. When these measures have been attempted, the results have indicated that people are not only at least as disapproving as before, and probably a little more so, but that their disapproval has become more visceral and deep-seated (Hibbing and Theiss-Morse, 1998). It is this sentiment that has led to the intense popular disdain for Congress often encountered on talk radio, in focus groups, in letters to the editor, at the workplace, and at family reunions. The mass media are more than willing to feed this monster; attitudes in the fourth estate have moved, according to one observer, "from healthy skepticism to outright cynicism" (Rozell, 1994, p. 109).

Earlier public attitudes toward Congress, while not clearly favorable, seemed to be less overtly hostile. In fact, Bowman and Ladd (1994) may be on the right track when they point out that "most of the public did not think much about Congress . . . until recently" (p. 45). There is a difference between not thinking much *about* Congress and not thinking much *of* Congress; the latter phrase certainly comes closer to capturing the mood of the 1990s. Long ago, if people did think about

Congress, it was usually in the context of party, with supporters of the majority party in Congress expressing pleasure and opponents expressing displeasure. This partisan component to congressional approval has not entirely vanished. When the Republicans became the majority party in Congress in 1995, approval of Congress among Democrats dropped from 41 percent (in 1992) to 14 percent, and approval of Congress among Republicans increased modestly from 32 percent (in 1992) to 34 percent. But the significant finding here is that even for those who belong to the party controlling Congress, it is far more common to disapprove of Congress than to approve. Today many people *do* think about Congress, and when they do, they usually become deeply angry regardless of which party is in the majority.

Causes of Public Disgust with Congress

Nothing in the preceding section should be construed to mean that Congress, after all is said and done, has no problem with the public trust. My point is only that if we hope to garner a true understanding of the situation, it is important to keep it in perspective. As we search for the causes of the low opinion so many Americans have of Congress, we must not look for something that came on the scene only in the early 1990s and that applies only to Congress. We must look for something that, while present for much of the country's 225-year history, was clearly exacerbated by events and trends beginning in the 1960s. We must look for something that acknowledges the decline in trust visited upon most institutions even as we recognize that Congress has borne the brunt of this decline more than other institutions. And we must look for something that accounts for systematic variation across different aspects of Congress and across different types of people. It is to the task of finding a cause that fits these demands that we now turn.

Other contributors to this volume do an admirable job of discussing potential causes of Congress's low standing with so much of the public. There are many possibilities, some of them external, such as a mudslinging media corps and an informationally malnourished public, and some of them internal, such as convoluted legislative procedures and a slightly irrational committee system. Their good work on the many possible causes frees me to focus on an explanation of a somewhat different sort. I do not mean to imply that the trouble Congress has with the public can be attributed to a single cause. This is almost certainly not the case. But it is true that the explanation I describe fits well with the patterns outlined in the previous section.

Americans' Dislike of Democratic Processes

Observers are fond of tracing the public's unfavorable view of Congress to the frequently shallow media presentations that beset the institution, to scandal-prone members, to presidential aggrandizement of the airwaves at the expense of Congress, to members being oblivious to or hostile toward the public relations needs of the body, or to a public that is poorly versed on congressional procedures and recent actions. The implication is that if we could just get the media and the people to care about substantive issues instead of peccadilloes and horse races, if we could just get members to behave and to speak glowingly of the institution, or if we could just reorganize Congress in some way, then the public would lose much of its negativity toward Congress and everything would be okay.

Without denying the validity of any of these possible explanations, I fear that they do not cut to the root of the problem. I contend that even if Congress were reorganized and reoriented, even if the media covered issues, not fluff, in mind-numbing detail, even if Congress hired the best public relations firm on the planet, and even if people cared about substance more than scandals, the modern Congress would still be suffering from public disapprobation. Why? Because the public does not like to witness conflict, debate, deliberation, compromise, or any of the other features that are central to meaningful legislative activity in a polity that is open, democratic, heterogeneous, and technologically sophisticated.

People need to be more openly accepting of the fact that Americans are bitterly divided over how to tackle nearly every major societal problem. Examples of this divisiveness abound, but just to provide a sample, recent surveys have asked respondents whether they believe the Democrats or the Republicans to be better at balancing the budget; whether they worry that welfare reform will go too far or not far enough; whether they support a constitutional amendment to ban desecration of the flag; and whether they support a continuing U.S. military presence in Bosnia. Tellingly, opinion is split virtually down the middle on each of these issues (among those who were willing to venture an opinion). Yet many Americans simply do not appreciate the extent to which we live in a politically divided society. Perhaps because there is general agreement among the people with whom they interact on a day-to-day basis, or perhaps because there is general agreement on the *goals* of public policy (low crime, high-quality educational opportunities, a prospering economy, and so on), people seem reluctant to acknowledge the deep divisions of opinion on the proper means of accomplishing these ends. Thus, when H. Ross Perot says repeatedly that he will "just fix" the country's problems, people respond enthusiastically. They do not recognize that the way one person wants to fix these problems is very different from how another person wants to do it.

Since people do not recognize the extensive disagreement among the rank and file on difficult issues, they do not see a need for elaborate political institutions to mediate these disagreements. It is not that they want authoritarian government, it is just that they believe the people themselves have the final answer, so democracy can be maintained without lots of debate, committees, parties, interest groups, and compromise. If public officials would just listen to the people, they would know how to fix our problems. Who needs an extensive governmental infrastructure? Who needs careerist politicians? Who needs staffers? These features can only get in the way of vox populi.

Those who harbor these populist views—as do nearly three out of every four adults in the United States—always see debate as bickering, and compromise as selling out; disagreement, in this view, occurs because one of the parties (and probably both) is "playing politics," and few things are worse than playing politics. Since the people believe that they themselves have the answers, disagreement among politicians must be due to the fact that at least some of the politicians are not listening to the people. Ergo, they must be listening to somebody else—like special interests. People conveniently ignore the fact that they are at least as confused and divided as the politicians in Congress. Hence, what they really dislike about Congress is that it showcases political disagreement and conflict. What they really dislike about Congress is that it is a visibly democratic institution. What they really dislike about Congress is that it is doing its job—that is, its members are representing the incredible range of beliefs held by their assorted constituencies.

The Evidence

These are serious charges against the American public and have, accordingly, been somewhat controversial. If true, they suggest that the real reason for Congress's lack of popularity is not any shortcoming on the part of the members of Congress; it is not that some of them kite checks, fondle congressional pages, take junkets, and worry more about fund-raising than about good public policy. Rather, the real problem is a shortcoming on the part of the American public, and a serious shortcoming at that—a lack of appreciation for the core features of democratic processes. This is a message that people, quite understandably, would rather not hear, so the burden of proof is on those pointing a finger at the public.

To make matters worse, the only evidence that can be marshaled is not direct. It is difficult to demonstrate conclusively that most people either do or do not appreciate democratic processes. Unlike voting intention or party identification, openness to democratic processes is not something that can be measured directly in surveys. We must make inferences, and no doubt the most determined apologists for the sensibilities of the American public will not be convinced. But I will now present the evidence, circumstantial as it is, for the contention that Congress is unpopular because it is required to reflect the political conflict that people hate so much to see.

Focus-Group Evidence.   Given the inability of closed-ended survey responses to get at an issue of this complexity, one option is to turn to focus-group sessions in which people are given the opportunity to discuss at length their feelings and attitudes. In the project mentioned earlier, eight focus-group sessions were held around the country in 1992. Each session brought together nine to twelve people for approximately two hours of loosely structured discussion of their feelings toward Congress and other political institutions (for details, see Hibbing and Theiss-Morse, 1995). Many of the comments elicited in those sessions were consistent with the interpretation described earlier. Consider the following:

> It seems the Democrats and Republicans are always fighting. I mean, they want the same thing. I hope anyway.... [They should] concentrate on the problems and work together to solve them. (Roger)

> There are too many lobbyists in Washington, and as far as I am concerned, they should be outlawed because they are not representing the entire country. (Naomi)

> We need [members of Congress] who are going to work with the president instead of doing their own thing. (Kerri)

> If you are all working for the same goal . . . [there shouldn't be a problem]. We have millions of plans or whatever all over. . . . I mean, out of all these plans there should be at least one thing they should all agree on. . . . Something has to be done. And not just talk, action. (Roger)

These comments are typical of people's dissatisfaction with conflict. Parties are "always fighting," interest groups "are not representing the entire country," and members of Congress are "doing their own thing." The people do not like this divisiveness. How exactly the people believe politicians should incorporate diverse preferences into a policy solution is unclear. Roger's suggestion, born more of frustration than logic, is probably typical. He says, just find a plan, any plan, that can be agreed upon. At root, the people want conflict, whether it stems from interest groups, political parties, or the separation of powers, to go away. When asked about the primary reason she was upset with government, Delores said simply, "There is no cooperation." How did we end up with all this contentiousness when we should be getting the cooperation that Delores and so many others desire? The following exchange is instructive of the answer that ordinary people provide:

> BOB: When the president says, "I think we need to do this for the country, blah blah, and all that," [members of Congress] ought to see if they can do it rather than work hard not to do it and kill it, right?
> DELORES: But that started a long time ago when they allowed the protesters and the demonstrations to come in front of the White House or wherever. They pitch their little thing and confuse the whole issue. And then everybody gets all excited, and this has to be acted on.
> BOB: The government has to listen to the ten people who feel this way, but that's only ten out of millions.

LINDA: Those ten people that get up there and protest are the ones that are
    listened to because they are protesting.
BOB: We are the silent majority.

This is a commonly expressed notion. People believe there really is a popular
consensus out there, but "protesters" or parties or special interests "confuse the
whole issue" and get everybody "all excited." As a result, the "silent majority" gets
ignored in favor of a noisy and distinctly atypical minority. The sentiment in this
exchange seems to be that somehow this noisy minority should be ignored, but
in the following passage George wrestles more seriously with the issue of representing minority positions. His comments are not the most articulate, but he is
at least addressing the issue in a more reflective fashion.

> It's like we can vote any way we want to. Somebody's goin' to win by 60 percent. What
> about the other 40 percent of the people that are still not happy? And that's where I
> think a lot of the frustration comes from, too. It's like my vote didn't count; he lost.
> There's 40 percent of . . . just take 100,000 people: that's 40,000 people that are un-
> happy about who is, you know, representing them. You know, two people in there
> running for something, unless it's a landslide, ninety to ten, [it's] 51 to 49, and this
> guy wins, then like 49 percent of the people are not happy. That's big, that's frustrat-
> ing, that'll frustrate a lot of people into saying, you know, "My vote doesn't count."
> You know, I don't know how to change that either.

Debbi expressed a similar assessment of the source of dissatisfaction and concluded that "when we demand something, we still don't get it. . . . That is why we
get disgusted and stop voting." Traci sounded somewhat like Rodney King when
she said plaintively, and in reference to government in general, that "it should all
work together."

It is clear from many of these comments that people are not convinced that
conflict has to be tolerated in the modern democratic political arena. Perhaps
with the exception of George, who "does not know what to do" about giving
minority viewpoints some representation, the consensus is that if the people in
government would only "work together," there would be no conflict. The people endorse divided government in the abstract, but this does not mean they
like to see actual contention. Whether government is divided or unified, the
people believe politicians "should all work together." No need for talk, just give
us action—action consistent with the desires of the entire country, not just a
part of it.

How could an institution like Congress hope to be popular when it has to operate in this milieu? Congress is designed to give full voice to diverse interests—
even those of ten protesters. Congress is designed to hash out the issues in clear
view and to fight with other branches of government to keep any of them from

gaining too much power. Do the people really want Congress to accept blindly the policy proposals of the president, as is implied in these comments?

Longitudinal Evidence. It would appear so. If we shift from these focus-group comments—which, after all, may not be representative of true national sentiment—to other, more systematic kinds of evidence, we discover findings that are perfectly consistent with this interpretation. One way to approach this problem is to determine when Congress is more popular and when it is less popular. If popularity is inversely related to the presence of conflict, support is given for the interpretation offered here.

Davidson, Kovenock, and O'Leary (1968) find just such a pattern. Their evidence from the mid-1940s to the mid-1960s supports the conclusion that "public approval is usually highest when domestic political controversy is muted. . . . When partisan controversy is especially acrimonious, or when Congress seems slow in resolving legislation, public disaffection increases" (pp. 52–53). The jarring events of Watergate provided an even clearer indication of the people's proclivities on such matters. It might be thought that Congress would be given some credit for the way it handled Watergate. In the eyes of many sophisticated political observers, Watergate indicated that the system worked, that if one branch of government was not playing by the rules the other branches would be there to do the dirty work of restoring an equilibrium. Watergate was not easy for members of Congress, particularly Republicans, but most handled the affair with dignity, fairness, and a sense of history. Yet there was no post-Watergate bounce in public confidence in Congress. The Supreme Court received such a bounce (up to 40 percent in 1974), but Congress did not (down to 18 percent in 1974). Watergate was divisive, and there is no way Congress wins when it is seen as embroiled in conflict.

Durr, Gilmour, and Wolbrecht (1997) have also analyzed longitudinal evidence. They use an elaborate technique of combining many different questions pertaining to the public's attitudes toward Congress. This procedure is vital given the spotty pattern to how the individual questions have been posed. Their key conclusion is that

> when Congress acts as it was constitutionally designed to act—passing major legislation and debating the issues of the day—it is rewarded by the public with lower levels of approval. . . . While pundits and polls often portray declines in Congressional approval as indications of that body's failings, if not a crisis of the political order, our research suggests that decreases in Congressional approval are, in part, simply a reaction to Congress doing its job. (p. 199)

Durr and his colleagues used a data set that ends in 1991, but if it had continued, events later in the decade would have provided additional confirmation of their conclusion. As alluded to previously, even though economic conditions soared to new heights in late 1992 and stayed there for most of the rest of the decade, public approval of Congress (and government generally) remained in the dumps until mid-1997. What marks that particular time as unusual was not any further growth in the economy but rather the perception that Congress worked together with the president to solve an important national problem—the budget deficit. Such cooperation is what the public wants from government. All told, fluctuations in congressional approval over time fit very nicely with the thesis that the people dislike conflict and that they dislike Congress because it displays political conflict when performing its constitutionally assigned role.

Other Evidence.   Still other evidence is consistent with this notion. Elections are the embodiment of conflict (if they are meaningful); therefore, if the people dislike conflict, elections should have a negative impact on public approval of Congress. Findings reported by Gary C. Jacobson and Thomas P. Kim (1996) suggest this is exactly what happens. They show that in the 1990s each congressional election campaign has brought marked decreases in congressional approval. After the election, approval temporarily increases in a fashion reminiscent of the presidential honeymoon effect (p. 7). The period after the conflict of the election, but before the conflict of governing, seems to afford a rare chance for Congress to be popular.

Since postelection surveys are usually spread out over a period of several weeks, it is possible to determine whether respondents interviewed close to the time of the election are less approving of Congress than respondents interviewed later, well after the sturm und drang of the election. The "people dislike conflict" thesis expects just such a pattern, and Jacobson and Kim discovered that expectation meets reality—or at least it did in 1994. They found that, other things being equal, merely the timing of the interview could produce a six-point change in approval of Congress, with greater temporal distance from the election creating greater approval of Congress (p. 6).

Finally, it is useful to compare the institutions eliciting the most public confidence with those, like Congress, eliciting the least. According to the 1996 Gallup results, the institutions in which the American public had the most confidence were, in order from first to fourth, the military, the police, organized religion, and the Supreme Court. This pattern has actually been reasonably stable for several years now. What is interesting is that none of these top four institutions is known for its democratic operating procedures. The military, the police, and organized religion are classically structured, hierarchical institutions in which orders come from the top and are passed down. Questioning the chain of command is viewed as untoward, perhaps an indication of a lack of faith or a desire to weaken the fabric of authority that is believed to hold society together. The Supreme Court, while technically not hierarchical, has done a marvelous job of hiding the debate, compromise, conflict, and politicking that characterize its decisionmaking procedures. The Court's "bickering," "horse-trading," and "selling out" all occur behind closed doors, well out of public view. Decisions are announced later, and any dissent is buried in obscure documents that few ordinary citizens ever encounter. So the most approved institutions all tend to cloak their internal conflict in some fashion, in direct contrast to Congress.[2]

The Timing of the Decline in Public Approval of Congress

But why would this frustration with conflict become more noticeable in the late 1960s and early 1970s? Presumably people have always been conflict-averse, so how could the thesis explain the decrease in approval beginning in the late 1960s? Because it was only then that dissenting voices were heard and taken seriously— that people were made aware of the country's true diversity. If, as was the case to a certain extent in the 1950s and early 1960s, the only voices heard are those of white, heterosexual, Christian, middle-class, male-dominated, stable-family, company-man America, democratic processes do not seem messy. There would often be no need for debate and compromise on delicate issues because these issues were either screened from the agenda or treated in such a way that nonmainstream voices were not heard.

Many of the democracies of the past have not been true democracies in that potentially dissenting voices (women, slaves, nonproperty owners, and so on) have not been heard. In more recent times, opposing voices have become plentiful, and the media now love to report on clashes of various sorts. This exposure has a negative impact on many institutions, but especially on those showcasing disputes. The people have had to adjust to seeing conflict and to acknowledging the presence of diverse interests. Moreover, democracy requires us not only to recognize the existence of these other voices but to give them a place at the bargaining table, to discuss with them and compromise with them (that is, to give them some of what they want in order to get some of what we want). This is bitter medicine for people to swallow.

The increased diversity and number of voices have been described at some length by Robert Dahl (1994) and Jonathan Rauch (1994). Dahl observes simply that the new American political order is one in which "government policies are made in response to a greater number and variety of conflicting and substantially independent interest groups" (p. 1). He worries about how political institutions can weight these competing claims or evaluate the extent to which they represent the larger polity. Rauch's (1994) concerns run even deeper. He believes that the welter of interest groups has created "demosclerosis," a situation in which there are so many voices clamoring to protect their own interests that modern government loses its ability to adapt (p. 17).

Whether or not the situation is as dire as Rauch believes, people do not like the results. The political process becomes quite unruly, and many citizens conclude that the political process must therefore be flawed somehow. Nobody is satisfied with the half-a-loaf results. Some withdraw from the political process altogether, believing it is beneath them and beyond hope. The thinking seems to be, "If I do not get my way on a policy decision, then something must be wrong." Remember the dismay that Debbi expressed in one focus-group session: "When we demand something . . . we still don't get it." Democracy requires people to face up to the fact that they will not get many of their demands, particularly given the fixed-pie, zero-sum, multiple-actor nature of modern politics. People need to recognize that democracy does not provide them with a guarantee that they will always be on the winning side. Just because we disagree with the other side does not mean we can pass them off as wild-eyed "protesters in front of the White House or wherever," or imply that there are only a few of them compared to the millions who are on our side. But denigrating opposing views or, more to the point of this chapter, denigrating the entire governmental process is easier than acknowledging that the views of those ordinary people with whom we disagree are in fact just as valid and legitimate as our own and that a truly democratic governing process must guarantee that opposing voices will be heard.

Congress's growing problems with the public trust do not stem merely from C-SPAN, a more investigative press, or a more educated public, although all of these no doubt play some role. Mostly they stem from the increasingly conflict-laden age in which we live. As painful as it may be to see Congress-bashing in epidemic proportions, it may be of some comfort to realize that much of the bashing is now occurring because we have a more inclusive polity. It is possible to make Congress more popular, but doing so would require us to make the institution much less open and much less democratic than it is now.

Teaching People to Appreciate the Messiness of Democracy

There is no denying that the legislative process could be improved and that elected officials could act with more dignity, but there is also a real possibility that if Congress were suddenly devoid of professional politicians, lucrative salaries and pensions, staffers and perquisites, campaign finance scandals, and other all-too-common embarrassments, it would still be a less than popular institution. The truth of the matter is that people need to accept the existence of honest policy disagreements among ordinary people. Once they did so, much of the rest would fall into place. People would then be able to see that debating, compromising, and otherwise working through honest disagreements is not pretty and takes time. People would then understand that elected officials are not constructing conflict but rather reflecting it. If people could be made to see that an unruly political process is not necessarily a flawed political process, they would then become more understanding and supportive of it. The key to improving Congress's public standing is imbuing the public with more realistic notions of what legislatures in large, complex, heterogeneous societies look like (for more on the importance of expectations, see Kimball and Patterson, 1995).

How might this more realistic public understanding be fostered? Admittedly, there are no clear answers. One possibility is to make a more concerted effort to teach school-age children about the extent of issue disagreement in our society and about the resultant, inevitable messiness of democracy. Students still need to be taught how the political system works, the nuts and bolts, as well as the intricacies of major issues of the day. But some time should be set aside to show students what happens when people disagree and they struggle to resolve their differences through democratic processes. This message can be delivered through in-class simulations, computer simulations, participation in the actual political process, class projects, analysis of group surveys, and countless other potential techniques, but somewhere along the line students must come to terms with the realities of the democratic process—and therefore the reality of congressional practices.

As I noted earlier, other things being equal, people with more education are *not*, apparently, more understanding of the conflict they see in Congress. It would seem, then, that our educational system, as it is currently constituted, is not structured to teach people democracy appreciation. Music appreciation and art appreciation courses are offered, but not democracy appreciation. Instead, students are fed standard civics fare, with accolades, many definitions, and sterile constitutional detail. Most secondary-level texts do little to familiarize students with the rough-and-tumble of democratic politics in a society such as ours. This must be changed if we hope to make lasting improvements in the public's views of Congress and government (see Hibbing and Theiss-Morse, 1996; for similar sentiments, see Bennett, 1997).

There are those who disagree with the suggestion that appreciating political diversity is the way to solve our problems. They advocate various methods of diminishing the appearance of disagreement. Some believe that, rather than teaching students about all the people who disagree with us, we should shield students from this information by placing them in enclave schools until they are old enough to handle differences (see Chabot, 1996). Others advocate that we devolve decisionmaking to state- or even community-based settings. Of course, the attraction here is that states and, especially, local communities tend to be much more homogeneous than the country as a whole. It may be tempting to give up on the ability to make tough decisions in national institutions that then produce policies to be applied to national constituencies, but we must not. Community-based decisions reduce the sense of collectiveness that makes a country and amount to little more than a cop-out. We must instead face up to the need to compromise with people with whom we disagree. Even communitarians recognize that decisions involving foreign policy, protection of fundamental rights, and air pollution must be handled nationally. Fooling ourselves on some issues only to be jarred back to reality by the big issues is not the recipe for happy government. Indeed, dissatisfaction with the federal government and especially Congress would almost certainly intensify if the communitarians had their way. The easy, locally contained decisions would be made by each community's like-minded citizens, and the federal government would be left to carve out compromises and secure popular support from people accustomed to the lesser levels of disagreement afforded by the homogeneous nature of their community and their local issues. Neither isolating children in enclave schools nor isolating adults in communities constitutes an appropriate solution to the difficulties of Congress and the larger government of which it is a part.

Conclusion

I could not disagree more with Herb Asher and Mike Barr (1994) when they claim that "the primary responsibility for improving the reputation of Congress rests with the members themselves" (p. 36). Of course, I wish scandals would go away and the legislative process would lose some of its barnacles, but these matters do not address the core of the problem. Congress sans scandal is still quite likely to be Congress sans popularity. What is my advice then? We should entertain the possibility of visiting sensible reforms upon Congress, but not under any illusion that politics can be disgorged from Congress. The evidence suggests that Congress would be more popular with the people if it never disagreed with the president, if members never disagreed with each other, and, in fact, if members ignored any evidence that ordinary people disagree with other ordinary people. This ersatz consensus would then allow Congress to divest itself of the debates and compromises that many people find so distasteful.

The problem is that this new system of government would be anything but democratic, and if we have to choose between no democracy and a reasonably popular Congress or democracy and an unpopular Congress, the choice is obvious. The shame of it all is that, if we took a somewhat retooled approach to educating our youth and more of us made a concerted effort to recognize the challenges facing open government in an incredibly heterogeneous culture, we could have both democracy and a reasonably popular Congress—well, at least a Congress that had not lost a major portion of the public trust.

REFERENCES

Asher, Herb, and Mike Barr. 1994. "Popular Support for Congress and Its Members." In *Congress, the Press, and the Public,* ed. Thomas E. Mann and Norman J. Ornstein (pp. 15–44). Washington, DC: American Enterprise Institute/Brookings Institution.

Bennett, Steven E. 1997. "Why Young Americans Hate Politics, and What We Should Do About It." *PS: Political Science and Politics* 30 (March): 47–52.

Born, Richard. 1990. "The Shared Fortunes of Congress and Congressmen." *Journal of Politics* 52 (November): 1223–1241.

Bowman, Karlyn, and Everett Carll Ladd. 1994. "Public Opinion Toward Congress: A Historical Look." In *Congress, the Press, and the Public,* ed. Thomas E. Mann and

Norman J. Ornstein (pp. 45–58). Washington, DC: American Enterprise Institute/Brookings Institution.

Broder, David, and Richard Morin. 1994. "Why Americans Hate Congress." *Washington Post,* national weekly edition, July 11–17, pp. 6–7.

Caldeira, Gregory A., and James L. Gibson. 1992. "The Etiology of Public Support for the Supreme Court." *American Journal of Political Science* 36 (August): 635–664.

Chabot, Dana. 1996. "The Education of Skeptical Citizens." Unpublished paper, University of Indiana, Bloomington, IN.

Congressional Ethics. 1977. Washington, DC: Congressional Quarterly Press.

Dahl, Robert A. 1994. *The New American Political (Dis)Order.* Berkeley, CA: Institute of Governmental Studies Press.

Davidson, Roger H., David M. Kovenock, and Michael O'Leary. 1968. *Congress in Crisis: Politics and Congressional Reform.* Belmont, CA: Wadsworth.

Delli Carpini, Michael, and Scott Keeter. 1996. *What Americans Know About Politics and Why It Matters.* New Haven, CT: Yale University Press.

Dennis, Jack. 1973. "Public Support for American National Political Institutions." Paper presented at the Conference on Public Support for the Political System, Madison, WI (August).

Dionne, E. J., Jr. 1991. *Why Americans Hate Politics.* New York: Simon & Schuster.

Durr, Robert H., John B. Gilmour, and Christina Wolbrecht. 1997. "Explaining Congressional Approval." *American Journal of Political Science* 41 (January): 175–207.

Fallows, James. 1996. *Breaking the News: How the Media Undermine American Democracy.* New York: Pantheon.

Fenno, Richard F., Jr. 1975. "If, as Ralph Nader Says, Congress Is 'the Broken Branch,' How Come We Love Our Congressmen So Much?" In *Congress in Change: Evolution and Reform,* ed. Norman J. Ornstein (pp. 277–287). New York: Praeger.

Hibbing, John R., and Elizabeth Theiss-Morse. 1995. *Congress as Public Enemy: Public Attitudes Toward American Political Institutions.* New York: Cambridge University Press.

_____. 1996. "Civics Is Not Enough: Teaching Barbarics in K-12." *PS: Political Science and Politics* 20 (March): 57–62.

_____. 1998. "The Media's Role in Public Negativity Toward Congress: Distinguishing Emotional Reactions and Cognitive Evaluations." *American Journal of Political Science* 42 (April): 475–498.

Jacobson, Gary C., and Thomas Kim. 1996. "After 1994: The New Politics of Congressional Elections." Paper presented at the annual meeting of the Midwest Political Science Association, Chicago (April).

Kimball, David C., and Samuel C. Patterson. 1995. "Living Up to Expectations: Public Attitudes Toward Congress." Paper presented at the annual meeting of the American Political Science Association, Chicago (September).

Lipset, Seymour Martin, and William Schneider. 1987. *The Confidence Gap: Business, Labor, and Government in the Public Mind.* Baltimore: Johns Hopkins University Press.

Locke, John. 1947. *Second Treatise on Civil Government.* In *Social Contract,* ed. Ernest Barker (pp. 3–143). London: Oxford University Press. (Originally published in 1690.)

Madison, James. 1987. *Notes of Debates in the Federal Convention of 1787.* Bicentennial edition. New York: Norton. (Originally published in 1840.)

Mann, Thomas E., and Norman J. Ornstein. 1992. *Renewing Congress, A First Report.* Washington, DC: American Enterprise Institute/Brookings Institution.

Parker, Glenn R. 1981. "Can Congress Ever Be a Popular Institution?" In *The House at Work,* ed. Joseph Cooper and G. Calvin Mackenzie (pp. 31–55). Austin: University of Texas Press.

Patterson, Samuel C., Ronald D. Hedlund, and G. Robert Boynton. 1975. *Representatives and Represented: Bases of Public Support for the American Legislatures.* New York: Wiley.

Patterson, Samuel C., Randall B. Ripley, and Stephen V. Quinlan. 1992. "Citizens' Orientations Toward Legislatures: Congress and the State Legislature." *Western Political Quarterly* 45 (June): 315–338.

Polsby, Nelson W. 1968. "The Institutionalization of the U.S. House of Representatives." *American Political Science Review* 62 (March): 144–168.

Prothro, James, and Charles Grigg. 1960. "Fundamental Principles of Democracy: Bases of Agreement and Disagreement." *Journal of Politics* 22 (May): 276–294.

Putnam, Robert D. 1993. *Making Democracy Work: Civic Traditions in Modern Italy.* Princeton, NJ: Princeton University Press.

Rauch, Jonathan. 1994. *Demosclerosis.* New York: Times Books.

Rozell, Mark J. 1994. "Press Coverage of Congress, 1946–1992." In *Congress, the Press, and the Public,* ed. Thomas E. Mann and Norman J. Ornstein (pp. 59–130). Washington, DC: American Enterprise Institute/Brookings Institution.

Sniderman, Paul. 1981. *A Question of Loyalty.* Berkeley: University of California Press.

Young, John T., and Kelly D. Patterson. 1994. "Political Knowledge and Public Opinion About Congress: Does What Citizens Know Matter?" Paper presented at the annual meeting of the American Political Science Association, New York (September).

NOTES

1. Moreover, the parts of Congress identified earlier that receive public support are themselves related, even though some, like the members of Congress, receive much lower marks from the people than others, like one's own member of Congress. For details, see Born, 1990; also see Asher and Barr, 1994.

2. Thanks to my colleague Kevin Smith for bringing this point to my attention.

4

Congress and Public Trust

Is Congress Its Own Worst Enemy?

ROGER H. DAVIDSON

Belittling Congress is a venerable national pastime. Lord Bryce observed in the nineteenth century that "Americans are especially fond of running down their Congressmen." The colorful literature of congressional denigration extends from Mark Twain and Will Rogers to Jay Leno and David Letterman. Thus, the recent public displeasure with our national legislature has a long line of antecedents.

In the early 1990s Congress bore the brunt of public anger and discontent, although other institutions were by no means spared. At the height of what one lawmaker called a massive "civic temper tantrum," in the spring of 1992, only 17 percent of those questioned in a national survey approved of the way Congress was doing its job; 54 percent approved of their own representative's performance (Morin and Dewar, 1992). Both figures were all-time lows.

Although the public's anger subsided in time, Congress normally receives tepid reviews. In thirty-three Gallup polls taken between 1974 and 1995, an average of only 29.6 percent of the respondents rated Congress's performance favorably (Cook, 1995). Incumbent presidents over the same time period posted, on average, much higher ratings; only Richard Nixon, mired in the Watergate affair, sank below that level toward the end of his presidency in 1974 (Brace and Hinckley, 1992, p. 21). A more recent example was Bill Clinton, who continued to enjoy job ratings far higher than those accorded Congress despite repeated attacks on his personal and public life.

Although citizens tend to rate their own incumbent representative higher than Congress as a whole, they are not impressed with the people who make up Congress. In a recent survey, respondents agreed by a nearly two-to-one margin that the majority Republicans in Congress were out of touch with the American people (Kondracke, 1997). When asked whether most members of Congress spend more time trying to make the country better or trying to make themselves look better, the public voted four to one in favor of members' self-promotion (*National Journal*, 1997a).

Determining the source of the public's sour view of Congress is an intriguing and important question. Already a long list of suspects have surfaced in this detective story—including economic worries, campaign funding revelations, public scandals, declining "social capital," media hostility, poor leadership, Capitol Hill careerism, and on and on. Scholars and commentators are busily engaged in examining all these causes. The outcomes of their sleuthing will certainly be consequential, but it is not likely that we can do much to resolve or even alleviate the elements on which they may pin the crime.

So let us look carefully and critically to the institution of Congress itself. Is it possible that Congress's own characteristics alienate the American people and validate their feelings of distrust and even cynicism? Is Congress's way of organizing itself and doing its business responsible in part for the ambivalence so many citizens display toward it? Has Congress been careless or inattentive in setting and maintaining high standards of efficiency and ethical conduct and in policing itself and those who transgress them? Have the members of Congress—either collectively or individually—failed to explain their actions clearly and effectively to Congress's various publics?

Accordingly, let us review several of the core organizational and procedural attributes of the U.S. Congress. Our purpose is not to describe in detail how Congress and its members cope with their legislative and representational tasks. That is the job of textbooks and reference works. Rather, we need to remind ourselves of the essential characteristics of the institution with an eye to how these are likely to be conveyed to, or understood by, the average citizen.

A Complex Institution

Although extensively reported in the media, Congress is not well understood by the average American. Partly to blame are the size and complexity of the institution, not to mention the arcane twists and turns of the legislative process. The president appears as a single person who speaks and acts in a glare of publicity. Close observers know how faulty this picture can be: Internally, the White House organization is a veritable hornet's nest of contending personalities, interests, and viewpoints. The Supreme Court deliberates in private and delivers in public only the outcomes of its deliberations. Again, students of the Court dissect the opinions and other pieces of evidence to discern the justices' diverse views and frequent misgivings concerning the issues at hand.

On Capitol Hill, however, all the vagaries of interpersonal politics and policymaking are not only present but on continuous public display—the clashing egos, the sharp controversies, the self-serving rhetoric, the very messiness of it all. These very attributes of lawmaking may be what many citizens find distasteful.

Although we talk about "the Congress" as if it were a single entity, Congress is divided into two very different chambers that have similar but by no means identical internal structures. Despite claims that one or the other chamber is more important—for instance, that the Senate has more prestige, or that the House pays more attention to legislative details—the two houses staunchly defend their equal status and guard against intrusions by "the other body." On Capitol Hill, there is no "upper" or "lower" chamber.

As complex organizations faced with a demanding workload, the Senate and the House have evolved elaborate procedures for processing legislation. The typical course of a piece of legislation is long and circuitous. Many hurdles must be overcome; numerous votes must be won. Even seasoned observers are often confused about the process. Is this decision final? Will this vote later be overturned? How will the process eventually turn out? And will it ever end?

The Multiplicity of Work Groups

Both the Senate and the House of Representatives boast a large number of work groups—committees, subcommittees, task forces, party committees, informal caucuses, and factional groupings. A small number of joint bodies exist as well. In the 105th Congress (1997–1999), for example, the House had nineteen full committees and ninety-two subcommittees; the Senate had sixteen committees and sixty-eight subcommittees. There were also four joint House-Senate committees. (Two new special committees—one in each chamber—were created in 1998.) That added up to some two hundred formal work groups, containing more than three thousand members. The average senator served on nearly ten panels: three or more full committees and at least six subcommittees. Representatives claimed five assignments—two committees and three subcommittees.

Informal caucuses or voting-bloc groups outside the committee system allow members to involve themselves further in policies that interest them or affect their constituents. At least 176 informal groups and congressional member organizations operated during the 105th Congress (*Congressional Yellow Book,* 1997, pp. 1–4). Some of these are well-established organizations: for example, the Congressional Black and Hispanic Caucuses, which date from 1971 and 1976, respectively. Others, such as the Senate Footwear Caucus or the House and Senate Great Lakes Task Forces, are relatively obscure.

There are also many party committees and task forces that sometimes shape legislation. A preliminary inventory of task forces in the 105th Congress counted fifty-four of these informal groups (Oleszek, 1997). Thirty-three of these were formed by House Republicans, who even had a task force in charge of liaison with the entertainment industry (chaired by Representative Sonny Bono of California until his untimely death). "Too many!" exclaimed Majority Leader Richard Armey when I once asked him how many such groups had been formed.

On any given subject, therefore, not one but many work groups may be involved. Not too many years ago, outsiders could count on a handful of senior lawmakers—usually the chairmen of the relevant standing committees—to exert leadership in crafting major legislation and to carry the word to their colleagues.

Today a number of work groups, voting blocs, and individual members—not excluding the most junior ones—may leave their fingerprints on a piece of legislation.

The Tortuous Path of Lawmaking

As a result of the proliferation of work groups, the path of legislation through the House and Senate—always subject to twists and turns—has become even more convoluted and nearly impossible to describe to outsiders. Rather than simple bills addressed to a single purpose, today's bills are apt to be bulky, multipurpose vehicles considered by several committees. Bills may be passed without committee deliberation or even referral; jurisdictions are often stretched or trespassed; bills reported by committees may be completely reshaped by party leaders, perhaps in talks with the White House; parliamentary rules can be ignored or waived; even constitutional provisions can be circumscribed. Of 158 major bills in three recent Congresses, Barbara Sinclair (1997, pp. 72–73) found that nearly eight out of ten were subject to special procedures or practices. These "unorthodox" features included multiple referral, omnibus subject matter, a legislative-executive summit, bypassing of committees, postcommittee adjustment, and consideration under a complex or closed rule. Only one bill in ten followed the textbook process: legislation that covered a single topic, was reported by one committee, was not subject to legislative-executive summits or postcommittee changes, and was considered on the floor under an open rule. Over in the Senate, nearly half of these bills encountered at least one special or "irregular" procedure. She concludes: "The 'regular order' is no longer the norm; on major legislation it has become the exception" (p. 73).

Simple, single-purpose bills, to be sure, still tend to follow the traditional, straightforward path: from committee to floor, from House to Senate. But controversial or omnibus bills face a more unpredictable and convoluted route to passage. The ratio of the latter to the former, moreover, has shifted. Several types of minor bills—for example, private bills and commemoratives—have been curtailed; other routine bills are often loaded down with controversial provisions embodying "hot-button" political issues. Thus, recent Congresses have enacted fewer but lengthier laws than in the past. In the 80th Congress (1947–1949), more than nine hundred laws were enacted, averaging two and a half pages in length; fifty years later, only half as many laws were enacted, but their average length was more than nineteen pages (Ornstein, Mann, and Malbin, 1998, p. 167).

Thus, those familiar classroom diagrams of "how a bill becomes a law," a feature of every textbook and encyclopedia treatment, are about as accurate a guide to the legislative landscape as the Renaissance explorers' maps of the New World. The major land masses are identified and labeled, but the detailed features—of contours, distances, and alternative routes of travel—are often ignored or badly distorted. So it is with charts of the legislative process: The main features are readily conveyed to armchair travelers, but the byways and shortcuts are rarely understood, much less written about. If the diagrams still roughly capture the process for routine bills, they fail to convey the complex course followed by major or controversial legislation.

The twists and turns of federal funding for the arts for the fiscal years 1998 and 1999 illustrate a recent case in point. The National Endowment for the Arts (NEA), created in 1965, is a perennial flashpoint of controversy. To many, the NEA's annual spending (which peaked at $176 million in 1992) wastes taxpayers' money and supports controversial projects. But government support for the arts has many supporters, in local communities as well as on Capitol Hill: Most Democrats have voted for it, as have a number of Republicans, many of them northeastern moderates. The House Republican leaders who came to power in 1995 had promised conservative militants they would eliminate the NEA the very next year. They slashed its funding by 40 percent for the fiscal year 1996. When two years later the House's $13 billion Interior appropriations bill for fiscal 1998 included no funds for the agency (other than $10 million to close down operations), the stage was set for a dizzying sequence of legislative events (Freedman, 1997):

1. The "rule" permitting debate on the Interior bill was approved by a 217–216 vote only after GOP leaders spent all day twisting arms and persuaded one member to change his vote from no to yes. NEA supporters—who believed they could save the agency in an up-or-down vote—opposed the rule because it did not allow such a vote. (Fifteen Republicans and all but five Democrats voted against the rule.)
2. The next day the House rejected, 155–271, a compromise vote that the jittery leadership had included in the rule: an amendment by Representative Vernon J. Ehlers (R-MI) to eliminate the agency but send $80 million to the states in arts and education grants.
3. Four days later the House passed the Interior funding bill 238–192; many members opposed it because it eliminated the NEA. A sister agency, the National Endowment for the Humanities (NEH), would receive $110 million. (An amendment to eliminate the NEH was defeated.)
4. Later in the month the Senate Appropriations Committee voted 28–0 to approve its version of the Interior bill, which included NEA funding of $100 million.
5. The House and Senate had to come to agreement on the bill before it could be sent to the president—after the August recess. House Republican leaders were under pressure from the party's militants to hold firm. The NEA enjoyed widespread Senate support from both sides of the aisle, and its leaders sought a way to avoid a House-Senate conference. With senators coming to the rescue, the NEA's final appropriation was $98 million.

6. The following year saw a similar sequence of events for the 1999 fiscal year appropriations cycle. Again the House committee axed NEA funding and the Senate prepared to rescue it. This time, however, a House floor vote of 253–173 reversed the committee action and ensured that one way or another the agency would continue its previous year's level of funding (Seelye, 1998).

These maneuvers are not unusual for controversial issues on Capitol Hill. What was unusual was the extensive press coverage. Not a few reporters, by the way, made errors in recounting the details.

Members of Congress: Committed Partisans

The members of Congress are by and large men and women with a long-term attachment to their political party. It is, of course, possible to run as an independent, but few have been elected. In recent decades only one independent, Vermont's Representative Bernard Sanders, has served.

Like most members of the political elite in this country, members of Congress are far more fervent partisans than the people who elect them. Americans claim to spurn political parties, but the facts are somewhat more complicated. The 1996 elections found the electorate divided roughly in thirds among Democrats (34 percent), Republicans (36 percent), and independents (35 percent) (Dougherty et al., 1997, p. 58). Many who claim to be independent are in fact "closet partisans" who lean toward one party or the other. Adding these to the ranks of the two parties gives the Democrats a slight edge (47 to 42 percent), with about 11 percent being true independents. These preferences have remained surprisingly stable over the last several elections, despite short-term fluctuations.

Although many profess to be disenchanted with the two major political parties, voters recently have been following party lines. In 1996, a very partisan year, better than nine out of every ten Democrats and Republicans voted for their party's candidates. Independents' votes split fifty-fifty (Dougherty et al., 1997, p. 58). And despite rampant ticket splitting over the past three decades or so, only about 9 percent of voters in the last two presidential elections cast their ballots for the other party's candidates for president and the House of Representatives.

Once they arrive on Capitol Hill, newly elected members become immersed in an intensely partisan community. Congress is organized and led by its political parties. (There are four parties on Capitol Hill: House and Senate Republicans and Democrats.) The parties sponsor briefings for their new members. More important, the parties award committee assignments to their members. The majority party provides chairmen for all the committees and subcommittees; no minority-party members need apply. Especially in the House, the majority party draws up the rules and dictates the committees' party ratios. Although the Senate is less partisan, it too is led by the majority party leadership in tandem with the minority leadership.

Even though the American public professes disdain for party labels and resentment of excessive partisanship, the people they send to Washington are partisans who behave in a partisan fashion. In the 104th Congress (1993–1995), for example, more than six out of every ten floor votes in the House and Senate were party-line votes (that is, a majority of one party arrayed against a majority of the opposing party). The average Republican member followed his or her party on nine out of ten floor votes, and the average Democrat on eight out of ten (Carr, 1996).

People are correct when they perceive a heightened level of partisanship on Capitol Hill. Measures of party loyalty—for example, the number of party-line votes and individual members' party loyalty scores—have risen more or less steadily over the last generation. Because demographic shifts have altered their electoral bases, the parties have grown more distinct in their positions, and more militant in their policies and ideologies. One organization that has measured members' voting records over a long period is the liberal Americans for Democratic Action (ADA). In 1995—the year they took over Congress—House and Senate Republicans scored 8 and 7 percent, respectively, on the ADA's voting scale. Senate and House Democrats scored 89 and 83 percent, respectively (*Roll Call,* 1996).

One outgrowth of this robust partisanship has been the advent of congressional party "platforms," especially if the party does not control the White House (Bader, 1996). These documents lay out an agenda for legislative action with an eye to attracting voters and proving the party worthy of occupying the Oval Office. Former Speaker Jim Wright (D-TX) took charge of writing House Democrats' platforms as early as 1975. On becoming speaker in 1987, Wright announced a twelve-point agenda embracing highway construction, clean water, aid to the homeless, farm disaster relief, catastrophic health coverage, and trade legislation. He called his committee chairmen together and demanded that they report key bills on a set schedule. No modern speaker has compiled such a spectacular record. Working with his Senate counterpart, Majority Leader Robert C. Byrd (D-WV), Wright saw all but one of his major initiatives signed into law or otherwise adopted. In 1994, Republican Whip Newt Gingrich (GA) conceived and oversaw the celebrated "Contract with America," which formed the GOP agenda for the 104th Congress's first one hundred days.

Another outcome of partisan repositioning has been a shrinking ideological middle ground in the two chambers. The proportion of centrists hovered around 30 percent in the 1960s and 1970s. (Conservative Democrats and moderate Republicans, centrists are members who are closer to the ideological midpoint between the two parties than to the ideological center of their own party.) Only about one in ten of today's lawmakers fall into the centrist category (Binder, 1996). Conservative Democrats, the larger of the two centrist groupings, once accounted for one-third or more of their party's members—many of them southern "Boll Weevils." Today no more than a handful remain. Moderate to liberal

Republicans, too, account for no more than 6 percent of all House GOP members and 15 percent of GOP senators.

These partisan and ideological chasms result not only in sharp divisions in floor votes but also in harsher language and "take no prisoners" political tactics. Faced with mounting resistance within their respective parties, centrists especially have retired in droves. "I thought the essence of good government was reconciling divergent views with compromises that served the country's interests," wrote Senator Warren B. Rudman (R-NH), who retired in 1992. "But that's not how 'movement conservatives' or far-left liberals operate. The spirit of civility and compromise is drying up" (Rudman, 1996, p. 243). Many recent retirees have echoed Rudman's complaints.

Representing People, for Better or Worse

Despite the impression of some that Congress is remote and unresponsive, it is more than ever affected by the activities of individuals and groups. A plebiscitary quality has seeped into legislative life. There are simply more direct avenues of communication between constituents and lawmakers than ever before. Faxes, e-mail, the Internet, electronic "town halls," radio talk shows, and other vehicles enable citizens to engage in dialogue with their lawmakers. A better-educated electorate appears to want more opportunities to sway policy decisions. As Lawrence Grossman (1995) put it: "The people are becoming the fourth branch of government, alongside the president, the Congress and the courts. No longer is any major step taken without first testing the public's opinion; a permanent electro-cardiograph seems hooked up to the body politic" (p. 13A).

The presidency evokes images of greatness (Washington and his more illustrious successors) or obloquy (certain presidential failures). The Supreme Court deliberates in secrecy and symbolizes magisterial judgment. In contrast, the Congress is, and always has been, associated with just plain elected politicians, whether good or bad. As one former member of Congress expressed it, "Congress is a mirror in which the American people can see themselves" (Ornstein, 1993).

"People shouldn't expect those in office to be at the forefront of new developments," observed Representative Barney Frank (D-MA). "The best we can do is to be adapters. No one has the intellectual energy to be an elected official and simultaneously break new intellectual ground" (*Working Papers*, 1982, p. 43).

Reflecting the Student Body–Plus

Like any diverse group of people, the members of Congress differ in their abilities, their diligence in performing their public duties, and even in their public and private standards of conduct. Think of the houses of Congress as large-scale equivalents of a local high school or junior high class. (Except that almost all of them were inveterate student-body politicians!) There are the socialites, who are impressed by the status of their jobs; there are the jocks, the grinds and nerds, and even the class clowns. I will not name names.

The vast majority of lawmakers are earnest and ethical in their behavior, and there is no reason to think that overall ethical standards are not as high as, or higher than, at any time in history. As Norman J. Ornstein (1993) points out, "Most observers would suggest that real corruption on the Hill has in fact declined significantly over the past twenty or thirty years, whether the misbehavior is licentiousness or bribery or financial chicanery" (p. 16). Among the reasons he cites are the rising quality of members, broader scrutiny by the public, and reforms in campaign finance, disclosure, and ethics procedures.

Many people, even some who are seasoned observers, lament the low quality of public officeholders. Recently James K. Glassman (1997), former editor of the Capitol Hill newspaper *Roll Call,* bluntly voiced this viewpoint:

> Public officials, in both Congress and the executive, are of a distinctly lower quality than in the past. They have less breadth of experience, less depth and less intelligence. I don't need to name names and embarrass anyone. You know it's true. There's no Henry Stimson on the scene today; no Scoop Jackson or Sam Rayburn. (p. A15)

To be sure, recalling the glories of a past "golden age" is a recurrent theme among nostalgic pundits, cultural no less than political. But the above judgment flies in the face of thoughtful assessments of those whose memories are fortified with firsthand experience. My own close-range observation of House and Senate members goes back some thirty-five years, beginning with a doctoral thesis on the lawmaking process and, in the mid-1960s, a research project involving interviews with some 102 representatives. I encountered some legendary public servants. The first was Senator Paul H. Douglas (D-IL)—one of the Senate's giants and the principal author of the legislation I was studying. Speaker Sam Rayburn (D-TX) was no longer around, but our interview sample included the likes of former Speaker Joseph Martin (R-MA), Minority Leader Gerald R. Ford (R-MI), and Representatives Albert Rains (D-AL), Wilbur Mills (D-AR), Thomas Curtis (R-MO), and Richard Bolling (R-MO). All of these—and many more who are scarcely remembered today—came under our scrutiny.

To be sure, there were a number of far less distinguished members. Some were southerners elected from one-party districts and returned uncritically by their voters—so long as they protected local agricultural interests and engaged in a bit of race-baiting. There were also the emissaries of urban party machines, sent by their bosses to do their bidding in the nation's capital—or merely to get them out of the way. Again, I will not name names. However, Alan Ehrenhalt (1981), editor of *Governing* magazine, has given us a memorable portrait of one of them in writing about the Chicago of his boyhood: Representative John Fary of Chicago's Fifth District. When the incumbent died in 1975, Fary, a state representative, "was called into Major Richard J. Daley's office. At sixty-five, Fary had been a faithful servant of the machine, and he thought the Mayor was going to tell him it was time to retire. Instead, he was told he was going to Congress." He did, declaring on the night of his special election victory, "I will go to Washington to help represent Mayor Daley. For twenty-one years I represented the Mayor in the legislature, and he was always right" (p. 333). In Washington, Fary continued his faithful service, usually following unquestioningly the directions of House Democratic leaders. (When he ignored his party's request that he retire in 1982, he was crushed in the party's primary election.)

Few such members remain on Capitol Hill. As one member explained not long after Representative Fary arrived in the House:

> You can look around the floor of the House and see a handful—twenty years ago, you saw a lot of them—today, you can see just a handful of hacks that were put there by the party organization, and there are very, very few of them left. It is just mostly people who went out and took the election. (Bibby, 1983, p. 43)

Ethical Questions

Questions about members' personal ethics have been widely covered in the press and have colored citizens' views about the legislative branch. Why, then, do ethical problems continue to loom so large in public and media commentary about members of Congress? There are many possible answers to this question. One is that a network of laws and regulations has been erected to curb abuses by members and staff aides. More rules lead to more infractions, some of them inadvertent or careless. Second, changing standards of behavior have cast new light on issues of personal habits and conduct. Sexual misconduct and substance abuse, for example, are less tolerated today than they were a generation ago; certainly, colleagues and journalists are less inclined to look the other way. Third, the rise of investigative journalism over the past generation has increased the likelihood that ethics violations—or even allegations—will become headline news. Finally, ethics charges themselves can be weapons of political combat. Electoral foes, regulators seeking partisan advantage, or ambitious prosecutors can help elevate ethical issues in the public mind. For example, whatever the truth of the charges leveled against former House speakers Jim Wright and Newt Gingrich, it is clear that the allegations against them were raised and sustained by their political enemies for reasons of political advantage. In other words, ethics charges and countercharges have become another means of waging political warfare.

Congress Does Not Speak Up for Itself

As indispensable elements in our system of self-government, representative assemblies must communicate information about their work so that it is understood (if not always approved) by interested citizens. Although individual lawmakers communicate ceaselessly with their constituents, Congress as an institution invests little effort in making its work accessible to the public.

Congress is, of course, covered by a large press corps containing many of the nation's most skillful journalists. Capitol Hill is, after all, the best news beat in Washington. But neither reporters nor their editors seem able to convey in the mass media the internal subtleties or the external pressures that shape lawmaking.

National reporters maintain a cool, wary stance toward news sources on Capitol Hill. Following the canons of investigative journalism, many are on the lookout for scandals or evidence of wrongdoing. To the extent that they reveal bias in their work, it is the bias of the suspicious adversary (Parker, 1994). Thus, national reporters tend to be "tough" on Congress, especially through in-depth or interpretive stories. Ethical problems, congressional pay and perquisites, and junkets abroad are frequent subjects for their stories. Representative Barney Frank voiced what many of his colleagues think privately but dare not say about the media: "You people celebrate failure and ignore success. Nothing about government is done as incompetently as the reporting of it" (Aronson, 1997, p. A21).

Former Speaker Thomas S. Foley (D-WA) tells a story about press coverage of his remarks to a new member orientation session to illustrate how reporters now cover Capitol Hill (Aronson, 1997). Foley advised the freshmen to avoid the mistake of some former members who had promised perfect attendance for floor votes. You're going to miss a procedural vote now and then, he said; get it over with and don't drive yourself crazy trying to make every vote. The speaker also counseled that foreign travel, though a cheap political target, was a good way to learn about world conditions and, incidentally, get acquainted with colleagues from the opposing party. The next day's headline in his district proclaimed: "Foley Tells Freshmen: Take a Junket, Miss a Vote."

The two chambers were slow to permit direct radio or television coverage of their proceedings on a regular basis. Selected committee hearings of historical importance had, of course, been offered—for example, Senator Estes Kefauver's (D-TN) organized crime investigations (1950–1951), Senator Joseph McCarthy's (R-WI) hearings on Communist infiltration of the army (1954), and Senate and House hearings on the Watergate affair (1973–1974). Joint sessions of Congress, too, were often broadcast or televised. But live coverage of House floor proceedings dates only from 1979; Senate coverage began seven years later. In both instances, chamber staffs handle the production and camera work, with the signal transmitted to the Cable-Satellite Public Affairs Network (C-SPAN), which offers gavel-to-gavel coverage to its cable subscribers. Commercial and public radio and television outlets may also make use of the coverage at any time.

However, the televised proceedings are offered with little explanation of what is happening and what it all means. The proceedings themselves, as we have noted, can be complex and convoluted. Simplification and clarification of floor procedures could help cultivate public understanding. For example, a number of critics have proposed "Oxford-style" debates highlighting the pros and cons of a single public issue; several such debates were tried in the 103rd Congress but have not been resumed. As for legislative proceedings, the opposing views could be presented with more extensive information and commentary than they are now. This could be accomplished in a variety of ways—with additional visual messages, voice-over explanations, or independent, nonpartisan, off-the-floor commentary on the proceedings.

In other ways Congress is demonstrating greater concern for meeting public demand for information. Both chambers and most individual members now have Internet websites. At the start of the 105th Congress, House rules were changed to require that committee reports and other documents be made available electronically. In 1997 the House opened its new Legislative Resource Center, which brings together several informational services in a central location convenient for staff and visitors.

Even as citizens profess indifference to their governmental institutions, they continue to make pilgrimages to the U.S. Capitol. Most visitors return home having gleaned a few interesting historical tidbits of information but little or no understanding of the nature or work of Congress. There is no central point where visitors can learn about the Capitol and receive information on how to get around and ascertain what interests them. Few Capitol Hill buildings have space devoted to attractive, informative displays. The tours of the U.S. Capitol itself are long on historical trivia and short on real explanation of the work that goes on in the building. A small stand (operated by the U.S. Capitol Historical Society) sells a variety of souvenirs but lacks the space to display a wider range of books, documents, and mementos. A Capitol visitors' center, still under consideration but years short of realization, may be the major positive outcome of the gunman's attack that took place in the Capitol Building in July 1998.

On a visit to Australia's New Parliament House in Canberra several years ago, I encountered many elements that could well be emulated on Capitol Hill. Knowledgeable guides talked about the legislative process as well as the physical features of the Parliament House. Several full-color brochures on Parliament House, the House of Representatives, the Senate, and the committee system were freely available. A well-stocked tourist shop offered not only T-shirts but many attractive pamphlets about government and a small but thoughtful selection of books on Australian politics and society.

Conclusion

Congress's unpopularity may well be rooted in its own structures and procedures. As we have noted, Congress is a complex institution; it is composed of ambitious and for the most part dedicated partisans; and it airs its conflicts and its dilemmas before the public in written electronic records. Moreover, at the same time that individual legislators proclaim their stewardship before their home audiences, many of these same members routinely denigrate the institution of Congress.

Can Congress simplify its organization and procedures? Can it make a better effort to convey its deliberations to various publics? The answer is yes. Although Congress cannot transform itself into a simple organization—it is too large and must respond to too many demands—it could significantly streamline the organization it has. Consolidation of committee jurisdictions and limits on memberships on those committees could simplify the committee structure and make its processing of legislation more understandable. Limiting members' seats on committees would channel their energies into their committees' subject matter.

Organizational fixes, however, will not go very far in improving the public's image of Congress. But the two chambers could redouble their effort to make their public deliberations more understandable and compelling to the average citizen. This might well mean restructuring debate on major issues and eliminating unnecessary delays in floor proceedings. Moreover, Congress could move to present itself more forthrightly to the citizens who visit Capitol Hill and to those who follow the deliberations over C-SPAN. The attitudes of such people are critically important to Congress's reputation. They must be engaged by congressional information and news if the institution is to revive its standing with the general public.

References

Aronson, Bernard. 1997. "Tired of 'Gotcha' Journalism." *Washington Post,* March 6, p. A21.

Bader, John B. 1996. *Taking the Initiative: Leadership Agendas in Congress and the "Contract with America."* Washington, DC: Georgetown University Press.

Bibby, John F., ed. 1983. *Congress off the Record: The Candid Analysis of Seven Members.* Washington, DC: American Enterprise Institute.

Binder, Sarah. 1996. "The Disappearing Political Center." *Brookings Review* 15 (Fall): 36–39.

Brace, Paul, and Barbara Hinckley. 1992. *Follow the Leader: Opinion Polls and the Modern Presidents.* New York: Basic Books.

Carr, Rebecca. 1996. "GOP's Election-Year Worries Cooled Partisan Rancor." *Congressional Quarterly Weekly Report,* December 21, pp. 3432–3435.

Congressional Yellow Book. 1997. Washington, DC: Leadership Directories (Summer).

Cook, Charles E. 1995. "Voters Sense Less Gridlock, Increase Congress Approval." *Roll Call,* February 9, p. 8.

Dougherty, Regina, Everett C. Ladd, David Wilber, and Lynn Zayachkinsky, eds. 1997. *America at the Polls 1996.* Storrs, CT: Roper Center.

Ehrenhalt, Alan, ed. 1981. *Politics in America: Members of Congress in Washington and at Home.* Washington, DC: Congressional Quarterly Press.

Freedman, Allan. 1997. "Elimination of NEA Squeaks By as House Passes Interior Rule." *Congressional Quarterly Weekly Report,* July 12, pp. 1616–1618.

Glassman, James K. 1997. "Washington's Irrelevance." *Washington Post,* July 29, p. A15.

Grossman, Lawrence. 1995. "Beware the Electronic Republic." *USA Today,* August 25, p. 13A.

Kondracke, Morton M. 1997. "GOP's 'Blade Runner' Disease: Programmed for Self-Destruction?" *Roll Call,* July 24, p. 5.

National Journal. 1997a. March 17, p. 524.

_____. 1997b. April 26, p. 842.

Morin, Richard, and Helen Dewar. 1992. "Approval of Congress Hits All-Time Low, Poll Finds." *Washington Post,* March 20, A16.

Oleszek, Walter J. 1997. "Task Forces in the House 104th Congress." Unpublished paper, Congressional Research Service.

Ornstein, Norman J. "Prosecutors Must End Their Big Game Hunt of Politicians." *Roll Call,* April 26, 1993, p. 16.

Ornstein, Norman J., Thomas E. Mann, and Michael J. Malbin, eds. 1998. *Vital Statistics on Congress, 1997–1998.* Washington, DC: Congressional Quarterly, Inc.

Parker, Kimberly Coursen. 1994. "How the Press Views Congress." In *Congress, the Press, and the Public,* ed. Thomas E. Mann and Norman J. Ornstein (pp. 157–170). Washington, DC: Brookings Institution.

Roll Call. 1996. "Vanishing Liberals?" February 8, p. 4.

Rudman, Warren B. 1996. *Combat: Twelve Years in the U.S. Senate.* New York: Random House.

Seelye, Katherine Q. 1998. "In Election Year, House Authorizes Financing of Arts." *New York Times,* July 22, p. A1.

Sinclair, Barbara. 1997. *Unorthodox Lawmaking: New Legislative Processes in the U.S. Congress.* Washington, DC: Congressional Quarterly Press.

Working Papers. 1982. "Lessons on Opposition" (interview with Barney Frank) (May–June).

5

How Good People Make Bad Collectives

A Social-Psychological Perspective on Public Attitudes Toward Congress

DIANA C. MUTZ

GREGORY N. FLEMMING

Just like Garrison Keillor's description of Lake Wobegon, we live in a country where all of our citizens, their families, their hometowns, and their congressional representatives are above average—or at least, so our perceptions suggest. At the same time, the public's level of trust in Congress is considered a national disgrace. As Senator William Proxmire (D-WI) observed, "I have yet to hear one kind word, one whisper of praise, one word of sympathy for the Congress as a whole" (*Congressional Record*, 1987, pp. S11918–11919).

This chapter explores the well-known disjuncture between the public's generally positive perceptions of its individual congressional representatives and its quite negative perceptions of Congress as a collective. Although this is well-trodden ground in the literature on attitudes toward Congress, our approach emphasizes a social-psychological perspective that arrives at a unique set of explanations. These ideas are not meant to contradict so much as to complement previous explanations that have been offered for this puzzle, and to offer new insights to academics, politicians, and political observers on how to understand and interpret this recurrent finding.

Most writing on what has become known as "Fenno's paradox"—people holding positive views of their individual members of Congress while professing more negative views of congressional members as a collective—suggests explanations that are Congress-specific. For example, in his original description of this puzzle, Fenno (1975) proposed that the disparity occurs because people use fundamentally different standards of judgment for individuals and institutions. Their expectations of their individual members are rooted in constituency service, whereas the body as a whole is expected to solve national problems—a far more intractable task. Members may work well individually in providing representation and/or constituency service yet still fail to produce the outcome expected of the collective unit as a whole (Asher and Barr, 1994; Cook, 1979; Ripley et al., 1992). In addition, Fenno (1975) noted the inherent complexity of Congress and its committee structure, and the fact that the public frequently changes its mind about the kind of Congress it wants. All of these considerations were suggested as contributions to differential satisfaction with Congress and individual incumbents.

Fenno's remarks were based on observations during his travels with ten House members during the early 1970s, but the passage of time and the accumulation of extensive polling data have only affirmed the robustness of those early observations. Figure 5.1 illustrates some of the more recent evidence of this ongoing disparity using identically worded national survey questions. Based on parallel questions from the American National Election Studies (ANES) from 1980 to the present,[1] people are consistently and significantly more positive toward their individual members of Congress than they are toward members of Congress as a collective. Although judgments of Congress's performance do predict individual members' reputations (see Born, 1990), the overall levels of support for these entities remain quite different.

In principle, there are three ways people can evaluate Congress and its members. First, they can think about their own representatives; second, they can think about all 435 members of Congress collectively; finally, they can think about Congress as an *institution*. But people seem to draw a relatively sharp distinction between Congress as an institution, which gets fairly positive ratings, and the 435 members of Congress collectively, who receive quite negative ratings (Hibbing and Theiss-Morse, 1995). This makes the initial paradox all the more puzzling, since approval of the aggregate of individual members should logically coincide with the average approval of members. As shown in Figure 5.1, it clearly does not.

In this chapter, we propose a complementary explanation for Fenno's paradox that is both simpler and far broader in its implications than those previously offered. Ultimately, this explanation tells us something important about how the public processes information about Congress and its representatives in today's media environment. It also illuminates how members of Congress from districts with different kinds of media environments face quite different challenges in cultivating constituent support.

The Generality of Fenno's Paradox

Our point of departure in this chapter is the observation that the pattern of positive attitudes toward things local and personal, combined with more negative attitudes toward aggregates of those very same entities, is not specific to Congress;

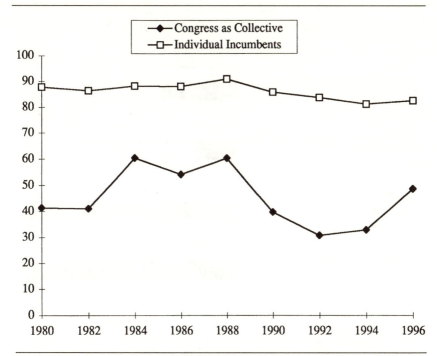

FIGURE 5.1   Trends in Approval of Incumbents and Congress as a Collective,
1980–1996

SOURCE: American National Election Studies, 1980–1996.
Congress as collective: "Do you approve or disapprove of the way the U.S. Congress has been handling its job?"
Individual incumbents: "In general, do you approve or disapprove of the way (U.S. House of Representatives incumbent) has been handling his/her job?"

it is part of a far more general social-psychological tendency with roots in how people process information. In fact, across a broad range of topics and in other countries besides the United States, positive evaluations of things personal and local are very consistently coupled with negative evaluations of those very same entities as large-scale collectives.

In other words, members of Congress are not alone in this regard. For example, people's assessments of their own doctors are systematically more positive than their assessments of doctors in general (Jacobs and Shapiro, 1994). Figure 5.2 shows the responses people gave when they were asked four identically worded questions about their own doctors and about their perceptions of other people's doctors. An overwhelming majority agreed that their own doctors spent enough time with them, but simultaneously claimed that doctors in general did not spend enough time with their patients. Likewise, a full 80 percent agreed that doctors were too interested in making money, but under half thought that their own doctors were too interested in making money. And though nearly 80 percent

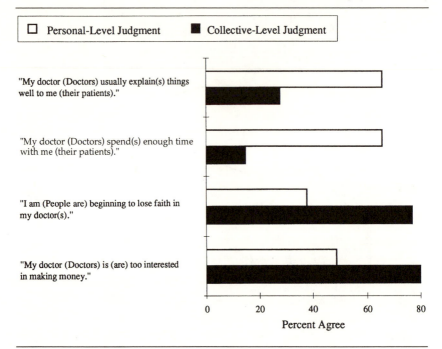

FIGURE 5.2   Personal- and Collective-Level Judgments about Health Care

SOURCE: American Medical Association, "Public Opinion on Health Care Issues," cited in Jacobs and Shapiro (1994). Words in parentheses correspond to collective-level wording of same question.

agreed that people were beginning to lose faith in doctors, under 40 percent agreed that they were beginning to lose faith in their own doctors.

This disjuncture between judgments made at the personal and collective levels has shown up again and again in patterns of public attitudes. Probably the most conspicuous and extensively documented examples come from the economic realm: People very consistently rate their own economic situation in a systematically more positive light than the national economic situation. Figure 5.3 illustrates one of many examples of this pattern drawing on two economic questions, one about the condition of the national economy and the other about the respondent's own economic situation. How can the collective logically be faring differently from the sum of its individual experiences? Despite its implausibility, across a wide range of studies with quite different purposes, this pattern maintains. Moreover, as with judgments about Congress, this disjuncture runs in a highly consistent direction, with perceptions at the collective level persistently more negative than personal-level judgments. Figure 5.3 summarizes over four hundred such comparisons from data collected between 1986 and 1996. At first glance, what is most striking about this series is its demonstration that over an entire ten-year period perceptions of collective conditions have consistently and without exception been more negative

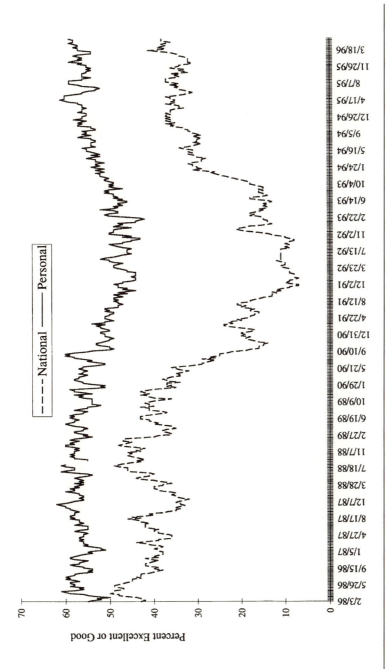

FIGURE 5.3   Rating of Personal and National Economic Conditions, 1986–1996

SOURCE: Based on weekly data from *ABC News/Money* magazine, four-week rolling averages.
National: "Would you describe the state of the nation's economy these days as excellent, good, not so good, or poor?"
Personal: "Would you describe the state of your personal finances these days as excellent, good, not so good, or poor?"

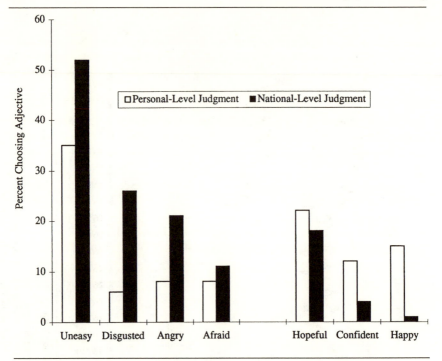

FIGURE 5.4   Personal- and Collective-Level Economic Judgments in the United Kingdom

SOURCE: Social Surveys (Gallup Poll) Ltd., April 15–21, 1993.
    "Please look at this card and tell me if any of the words on it describe your feelings about the country's general economic situation. If yes, which ones? Please look at this card again and tell me if any of the words on it describe your feelings about the financial condition of your household. If yes, which ones?"

than people's perceptions of their personal financial condition. In good economic times and bad, the gap remains. Although the majority of people have consistently rated national conditions as either "not so good" or "poor," more than 50 percent of the public consistently has rated their personal financial condition as "good" or "excellent." Not once during this entire ten-year period were people more pessimistic about their personal situation than about the nation as a whole.

Figure 5.4 presents evidence suggesting that this phenomenon is not even peculiarly American. When citizens of the United Kingdom were asked which adjectives described their feelings about their country's economy and which of these same terms applied to their feelings about the financial condition of their own household, a similar pattern appeared. On the left-hand side of the figure, four negative adjectives were systematically endorsed more often in the context of the national economy. The right-hand side of the figure shows that three positive adjectives were systematically endorsed more often to describe feelings surrounding people's personal financial condition.

The compartmentalization of personal and collective views also is consistent with a great deal of data drawn from noneconomic issues documenting the relative independence of personal- and collective-level judgments. For example, women's views about general discrimination in women's wages are not related to judgments about their own wages (Major, 1982). Likewise, estimates of the personal risk of rape have nothing to do with the number of rapes women perceive to be occurring (Gordon et al., 1980). Estimates of personal crime risks more generally also were found to be unrelated to judgments about the frequency or seriousness of crime in several major cities (Tyler, 1980); the same pattern has been replicated for other social problems as well (Tyler and Cook, 1984). In other words, studies of the psychological compartmentalization of personal and collective concerns have independently come to conclusions that jibe nicely with Fenno's paradox (for a review, see Tyler and Lavrakas, 1985): Perceptions of collectives often do not mirror the aggregate of people's personal experiences with the things that make up those collectives.

The same personal optimism extends to assessments of local entities. Regardless of whether one considers the issue of crime, racism, poverty, drug abuse, unemployment, violence, or declining moral standards, the consensus across the nation is that these problems are far more serious problems nationally than locally. As shown in Figure 5.5, respondents perceived seven of the nine issues to be between "a small problem" and "somewhat of a problem" for their communities, but somewhere between "a big problem" and "somewhat of a problem" for society as a whole. Like Fenno's paradox, this is obvious evidence of a logical inconsistency: Not all of the communities constituting the nation as a whole can be doing well while the collective is faring poorly.

The examples of this pattern are so numerous that not all of them need to be recounted here. Collectives of many different kinds tend to be perceived more negatively than the sum of their individual components. The point to be gleaned from these examples is that this phenomenon is sufficiently general that it may have relatively little to do with the peculiarities of Congress per se. For example, the idea that people have fundamentally different expectations of their local representatives (constituency service) and the collective body (policymaking) makes a great deal of sense and undoubtedly has some merit. But it is clearly not the whole story. For example, the same logic cannot easily be applied to the example in Figure 5.2: Doctors do not work as a collective in curing patients; thus, there is no easy explanation for the disparity between people's attitudes toward their own doctors and doctors collectively. Nor does it make sense that the economy could be in decline while the aggregate of people's personal economic situations is improving. Since the state of the economy is typically defined in terms of the collective well-being of the aggregate, plausible explanations are again lacking. Explanations for Fenno's paradox may have focused on the peculiarities of Congress and its complexity when more basic psychological processes are also at work. Indeed, if that were the only reason for this disparity, we would not see it in so many different areas of judgment.

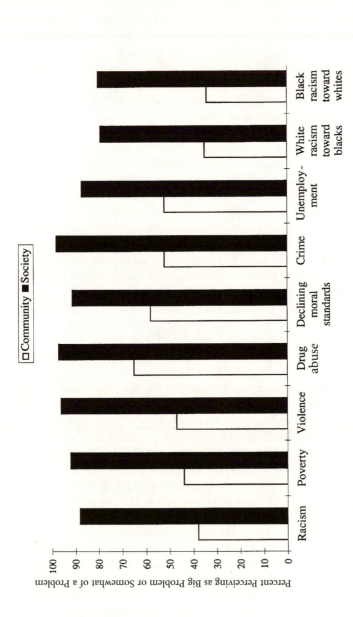

FIGURE 5.5   Perceived Severity of Community and Societal Problems

SOURCE: *Washington Post* national survey of 1,016 adults, June 28–July 2, 1996.
   Community: "What about in the community where you live? How big a problem is (the issue) in your community? Is it a big problem, somewhat of a problem, a small problem, or not a problem at all?"
   Society: "How big a problem are each of the following issues in our society today? How big a problem is (the issue) in our society today? Is it a big problem, somewhat of a problem, a small problem, or not a problem at all?"

How Good People Make Bad Collectives:
Origins of the Disjuncture

Having established the generality of Fenno's paradox and the fact that it is an exceedingly common pattern even outside of the congressional arena, we turn our attention to explanations for why this pattern of judgments occurs. How do people who are evaluated relatively positively as individuals become regarded far less admiringly as a collective? Given the generality of the pattern, one natural place to look is in basic human psychology, and particularly in what we know about how people process information. A second likely possibility is that the disparity is spawned by reliance on fundamentally different sources of information for what we know about things local and personal, on the one hand, and about large-scale phenomena, on the other. In the remaining portions of this chapter we discuss evidence pertaining to the role of perceptual biases and of information sources in altering levels of public esteem for Congress and its members.

The highly negative collective-level evaluations of Congress have received the most scholarly attention and have also been the focus of tremendous public hand-wringing. Members of Congress understandably prefer to focus on the more positive evaluations they receive as individuals. But theoretically this disparity could result from factors that bias attitudes toward Congress as a collective in a negative direction, from factors that bias attitudes toward individual members in a positive direction, or from some combination thereof. For this reason, we explore in turn each of these possibilities and its applicability to evaluations of Congress.

The Negative Perceptual Bias

An overly pessimistic outlook on Congress as a collective results at least in part from simple cognitive errors. For example, think about the mental processes that people might go through when asked to evaluate Congress as a collective. One possibility is that a person first makes separate judgments about each of the members, then mentally sums these up and divides by 435 to produce an average summary evaluation. Obviously, this procedure is ridiculously cumbersome at best. Instead, citizens are likely to use far more reasonable and economical mental procedures to arrive at a summary judgment. One likely alternative is that they mentally sample from a small number of individual cases, and then infer what the collective as a whole is like from the specific examples that they generate in their minds.

The problem with this procedure is that not all members of Congress are equally likely to spring to mind when someone is mentally generating examples. Media coverage is likely to make some members more accessible in memory than others. In particular, those who have received extensive national media attention are most likely to come to people's minds. To the extent that bad deeds receive more attention than good ones, this coverage is likely to be negative. And even if the media covered the good deeds of Congress as much as its scandals, the negative examples may be more likely to come to mind when people sample from what they know about Congress as a collective.

In other contexts, biased sampling has been shown to explain more negative evaluations of "average" or collective others of several kinds. People's mental samples of others who serve as the basis for judgments of this kind become more and more negatively biased the more vaguely these others are defined. In other words, when people are asked to evaluate vaguely defined "others," such as the collective members of Congress, they tend to think about prototypes of particular individuals who make up that body. In contrast, when people are forced to think about a specific other, the negatively biased perception disappears (Perloff and Fetzer, 1986).

All in all, this research suggests that the mental sampling that people do when evaluating the collective is simply not representative. Thus, a citizen can evaluate his or her own congressional representative relatively positively on the whole yet simultaneously evaluate the collective negatively because people tend to remember the same two or three well-publicized bad apples when they are generating their sample on which the collective evaluation is based.

The Positive Perceptual Bias

A negative perceptual bias in evaluating the collective is not the only likely source of Fenno's paradox. In fact, considerable evidence also suggests that assessments of things personal and local are biased in an overly positive direction. An unrealistically optimistic personal bias has been widely noted in perceptions of risk, and it is consistent across studies of a large number of potential hazards (Weinstein, 1980, 1989). For example, people judge themselves and those close to them to be less likely than others to be victims of diseases such as cancer, heart disease, pneumonia, and alcoholism. They also think they will live longer than the actuarial averages suggest, even when directly handed this information. People think they are less likely than average to get divorced, to be in an automobile accident, and so forth. This optimistic personal bias is not limited to potential hazards: People also think that positive events are more likely to happen to them personally—for example, that they are more likely than average to receive a raise.

Two general types of explanations have been offered for this positivity bias. Motivational explanations stress the idea that pessimism about things close to home threatens people's feelings of competence and self-worth, so they are compelled to make overly positive assessments either to shield themselves from fear or to protect their egos (Weinstein, 1989). For example, people generally exaggerate their uniqueness (Funder, 1980), and many psychologists argue that this tendency is a quite useful protective response with positive implications for mental health (Alloy and Abramson, 1980; Taylor, 1982). Likewise, there may well be psychological benefits in feeling that one's own city or neighborhood is uniquely friendly or pleasant, or that one's congressional representative is uniquely honest, competent, and well-meaning (Burger, 1981; Schlenker and Miller, 1977). We have a psychological vested interest in believing that we and those linked to us are above average, and our feelings about our congressional representative may be an outgrowth of that same motivation. When people evaluate themselves or things close to home, they generally engage in downward social comparisons, choosing others who make them look relatively better off.

As with the negative bias in assessing collectives, cognitive errors also may play a role in promoting positive assessments of one's own representative. When asked to evaluate one's congressional representative and how well he or she is doing, there is always an implicit comparison being made. Good compared to what? People may go about judging their own representative in a way that makes direct use of their perceptions of what other representatives are like. To the extent that we compare our representative with ones who have been involved in scandals or who have received negative national media attention, we are apt to see our own member as uniquely good.

A complete explanation of the gap between these types of evaluations probably requires a combination of ego-defensive motivations and cognitive biases, as when cancer patients make themselves feel better by constructing "hypothetical worse worlds" in their minds in which they are relatively well off (Taylor, Wood, and Lichtman, 1983, p. 31). So, too, people may be motivated to engage in downward comparisons when it comes to their incumbent congressperson. The local representative may not look particularly outstanding in a vacuum, but compared with the biased sample of members who come to mind—probably as a result of recent national press attention—he or she could look like a real standout.

In short, basic psychological processes are at work to create a disparity between attitudes toward Congress and attitudes toward congressional representatives. These processes produce a disparity between evaluations of things personal and collective in other realms and professions as well as with Congress. The bias toward greater positivity in evaluating things close to us probably serves an important ego-defensive function (Weinstein, 1987), but the disparity between evaluations of Congress and individual representatives probably also stems from a bias in the mental sampling procedures that people use when trying to summarize their attitudes toward all 435 members.

It is important to note that to date this type of research has been conducted entirely on topics other than Congress, but one can easily imagine parallel studies that would tap into the kinds of social comparison processes that people use when asked to evaluate Congress. The size and overall consistency of this ongoing gap makes it clear that even in the face of quite different objective circumstances, people tend to believe that their personal and local world is in better shape than the collective in which they share membership. In contrast, pessimistic biases are very rare at the personal level. Whatever the underlying causes, this pattern is exceedingly common.

Sources of Information About Congress

Perceptual biases undoubtedly play some role in creating and maintaining Fenno's paradox, but differences in the origins of information about one's local member of Congress and about Congress as a whole have also contributed to this gap. Information about the local incumbent comes primarily from local newspaper coverage and, to a lesser extent, from local television coverage. In contrast, information about members outside of one's own district and about Congress as a collective tends to originate with national news produced by journalists who work for a relatively small number of large media organizations. The amount of news about Congress generated by national media organizations is naturally far greater than the amount of news any local media outlet generates about any given individual congressperson.

The differential amounts of available information are reflected in the relative volatility of judgments about incumbents and Congress as a collective. Little information leads to relatively stable judgments, while heavy flows of information contribute to greater ups and downs. As the over-time trends in Figure 5.1 illustrate, evaluations of Congress have been subject to dramatic upswings and downturns in the last twenty years, while the public's evaluations of their congressional representatives have remained relatively stable over time in the aggregate, just as one would predict given the meager news attention that individual congressional representatives receive. It takes large amounts of information to alter people's judgments, and with a few notable exceptions, members of Congress do not garner that much attention on an ongoing basis.

Thus, for most Americans, information about the incumbent originates from completely different news sources than news about members outside the district and news about Congress as a whole. National coverage includes a good deal of coverage of the collective body and its conflicts and deliberations as well as coverage of individual members outside of the reader's or viewer's district. Since this same national information is distributed to even relatively small newspapers throughout the country, Americans in the 1990s receive basically the same national news regardless of where they live (see, for example, Mondak, 1995). The rise of wire services and of syndicated coverage of national affairs has promoted a great deal of homogeneity in coverage of national politics, even when it is relayed through local newspapers.

National news coverage about Congress as a collective has become progressively more negative in recent decades (see, for example, Lichter and Amundson, 1984; Patterson, 1994; Rozell, 1994). The very kind of conflict, disagreement, and debate that Hibbing (this volume) points to suits contemporary news values all too well (see also Robinson and Appel, 1979; Tidmarch and Pitney, 1985). The public may dislike hearing about endless conflict among members of Congress (Hibbing and Theiss-Morse, 1995), but for journalists the drama is the stuff of good news stories. Moreover, some recent evidence shows that approval of Congress as a collective declines in response to veto overrides, the passage of major bills, and intra-Congress conflict—in other words, when it is doing precisely what it is supposed to do as a representative and legislative body (Durr, Gilmour, and Wolbrecht, 1997). News coverage naturally seizes on the contentiousness and conflict inherent in resolving the views of representatives of a large and increasingly heterogeneous country.

When individual members receive attention in the national press, does it generally help or hurt their individual reputations? The pattern of results from recent studies is consistent with the idea that national attention to individual members is also becoming increasingly negative. For example, a study using data from 1970 and 1972 found some positive effects of national prominence on electoral support (Payne, 1980). But similar assessments from 1978 and 1980 found no consistent effects (Cook, 1987). The most recent effort to examine the effects of national coverage on support for individual members found no effects from 1982 through 1988, and then significant negative effects from 1990 through 1996 (Niven and Zilber, 1998). If national coverage was once a boon to the reputations of individual members, it may no longer be. National news attention appears to focus greater attention on the shortcomings of Congress's representatives than on the virtues of its star members. Since evaluations of Congress as a collective are subject to a strong sampling bias, national coverage that shows even a few individual members in a bad light can prime these examples in people's minds, thus producing a large effect on evaluations of the collective.

In contrast to the relative homogeneity of national news, the tone of local coverage varies from place to place and from newspaper to newspaper. In particular, large urban areas served by big-city newspapers are known to exhibit very different attitudes toward coverage of their public officials relative to small-town local newspapers. Local journalists often play a "booster" role, helping to promote their communities as wonderful places to live and work (Griffith, 1989, 1995; Kanis, 1991). Media in smaller communities also tend to report fewer conflicts and less social upheaval than newspapers in urban areas (Janowitz, 1952; Olien, Donahue, and Tichenor, 1968). In their study of small-town life, Vidich and Bensman (1968) acknowledged the newspaper's role in promoting perceptions of the superiority of local life:

> The newspaper always emphasizes the positive side of life; it never reports local arrests, shotgun weddings, mortgage foreclosures, lawsuits, bitter exchanges in public meetings, suicides or any other unpleasant happening. By this constant focus on warm and human qualities in all public situations, the public character of the community takes on those qualities and, hence, it has a tone which is distinctly different from city life. (p. 31)

Although many of the studies documenting relatively rosy local press coverage are somewhat dated, some more recent studies have corroborated these findings. For example, Stone, Hertung, and Jensen (1987) found local television news to be less negative than network news broadcasts. Likewise, Martin and Mutz (1997) found that residents of small towns were even more positive about the extent to which various social problems plagued their communities than the relatively low real-world incidence of these problems within their communities would justify. Although local communities are not all cut from the same cloth when it comes to the tone of local press coverage, bias tends to be in an overly positive direction.

In short, journalists in smaller communities are more reluctant to cover ostensibly "bad news" about their community, and this same attitude extends to coverage of their congressional representatives. The positivity of small-town journalists is not due exclusively, however, to boosterish attitudes. It also stems from the often meager resources that smaller newspapers have for digging up their own original news stories. Without the resources to generate an original, and potentially unflattering, story about the incumbent, small newspapers must rely on the information provided to them in news releases from the individual members, and this information inevitably casts the member in a positive light. It is for this reason that local media coverage is assumed to be highly attractive to House members (Cook, 1987, 1988). Television pays relatively little attention to local congressional representatives, so outside of direct mail efforts, newspapers provide the bulk of mass mediated information to constituents about their representatives.

Nonetheless, "local" coverage can mean something quite different for an incumbent in a large metropolitan area. In areas that support large media markets, the local paper may have the resources to do a great deal more investigative and enterprising reporting, resulting in less boosterish coverage. Figure 5.6 examines these assertions about the importance of local news sources to congressional approval, drawing on 1988 American National Election Studies data, the most recent data that include parallel approval measures for Congress as a collective and for individual incumbents, plus questions about the name of the newspaper that the respondent reads most often. These data allowed us to differentiate those who read large, typically urban newspapers from those who read small local newspapers.

In this figure, levels of approval for Congress as a collective are only negligibly different between readers of high- versus low-circulation papers. The small differences result from sampling error rather than any systematic difference between the information provided by these two types of newspapers. In other words, people are all getting roughly the same tone of information when it comes to news about the collective and about members outside of their own district.

In contrast, there is a highly significant difference in levels of incumbent approval for those who read low- as opposed to high-circulation newspapers. As anticipated, those reading smaller newspapers from more rural areas are significantly more positive in evaluating their incumbents than are those who get their

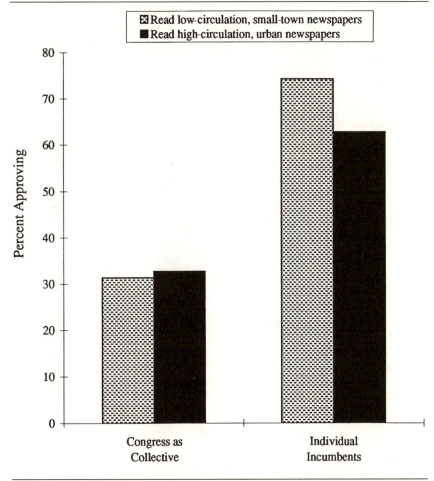

FIGURE 5.6   Approval of Congress by Newspaper Readership

SOURCE: American National Election Studies, 1988.

information from large urban newspapers. There is a gap in approval of more than ten percentage points between readers of these two kinds of newspapers.

Figure 5.7 shows that these differences are not a function of political party. As in the sample as a whole, there were no differences in how the two types of readers evaluated Congress as a collective, but there were large differences in how they evaluated their local incumbents. Consistent with the idea that smaller papers generally provide more positive coverage of their elected officials, among Republicans, Democrats, and independents, those reading small local newspapers were consistently more positive in their approval of their representatives. Of course, there are other differences between the kinds of people who read low- and

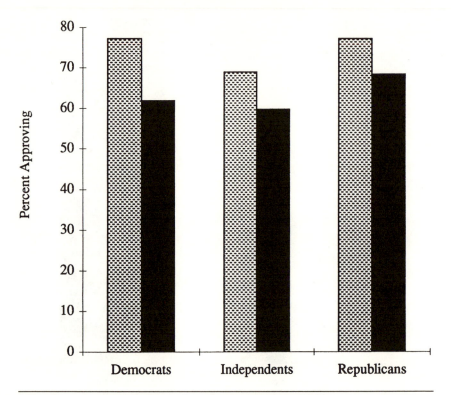

FIGURE 5.7   Evaluation of Incumbents by Newspaper Readership

SOURCE: American National Election Studies, 1988.

high-circulation newspapers that might account for these differences. Most obviously, education levels are generally lower in smaller towns and rural areas; thus, education might explain why those who read high-circulation newspapers are more likely to be critical of their incumbents. But this same pattern of differences between those reading high- and low-circulation newspapers holds up equally well among those with a high school diploma or less as with those who have received a college education. In other words, additional analyses suggest that this pattern of findings persists even when the usual statistical controls for demographic explanations are included.

Unless one buys the idea that members of Congress representing more rural areas are inherently more virtuous than those representing larger urban areas, where they are likely to be covered by high-circulation newspapers, then it is likely that the local newspaper's size and resources have a great deal to do with the challenges that face an incumbent attempting to cultivate support in his or her district. For those whose constituents rely primarily on small-town newspapers, the task is relatively easy. But for those who represent primarily urban districts, where many constituents rely on high-circulation metropolitan newspapers, it can be quite difficult to achieve the same levels of constituent approval.

The Implications of Compartmentalized Political Attitudes

This chapter has made two relatively simple observations about levels of public approval of Congress and its incumbents. Attitudes toward Congress are a function both of the type of information that reaches people and of how that information is processed by the individuals who receive it. The implications of human perceptual biases in the processing of information are fairly straightforward: Even if the national media were to become overwhelming positive in their portrayals of Congress, this probably would not erase the paradox that Fenno observed. The contemporary gap between approval of incumbent members of Congress and approval of Congress as a collective results at least in part from human perceptual biases. It is something that has probably been with us long before Fenno's observations or the first public opinion poll. How people process information about things close to them is fundamentally different from how they process mediated information about large, distant, and impersonal collectives.

Unflattering public attitudes toward political institutions may be more likely to arise in a country where the national media system is well developed and the organizations of government are large, complex, and distant from the affairs of day-to-day life. Evaluations of government and political leaders at the local level seem to support this idea. For example, people's ratings of local government tend to be systematically more positive than those of state government, which tend to be more positive than attitudes directed toward the federal government (Conlan, 1993). Likewise, the drop in confidence from the early 1970s to the early 1990s was greatest for the federal government (32 percent), smaller for state government (16 percent), and least of all for local government (4 percent).

To the extent that one feels that negative attitudes toward the collective are deleterious—and there are clear disagreements on this issue—one should probably also consider the negative public attitudes toward a variety of different kinds of collectives besides Congress. Indeed, the "hell in a handbasket" mentality regarding Congress is part of a broader fabric of compartmentalization that characterizes contemporary society. For example, in a Carnegie Foundation study of college seniors' views of the future, they reported the prospects for the state of the nation as very bleak: The ozone layer was being destroyed, nuclear war was going to break out, and so forth. When these same students were asked about the prognosis for their own future, the results were quite different: They were going to obtain good educations, prestigious jobs, make a lot of money, and live well—never mind the ozone layer or the pesky nuclear war (Levine, 1980).

The truth is likely to be somewhere in between the extreme negativity of judgments about the nation as a collective and our overly optimistic evaluations of things local and personal. Ideally we would like to bridge the gap between how people perceive their immediate lives and communities and how they perceive the nation and its institutions—in other words, to bridge the personal and the political. In order to do this, however, educational efforts need to consider not only *what* people know about Congress but also *how* they know it. Simply throwing more information at the problem is unlikely to work. For example, teaching *about* Congress—its conflict, messiness, complexities, and so forth—is probably not enough to bridge the gap because even that information will be processed as information about that distant and distasteful group in far-off Washington. As Palmer (1987) notes, for the most part students "have always been taught about a world out there somewhere apart from them, divorced from their personal lives; they have never been invited to intersect their autobiographies with the life story of the world. And so they can report on a world that is not the one in which they live" (p. 22).

Efforts to convince people that political conflict is an inevitable, acceptable, and even desirable part of the democratic process first need to confront the fact that Americans do not just dislike conflict and messiness in Congress, they also dislike it in their own lives. They regularly avoid face-to-face political discussions with those with whom they anticipate political disagreement (see, for example, MacKuen, 1990). Even civics classrooms seldom incorporate a great deal of open conflict, except of the variety where students are assigned to debate arbitrary positions that they are unlikely to feel particularly passionate about. It is only when conflict incorporates both the personal and the political that students learn the very difficult and unintuitive art of respecting those with whom they may passionately disagree. College students can vigorously support their school's athletic teams and rarely think that those who cheer for the opposing team are morally inferior. Yet that same logic is seldom extended among political adversaries of any age (Wineke, 1997). Instead, they learn that politics is one of those topics that is not supposed to be brought up in mixed company lest people become angry, offended, or forced to suppress their disagreement.

Learning through impersonal channels about how collective bodies resolve disagreement is unlikely to work as well as learning by experience. But it is also worth acknowledging that experiential education has its limits. For example, in theory, involvement in local politics provides the core civic education for democratic citizens. It is in this forum that we supposedly learn about how groups go about resolving conflict. But in practice, attending meetings of the local school board gives one little insight into the extent or complexity of the kind of large-scale problems facing Congress. The problems faced by national institutions are bigger and more complex, and the range of views that need to be reconciled far broader, than what we experience within the more homogeneous communities where we live and work.

Thus, even with increased local involvement, national political institutions may continue to seem remote and unresponsive, and most experience in classrooms or in community politics will not render them comprehensible and approachable. As Calhoun (1988) suggests, these large, bewildering institutions

> can be grasped well only through statistics, theories, cybernetic concepts and other intellectual tools which are both poorly distributed among the population, and also at odds with the direct understanding which people gain of their immediate surroundings. The lifeworld, by contrast, can be understood intuitively; it is a "lived reality," not an abstraction. (pp. 223–224)

These observations are not meant to suggest that improvement is impossible, or that attitudes toward Congress are unrelated to the ongoing activities of Congress and its individual representatives. But they do imply that perhaps our expectations are overly high. Although many factors no doubt contribute to low levels of trust in the U.S. Congress, few analyses have focused on more general explanations. Low levels of trust are to some degree an inevitable consequence of an extremely large, highly pluralistic society and of the kind of information-processing strategies that people in such a society use to assess large-scale collectives.

REFERENCES

Alloy, L. B., and L. Y. Abramson. 1980. "The Cognitive Component of Human Helplessness and Depression: A Critical Analysis." In *Human Helplessness: Theory and Applications,* ed. J. Garber and M.E.P. Seligman. New York: Academic Press.

Asher, Herb B., and Mark Barr. 1994. "Popular Support for Congress and Its Members." In *Congress, the Press, and the Public,* ed. Thomas E. Mann and Norman J. Ornstein (pp. 15–44). Washington, DC: American Enterprise Institute/Brookings Institution.

Born, Richard. 1990. "The Shared Fortunes of Congress and Congressmen: Members May Run from Congress, but They Can't Hide." *Journal of Politics* 52 (November): 1223–1241.

Burger, J. M. 1981. "Motivational Biases in the Attribution of Responsibility for an Accident: A Meta-analysis of the Defensive-Attribution Hypothesis." *Psychological Bulletin* 90: 496–512.

Calhoun, C. 1988. "Populist Politics, Communications Media, and Large-Scale Societal Integration." *Sociological Theory* 6: 219–241.

Congressional Record. 1987. 100th Congress, vol. 133 (September 10).

Conlan, T. J. 1993. "Federal, State, or Local? Trends in the Public's Judgment." *The Public Perspective* (January/February): 3–5.

Cook, T. J. 1987. "Show Horses in House Elections: The Advantages and Disadvantages of National Media Visibility." In *Campaign in the News: Mass Media and Congressional Elections,* ed. J. P. Vermeer (pp. 161–181). Westport, CT: Greenwood Press.

_____. 1988. "Press Secretaries and Media Strategies in the House of Representatives: Deciding Whom to Pursue." *American Journal of Political Science* 32: 1047–1069.

_____. 1979. "Legislature Versus Legislator: A Note on the Paradox of Congressional Support." *Legislative Studies Quarterly* 4: 43–61.

Durr, Robert H., John B. Gilmour, and Christina Wolbrecht. 1997. "Explaining Congressional Approval." *American Journal of Political Science* 41: 175–207.

Fenno, Richard F., Jr. 1975. "If, as Ralph Nader Says, Congress Is 'the Broken Branch,' How Come We Love Our Congressmen So Much?" In *Congress in Change: Evolution and Reform*, ed. Norman J. Ornstein (pp. 277–287). New York: Praeger.

Funder, D. C. 1980. "On Seeing Ourselves as Others See Us: Self-Other Agreement and Discrepancy in Personality Ratings." *Journal of Personality* 48: 473–493.

Gordon, M. T., S. Riger, R. K. Lebailly, and L. Heath. 1980. "Crime, Women, and the Quality of Urban Life." *Journal of Women in Culture and Society* 5: 144–160.

Griffith, S. 1989. *Home Town News.* New York: Oxford University Press.

_____. 1995. "Virtue, Enterprise, and Harmony: Booster Ideologies in Nineteenth-Century America." Paper presented at Davis Center Seminar, Villanova University.

Hibbing, John R., and Elizabeth Theiss-Morse. 1995. *Congress as Public Enemy: Public Attitudes Toward American Political Institutions.* New York: Cambridge University Press.

Jacobs, L. R., and R. Y. Shapiro. 1994. "Questioning the Conventional Wisdom on Public Opinion Toward Health Reform." *PS: Political Science and Politics* 27: 208–214.

Janowitz, M. 1952. *Community Press in an Urban Setting.* Chicago: University of Chicago Press.

Kanis, P. 1991. *Making Local News.* Chicago: University of Chicago Press.

Levine, A. 1980. *When Dreams and Heroes Died.* San Francisco: Jossey-Bass.

Lichter, S. R., and D. R. Amundson. 1994. "Less News Is Worse News: Television News Coverage of Congress, 1972–92." In *Congress, the Press, and the Public*, ed. Thomas E. Mann and Norman J. Ornstein (pp. 131–140). Washington, DC: American Enterprise Institute/Brookings Institution.

MacKuen, M. B. 1990. "Speaking of Politics: Individual Conversational Choice, Public Opinion, and the Prospects for Deliberative Democracy." In *Information and Democratic Politics*, ed. J. A. Ferejohn and J. H. Kuklinski (pp. 59–99). Urbana: University of Illinois.

Major, B. 1982. "Individual Differences in What Is Seen as Fair." Paper presented at the Nags Head Conference on Psychological Aspects of Justice, Kill Devil Hills, NC.

Martin, Paul S., and Diana C. Mutz. 1997. "Why Is the Grass Never Greener? Disjuncture Between Perceptions of Community and Society." Paper presented at the Midwest Political Science Association, Chicago (April).

Mondak, Jeffery J. 1995. *Nothing to Read: Newspapers and Elections in a Social Experiment.* Ann Arbor: University of Michigan Press.

Niven, David, and Jeremy Zilber. 1998. "What's Newt Doing in *People* Magazine? The Changing Effect of National Prominence in Congressional Elections." *Political Behavior* 20: 213–224.

Olien, C. N., G. A. Donahue, and P. J. Tichenor. 1968. "The Community Editor's Power and the Reporting of Conflict." *Journalism Quarterly* 45: 243–252.

Palmer, P. J. 1987. "Community, Conflict, and Ways of Knowing." *Change* 19: 20–25.

Patterson, T. 1994. *Out of Order.* New York: Vintage Books.

Payne, J. 1980. "Show Horses and Work Horses in the United States House of Representatives." *Polity* 12: 428–456.

Perloff, L. S., and B. K. Fetzer. 1986. "Self-Other Judgments and Perceived Vulnerability to Victimization." *Journal of Personality and Social Psychology* 50: 502–510.

Ripley, R. B, S. C. Patterson, L. Maurer, and S. V. Quinlan. 1992. "Constituents' Evaluations of U.S. House Members." *American Politics Quarterly* 20: 442–456.

Robinson, M., and K. Appel. 1979. "Network News Coverage of Congress." *Political Science Quarterly* 94: 407–413.

Rozell, Mark J. 1994. "Press Coverage of Congress, 1946–92." In *Congress, the Press, and the Public,* ed. Thomas E. Mann and Norman J. Ornstein (pp. 59–130). Washington, DC: American Enterprise Institute/Brookings Institution.

Schlenker, B. R., and R. S. Miller. 1977. "Egocentrism in Groups: Self-Serving Biases or Logical Information Processing?" *Journal of Personality and Social Psychology* 35: 755–764.

Stone, G., B. Hertung, and D. Jensen. 1987. "Local TV News and the Good-Bad Dyad." *Journalism Quarterly* 64: 37–44.

Taylor, S. E. 1982. "Adjusting to Threatening Events: A Theory of Cognitive Adaptation." Katz-Newcomb Lecture, University of Michigan.

Taylor, S. E., J. V. Wood, and R. R. Lichtman. 1983. "It Could Be Worse: Selective Evaluation as a Response to Victimization." *Journal of Social Issues* 39: 19–40.

Tidmarch, C., and J. Pitney. 1985. "Covering Congress." *Polity* 17: 446–483.

Tyler, T. R. 1980. "Impact of Directly and Indirectly Experienced Events: The Origin of Crime-Related Judgments and Behaviors." *Journal of Personality and Social Psychology* 39: 13–28.

Tyler, T. R., and F. L. Cook. 1984. "The Mass Media and Judgments of Risk: Distinguishing Impact on Personal and Societal-Level Judgments." *Journal of Personality and Social Psychology* 47: 693–708.

Tyler, T. R., and P. J. Lavrakas. 1985. "Cognitions Leading to Personal and Political Behaviors: The Case of Crime." In *Mass Media and Political Thought,* ed. S. Kraus and R. M. Perloff (pp. 141–156). Beverly Hills, CA: Sage.

Vidich, A. J., and J. Bensman. 1968. *Small Town in Mass Society.* Princeton, NJ: Princeton University Press.

Weinstein, N. D. 1980. "Unrealistic Optimism About Future Life Events." *Journal of Personality and Social Psychology* 39: 806–820.

———. 1987. "Unrealistic Optimism About Susceptibility to Health Problems: Conclusions from a Community-Wide Sample." *Journal of Behavioral Medicine* 10: 481–500.

———. 1989. "Optimistic Biases About Personal Risks." *Science* 246: 1232–1233.

Wineke, W. 1997. "Disagree with Governor, Admire Him." *Wisconsin State Journal,* November 15, p. 1C.

Notes

1. The ANES provides some of the most reliable data derived from asking parallel questions about approval of Congress and its incumbent members. However, one limitation on the ANES results is that the latter question was asked only about those running for reelection. Despite this limitation, it is still the best single source of data in which parallel collective and individual-level questions were asked of the same sample of people at the same point in time.

6

Congress, Public Trust, and Education

MARY A. HEPBURN

CHARLES S. BULLOCK III

In terms of accountability, Congress is the branch of national government closest to the people. To the average American, however, any number of executive agencies—the Social Security Administration, the Postal Service, the Occupational Safety and Health Administration, the Centers for Disease Control, the Veterans Administration, the FBI, or the president—may seem "closer" than Congress. Perhaps that's to be expected: Congressional debates and votes are not as obviously relevant to personal well-being as is the arrival of a social security check or an inspector from OSHA. Unfortunately, the American public is not all that attentive to or conversant with the nation's representative policymaking body, and that lack of understanding contributes to its remoteness and the public's scornful attitude toward it.

Representation and lawmaking are the vital center of American politics. How do we make them the vital center of civic education? This chapter addresses that and other questions: What are the strengths and deficiencies of what and how students are taught about Congress? Does the approach taken by texts prepare students for the conflict and compromise found in public policymaking in general and more specifically in Congress? What can educators do to promote an informed awareness of how Congress functions as a national policymaker?

Until the mid-1960s, secondary and introductory college government courses socialized students to uncritical support for government. The civil rights movement, the emergent youth culture, and especially the Vietnam War changed that. At the same time when many Americans came to distrust government's explanations and motivations in Southeast Asia, a movement in political science instruction to separate facts from values gained momentum. These two currents undercut the traditional boosterism that had characterized teaching and set off an aggressive debunking of myths about the wisdom and idealism of government leaders. When college teachers turned from praise to criticism, many considered it a corrective for the unalloyed positive images imparted in precollegiate civic education. Actually, the fact-value separation also made inroads in the secondary schools through the documentary realism of "the new social studies," which encouraged students to question policies of the past and present.

Today neither high school nor college texts or teachers play the cheerleader role. Political science education seems caught up in what Kees and Phillips (1994) call the "cranky age," this current period in which the public yells at the politicians, the press yells at politicians and the public, and the politicians yell at the press. Meanwhile, distrust increases among all groups based on little real understanding of the workings of government.

Our presumption is that a deep lack of trust is detrimental to the American polity and unhealthy for American society. Civic education in a democratic society must cultivate a certain degree of skepticism and critical, evaluative thinking, but such skills should rest on a knowledge of political processes and analysis of policy alternatives. We are convinced that the prevailing distrust coupled with narrow perceptions and little or no knowledge of the American political system is an unsound basis for democratic citizenship. Therefore, we must look to education to alleviate both the narrow perceptions and the distrust.

Informing the citizenry of the way Congress goes about shaping public policy requires recasting introductory American government courses to better explain the forces and processes that invigorate a democracy. Students need to know that a democracy permits and even encourages the articulation of multiple perspectives and competing demands. Toward this end, the study of public opinion should point up the range of preferences on salient policy issues such as balancing the budget, gun control, or abortion; interest-group studies should stress that widely varying views of what constitutes appropriate public policy will be urged on Congress and other decisionmakers; and the study of efforts by the president, the political parties, and interest groups to influence Congress should provide evidence that these players push legislators in different directions.

Civic education takes place not only in school. Students' homes and the popular culture also influence their attitudes about Congress. Therefore, we turn to the social context in which formal education takes place to get a sense of the perceptions that students bring to classroom discussions of Congress.

The Societal Context

The current state of public attitudes toward Congress is a scornful combination of low confidence, lack of trust, and low opinion. Princeton Survey Research Associates assessed the confidence that American adults have in seven U.S. institutions. When compared with the military, the Supreme Court, the medical profession, large business corporations, the Clinton administration, and the media, Congress received the lowest expression of confidence. Among the national respondents, 41 percent said they had "very little confidence" in Congress; 3 percent said they had "none" (Morin and Balz, 1996).

A Gallup Poll (McAneny, 1997), comparing public perceptions of the honesty and ethics of people in twenty-six occupations, found that only 14 percent rate members of Congress very highly. Pharmacists, clergy, doctors, and college teachers are more highly rated. But the 1996 data reported in this poll were an improvement over even lower ratings of Congress in 1994 and 1995.

The disapproving attitude toward Congress may have its roots in a broad public distrust of Washington politics. The 1994 American National Election Study reported that 80 percent of the over-thirty public believe that government in Washington is run to benefit "a few big interests looking out for themselves." Likewise, very low confidence was evident, with 79 percent saying that they did not trust the government in Washington to do the right thing (Bennett, 1997).

Hibbing and Theiss-Morse (1995) found that the public sees Congress as the most powerful institution of the federal government, with many judging it to be too powerful. Less than one-quarter approved of Congress. Meanwhile, political scientists believe the president has more power.

Sources of the Negative Attitudes Toward Congress

Popular disaffection with Congress is not new. A century ago, Mark Twain castigated the national legislature in a frequently repeated comment: "It could probably be shown by facts and figures that there is no distinctly native American criminal class except Congress." Elsewhere, Twain quipped, "Reader, suppose you were an idiot; and suppose you were a member of Congress; but I repeat myself" (Paine, 1912). Cartoonists of the late nineteenth century often depicted Congress as obese, avaricious, and eager to sacrifice public interest to curry favor with the rich and powerful, and some of these cartoons are readily found in today's history books.

Negative portrayal of Congress continues in talk show one-liners by comedians like Jay Leno and David Letterman and the songs and skits of such comics as the Capitol Steps and Mark Russell. Popular culture further reinforces the corrupt image of Congress in movies and on television. MTV, prime-time sitcoms, and *Dallas* reruns show members of Congress in a dark light. Popular depictions of Congress are more integral to civic education than in the past because young people get much of their information and many of their views from the electronic entertainment media. They are far more likely to view MTV, cable comedy, and *The X-Files* than to watch public television or C-SPAN.

Even best-selling novels reinforce the antithetic image of Congress. For example, in Clive Cussler's *Sahara* (1993), an adventure fiction on the *New York Times* best-seller list for fourteen weeks, the dedicated national director of an underwater and marine agency expounds his frustration with members of Congress who show no interest when he seeks support to battle a world-threatening environmental problem: "They're more concerned with maintaining their precious power base and promising the moon to get reelected. I'm sick to death of their endless stupid committee hearings. Sick to death of their lack of guts in standing for unpopular issues, and spending the nation into bankruptcy" (p. 101). Such assertions by the heroes of popular novels plant or reinforce a negative view of Congress.

Of course, the actual behavior of some legislators contributes to negative stereotypes. Contrary to Twain's picture of Congress, members of Congress may be no more inclined toward criminal activity than anyone else. However, the misdeeds of legislators receive far more widespread media coverage than their accomplishments do. Rarely does a member of Congress go to prison, but the arrest of a single member—for example, Representative Pat Swindall (R-GA) for perjury—feeds the perception of widespread dishonesty. The "Abscam" tapes that showed several House members grabbing stacks of currency fueled the belief that legislators are for sale. Stories about millions spent in campaigns by Senator Jesse Helms in North Carolina and by Michael Huffington in California create an image of a political system in which offices go to the highest bidder, even though high-spending candidates like Huffington often fail. Further besmirching Congress's reputation have been several sex scandals, such as Representative Gerry Studds's (D-MA) seduction of a male page and Daniel Crane's (R-IL) affair with a female page. Financial misdeeds, such as the misuse of the House post office by Dan Rostenkowski (D-IL) and issues of illegal fund-raising by Newt Gingrich (R-GA), receive the extensive media coverage that the dedication and hard work of many other Congress members do not receive.

Commercial news media coverage of national politics also places Congress at a disadvantage. Both television and print media tend to have a presidential orientation to national policymaking. The media often compare policy initiatives coming from the White House with multiple responses from members of Congress, presenting the latter as intrusive or intent on preventing quick action. When our government is "divided"—different parties control Congress and the presidency, as has been the case for all but six years since 1969—presidential proposals avoid challenges by one or both chambers only in a crisis. The news media often present the ensuing exchange of arguments to the American public as contentious and disagreeable, even implying that it is not in the best interests of the country. The Constitution, with its clear separation of powers, did not envision Congress as a rubber stamp. Yet the public seems quite unaware or unconvinced that the congressional role in policymaking invites disagreement with the president. Such give-and-take in the process is often played up as an unnecessary battle in news media coverage. In fact, as Parker (1977) noted, Congress is most popular when it does little to impair the realization of presidential objectives. Here again we have evidence of public discomfort with the process.

Members of Congress themselves tend to accentuate the negative. The norm of institutional loyalty widely shared by representatives and senators in the 1950s

(Matthews, 1960) has been replaced by a recognition of the norm of populist disdain. Many challengers and an increasing number of incumbents run for election against the institution—castigating alleged self-serving actions, unwise use of federal funds, and a lack of responsiveness to the public. Such campaign behavior does not engender trust.

Congress and the national government have been criticized from both ends of the political spectrum. Conservatives, who have held the upper hand in the legislature since 1995, challenge the wisdom of policies that provide social welfare benefits, assist the arts community, encourage affirmative action efforts, and enact redistributive policies. Liberals have done little to defend Congress, instead criticizing the institution for not doing enough to support a broader social agenda. Thus, the institution has been left without defenders.

The concept of government of, for, and by the people, if not properly explained, may feed unrealistic expectations about how Congress processes public preferences. Many people expect that government—and by this they often mean Congress—will be responsive and enact public wishes into law in a neat, uncomplicated way. What people often fail to recognize is that the American public does not speak with a single voice. People want the enactment of their preferences, but few realize that not everyone agrees with their wishes. Until a broad consensus emerges, new policies are not likely to be forthcoming—an irritation expressed by both the media and the public.

Young Americans' attitudes about Congress derive from this social context. Their lives are immersed in a popular culture conveyed by colorful, fast-paced mass media. Hours of television viewing, video games, video movies, radio talk shows, and glitzy magazines are part of the daily lives of young Americans. These media affect youth directly, and in their influence on family, social-religious, and peer groups, they affect young people indirectly (see Figure 6.1). Since the popular media typically provide little insight into policymaking and tend to hold Congress specifically, and government generally, in low esteem, we sought information about the dispositions of young people toward Congress.

Youth Awareness and Attitudes

Surveys conducted in the 1980s and 1990s indicate that young Americans (1) have little more than superficial knowledge of Congress, (2) have shown shifts and changes in trust, and (3) have little inclination to follow politics or get involved. Data from the 1988 National Assessment of Educational Progress (NAEP) show that high school seniors had a very limited knowledge of Congress (Niemi and Junn, 1998). However, the structure of Congress was better understood than the process of electing congressional representatives or the lawmaking process. For example, 77 percent knew that Congress consists of the House and the Senate, 72 percent knew that checks and balances involve the powers of the three branches as they relate to each other, and 68 percent were aware that the number

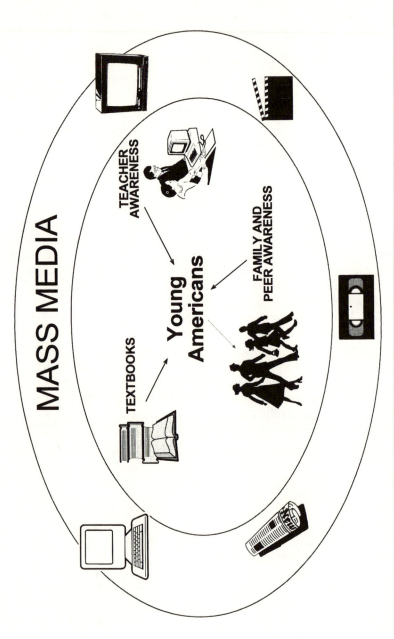

FIGURE 6.1 Influences on Learning About Congress

SOURCE: Hepburn, 1998.

of representatives in the House varies by state population. When we look at processes, however, students show little understanding of how candidates are nominated in party primaries and then run for office. Only 40 to 55 percent could correctly answer questions about the nomination process, and only 40 percent were aware that the parties organize the procedures. Just 54 percent knew that a two-thirds vote of both houses is required to override a presidential veto. Only 39 percent knew that Congress can raise the income tax. Even fewer (36 percent) knew that the House can impeach a president and that the Senate would then conduct the trial. Students viewed lobbying as a way to change laws (84 percent), but other responses showed a weak understanding of political action committees. On NAEP items testing reasoning skills, students did not fare well either. For example, on an item that required students to look at polling data and interpret it, only half could do so. From the 1988 study we can see that high school students lacked any depth of knowledge of Congress. Given the context discussed earlier, we suggest that attitude may be contributing to low levels of knowledge.

The last survey of student political attitudes by NAEP was conducted in 1976. It had few attitude items, and none were on Congress. One set of questions assessed "willingness to participate in the political process"; these results showed that about half of the seventeen-year-old students believed they could influence both national and local government (National Assessment of Educational Progress, 1978). A 1983 survey of students in grades 7 through 12 commissioned by the National Association of Secondary School Principals (1984) examined youth attitudes in more detail and compared the results with a 1974 study. In 1974 three-fourths of the students had felt that corruption and dishonesty in government were widespread; by 1983 just over half took that stance. The report concluded that Watergate-era mistrust of government and politics was declining.

A more recent national attitude survey of students aged thirteen to seventeen (Horatio Alger Association, 1996), however, showed a rebound in negative attitudes toward government. A full 76 percent said they believed that government corruption and dishonesty are widespread, and a 55 percent majority felt that being rich is necessary to get elected to high office—perhaps an indication of growing dollar realism in current student attitudes.

College freshmen are surveyed each fall in a large national study (Cooperative Institutional Research Program, 1996, 1997). One question taps attitudes about the importance of keeping up with politics. Since the survey began in 1966, positive attitudes have been in decline. In the 1996 presidential election year, just 29 percent of college freshmen thought politics was important, and only 16 percent discussed the subject often. The lowest level of political interest was found in 1997: Only 27 percent of freshmen responded that it is important to keep up with political affairs, and a meager 14 percent said they discuss politics frequently.

The picture that emerges from this collage of evidence on the knowledge and attitudes of youth is not encouraging. Although students learn certain basics about the structure of American government, they acquire a very limited knowledge of the procedures and workings of the American political system. They seem to have a very narrow understanding of the processes of electing members of Congress and of making laws. Compounding the knowledge deficiencies are disapproving attitudes. Today an overwhelming majority of youth distrust the honesty of politicians in office and feel that only monied people can get elected to high office. Moreover, students openly express their disinterest in political matters. These circumstances make educating them about Congress and the rest of the political system highly critical, but it is clearly no easy task.

Secondary Education:
Government and Civics for All?

Surveys reveal that young Americans have surly attitudes toward government and attribute little importance to political life. If the NAEP's forthcoming 1998 assessment of civic knowledge reaffirms the low levels of knowledge of political processes found in 1988—and we suspect it will—then American civic and political science educators must contend with the looming issue of failed education for responsible democratic citizenship. Since nearly every American attends secondary school, concern about improving education about democratic political processes and institutions, including Congress, should begin there.

For secondary school students to gain a practical understanding of both the principles and processes of American democracy (focusing on congressional studies), it is our assumption that several educational components must converge: (1) adequate time and attention in the school curriculum; (2) teachers who themselves are educated in the processes of democratic governance; (3) instructional guidelines that provide a realistic conceptualization of how democratic government works; (4) textbooks that not only contain solid, well-presented substantive material on the framework and fundamentals of government but also support the analysis of public issues; and (5) accurate supplemental instructional material attuned to the listening-viewing-learning styles of today's students. These elements of an ideal civic education in secondary school would seem to be attainable. However, there are significant problems in the conceptualization of civic education in schools, and there are institutional barriers as well.

Critical Conceptual Issues

Several political scientists have offered persuasive critiques of the conceptualization of civic education in the schools. Three of them touch on areas of school curriculum and instruction that we find especially problematic in the overall effort to reform what is taught about Congress and American politics.

Hibbing and Theiss-Morse (1996) contend that curriculum and instruction are overly focused on "abstract governmental arrangements" at the expense of teaching how government actually operates. They argue that the study of "clean" constitutional structure is inadequate if the more tumultuous process of grinding out policies from diverse views is not understood. Their research (1995) has shown that the public generally misunderstands the fundamental disagreement, debate, and argumentation that goes on, and should go on, in the governing process, and that many Americans consider it to be petty bickering. The bargaining and compromise that are part of forging public policies are often viewed as "selling out." Counter to the conventional wisdom of political science was the low opinion of Congress expressed by some better-educated people—those who knew little about the process and were uncomfortable with the contention, argument, and compromise in lawmaking (Hibbing and Theiss-Morse, 1996). Two types of respondents were more supportive: those who had less education and those who combined more years of education with an understanding of the give-and-take that occurs in the legislature. As a corrective, Hibbing and Theiss-Morse (1996) propose that young people study the contentious aspects of public issues, learn that public opinion is divided on most public issues, and gain an understanding of the difficult and necessary work that Congress and the president perform in resolving them.

Bennett (1997) also argues that the controversy and compromise at the heart of democratic politics are not part of civic education and that students do not learn how political institutions work. In his appraisal, large numbers of young Americans cannot tolerate the political disagreement characteristic of the American democratic system. He calls for more realistic school education on "how public officials conduct the people's business." Bennett points up the television media's hold on the attention of young viewers and then underscores the mass media's distortion of political processes. He asserts that school instruction about the realities of politics must begin early and continue throughout the grades in order to balance the mass media's inadequate and overly negative coverage.

In a review of part of the National Standards for Civics and Government,[1] Merelman (1996) also finds evidence of discomfort with the contention and dissension in democratic politics. Analyzing the civics approach inherent in the standards on American political culture, he finds the assumption that conflict and disagreement are not healthy for democracy. He perceives in those standards an acclamation that American democracy, compared with the political systems of most other nations, does not have differing values and dissension. "Shared political values" and "cohesion" are praised in the standards for distinguishing American democracy from other political cultures. Analyzing the implications of this inaccurate conceptualization, Merelman writes, "Diversity apparently creates conflicts which threaten the constitutional principles of American political culture: when such conflicts occur, the proposed standards recommend that diversity give way" (p. 56).

These three critiques point up an underlying problem in how civic education is conceptualized and taught in schools. By avoiding the clash of viewpoints and values, civic education fails not only to tell the whole story but to breathe life into Congress and other political institutions. If civic education were reconceptualized to embrace the study of how public policy is wrought, then educational improvement would be under way. But we must consider the significant barriers to change with which schools as institutions must contend.

Institutional Barriers

Schools as public institutions present many barriers to instructional reform— some long-standing and others produced by present social conditions. Lack of priority has been a major problem for political science in schools in the past decade. Education about American government and politics has suffered from a public perception that it is not as necessary to the well-being of the nation as subjects such as math, science, and computer skills. Many adults over thirty-five remember a yearlong course on American government required sometime during their last two years of high school. In some states the required course was "Problems of Democracy," which focused student attention on policy issues and analysis of multiple viewpoints, but in most states the required government course consisted of a study of the structure and functions of the three branches of American government. Although structure may have been overemphasized, the study of American government and politics was accepted as necessary preparation for active citizenship. Equally important, the subject had a time and a place in the secondary school curriculum.

In the 1980s many school districts reduced or eliminated the requirement of a secondary American government course. The concern over the "nation at risk" in a competitive global economy probably fueled the decline, as did the concern over rising crime rates. Courses in economics and "law-related education" often replaced the traditional government course. The newer courses were viewed as more practical and useful by many school boards. Other social studies courses subsequently incorporated educational objectives related to citizenship. Curiously, neither American government nor civics was included in the original *Education Goals 2000* launched during the Bush administration. Only organized lobbying by educators and support from concerned members of Congress convinced administration officials to add the study of American democracy to the national effort to improve education.

National statements like the National Standards for Civics and Government attract some public attention and mobilize public and private foundation support that make it possible for professionals to work on real changes in schools. However, as a practical matter it should be understood that these national goals and national standards can be expected to have no more than a slow, trickle-down effect on local classrooms. As Merelman (1996) points out, such endeavors are largely symbolic. Educational policies applied in the school districts are determined by state or local educational planners, and state and local politics come into play. Some state educational leaders resist adopting or supporting *national* guidelines, considering them either too liberal or too conservative, or as a downright intrusion into state affairs. Teachers, on the other hand, are likely to be encouraged by their national professional organizations to work in groups to adopt national goals, guidelines, or standards, but they often do so selectively, based on local views. By the time state and local schools have worked over and assimilated selected national objectives into the local curriculum, the national government's education focus is likely to have changed. All too many reforms that are launched nationally "at the top" are adopted years later and only here and there across state and local districts. Hence, it would be unrealistic to expect national statements to accomplish real reform in civic education.

What about state requirements? It is difficult to determine the current patterns of course offerings in American government and politics even in states that have a fairly large degree of authority. Niemi (1995) sought to ascertain such patterns in a survey of state education departments. Some type of civics requirement was reported in forty-two states, but only twenty states required a separate course for graduation. We note, for instance, that in Oklahoma, local school systems have a degree of autonomy, and some do not include American government as a graduation requirement. In Georgia a list of state-recommended competencies includes knowledge and skills in government, but there is no requirement for a specific government or civics course, although American history is required. Apparently in many school districts around the country government and civics learning objectives are to be met in history and general social studies courses. Doubtless this means that high school graduates today have fewer opportunities and less time to study Congress and other institutions of American government in any depth.

Even if an American government course is required, the approach in textbooks and the attendant teacher's guides and course outlines can be problematic. Much can be learned about the content of American government courses from a perusal of the textbooks. We examined four secondary textbooks[2] used in a large metropolitan-area school district near us. The textbooks include a volume reputed to be the most widely sold for high school American government courses in the United States, a textbook similar to the best-seller that competes quite well with it, a textbook commonly used in advanced-placement government courses, and a textbook designed for students with lower reading ability.

Chapters on the structure of Congress as the first branch of government precede the executive and judicial branches. Each book devotes about 10 percent of total pages to Congress. In the most widely used textbook, the teaching plan for a one-semester high school course outlines a twelve-day program on Congress. Given the various intrusions of school activities into the best-laid plans of teachers and textbooks, it is probable that with this plan students would actually have no more than nine to ten classes on Congress. But time-on-task offers little assurance of students learning about how Congress works. The dominant approach in the books is deductive—generalizations and description followed by questions. One book aims to motivate some inquiry and inductive thinking by asking key questions at the beginning of the chapter, but even it does not sustain a probing, questioning approach.

We should clarify that compared to the American government textbooks of ten to fifteen years ago, the books we examined do offer more attractive and informative tables and graphs, a greater number of short case studies, and more analytical questions. If teachers have the competence and preparation time to use these improved text materials in an engaging way with motivated students, knowledge of the structure of Congress would increase. But the textbooks generally do not make Congress, its members, and the policy process come alive. There are a few exceptions: The book used with advanced students includes a chapter on past and present power struggles between the executive and legislative branches. Another textbook contains a feature on the pros and cons of term-limits legislation. But overall, only a very small portion of the textbook material focuses on the multiple actors, issues, and actions in lawmaking.

To bring about a change in the textbooks' approach would be difficult considering the state and local politics of textbook selection, adoption, and purchase. Lively discussions of issues and differing political views regarding alternative solutions are unlikely to be featured in large-circulation textbooks from national publishers for fear of stirring opposition from state or local adoption committees or the school boards that oversee them. Corporate textbook profits depend on quantity sales in multiple states, and the books favored are those that provide the fundamentals and disturb no groups with political clout. They are unlikely to illuminate what Hibbing and Theiss-Morse (1996) refer to as "the nitty gritty of democratic politics" (p. 60). Accordingly, national textbooks are another barrier to enlivening civic education in secondary schools.

Student indifference to learning about politics and government is another school problem. Beyond the exceptional students who come to school with a family-stimulated interest in government, there is a widespread problem of motivation. Part of that lack of motivation to learn about government stems from the negative societal perspective described earlier, but the problem is also related to the way in which courses and instruction (often based on textbooks) present government—offering the principles and the organization without insight into how national policies are wrought. Consider also that most secondary school students live in homes where television is on twenty-five to fifty hours a week. They are accustomed to vibrant sounds and colorful action as means to obtaining information. Many are not used to reading for information or pleasure. Hence, many will not complete reading assignments in a seven-hundred-page government textbook.

We talked about student motivation with an experienced government teacher, who has been praised by administrators and students as a "good teacher." She told us that students consider the well-written and well-illustrated textbook used in their school to be dull. She considers it necessary to use supplemental instructional materials (teacher-prepared print and video items) to stimulate students to read, think about, and discuss differing viewpoints on such governmental issues as term limits, reduction of the national debt, shifting welfare responsibilities to the states, and campaign finance. This teacher feels that only by involving students in legislative issues can she lead them into effective study of powers and procedures. Other well-qualified teachers make similar comments. Clearly they would not want to teach American government and politics without a textbook, but they find that textbooks *alone* do not engage students in learning how Congress and other institutions work. Adding short segments of videotaped debate, issue-focused print material, and simulations can help to overcome the initial lack of interest and make students aware of the wide range of public opinion, the pressures of interest groups, the influence of the chief executive, the effects of media coverage, and the intersection of all these factors with Congress in the drama of legislating.

Of course, the use of challenging materials is dependent on the efforts of a qualified and imaginative instructor. The teacher is the key to improving civic education. Educators with a strong background in political science who also understand the skills needed to communicate with secondary school students can make a big difference. However, there are few institutional or practical assurances that schools will have such well-prepared educators to teach government and civics. Impediments stem from an intricate mix of certification requirements, job availability, and the undergraduate programs for professional teachers. Most who will teach social science and history courses in the schools prepare for broad certification in "social studies." Normally they take only a few political science courses along with history courses and other social sciences. Their professional preparation is likely to be generic in the sense that they are being prepared to teach any of the social studies courses in the secondary curriculum. They usually will not know until they obtain a job just which of the social studies they will be called on to teach. Some who major in political science do become certified to teach only civics or government courses, but they risk not finding a job, so that alternative is not very popular.

A further problem in the undergraduate education of civics and government teachers is the limited opportunity to relate substantive course work in political science to instructional approaches and materials needed to teach high school. Few political scientists are concerned about how their research and college instruction will be applied to the education of secondary school students, and few social studies professors invite political scientists to address the needs of secondary education. Perhaps narrowing the gulf between political scientists and social studies education professors would not only open up avenues to improving civic education in school but also ultimately send better-prepared students to introductory college political science.

Once government and civics teachers are established in their subject area, they find very few opportunities to expand their knowledge and skill in teaching about Congress or other areas of American government. There is no consistent mechanism in school districts or college and university teacher education programs for updating and upgrading the civic-education preparedness of teachers. There are only a few in-service or graduate-level short courses designed for secondary civics or government teachers. Where else can practicing teachers gain the substantive background and professional skills to expand their treatment of American politics? Not many would undertake the change in approach on their own.

In civic education the climate of the school or school district often comes into play. Typically teachers of history and social science are very cautious about dealing with social-political conflict and controversy (see Beale, 1936; Hepburn, 1983). Well-publicized incidents of parental or school board interference generate apprehensions that objections will be raised to classroom discussion of public issues—even those issues that are being debated in Congress. Some teachers have learned how to explain the worth of unbiased investigation of public issues to parents and administration, and if they work in an open educational climate, they feel free to encourage issue discussions. But for the majority of school civic educators, special materials, training, and professional encouragement would be requisite to adding issue analysis to instruction on Congress.

What Can Be Done to Improve
Secondary Education on Congress?

For about half of the population, secondary school provides the last formal opportunity to learn about national policymaking, the final chance to study and discuss the role of Congress in shaping how we live. Consequently, exactly what is taught in American government and how well that instruction involves young people in learning are of major significance to democratic citizenship. Having identified the several components of effective civic education as adequate time in the curriculum, well-educated teachers, informed and realistic guidelines for teachers, improved textbooks, and quality supplemental instructional materials, we have further explained why existing conceptual and institutional barriers make change formidable. Nevertheless, not all of the barriers are impenetrable. Although the long-established textbooks that tend to avoid controversy will be difficult to change, and increasing the hours in the curriculum devoted to civics will likely be a slow, state-by-state process, there are accessible channels for improving the study of Congress. Education for experienced teachers, the preparation of practical instructional guidelines, and the development of supplemental print and electronic instructional materials are three realistic avenues for correcting misperceptions of Congress and enriching understanding of how our national legislature works.

Experienced Teacher Education

Teachers are the key to change. If an understanding of the branch of government closest to the people is to be gained by students in school, the pivotal factor will be teachers who know the subject matter well and have developed skills not only to teach fundamentals but to handle discussion of conflict issues adequately and fairly. Because social studies teachers typically have minimal undergraduate course work in political science, once assigned to teaching government and civics, they need opportunities to increase the depth of their knowledge of the subject. Knowledge of Congress is no exception.

In contrast to the current national support given to economics short courses by business and economics organizations, the state-by-state support of law-related education workshops provided by bar associations, and the geographic computer applications courses supported by national professional geographers' organizations, experienced teacher education in government and civics has lacked consistent annual support. The American Political Science Association (APSA) has been involved in curriculum advocacy and design since the early 1900s. Its programs for teachers have been sporadic but well focused; for example, the APSA assumed national leadership during the bicentennial period to promote teacher education and publications on enduring constitutional issues. In the 1990s, however, there has been less financial and professional support for teacher education in political science. Nevertheless, there are good prospects that secondary civic education will be strengthened through a program of the APSA Task Force on Civic Education for the Next Century to advance research and involve political scientists in improving civic education at all levels.

The Dirksen Congressional Center for six years has offered summer seminars to increase teacher understanding of Congress, but this program reaches only about thirty teachers per year. The Taft Institute, for approximately twenty-six years, offered summer seminars on American politics and government in numerous states—as many as thirty-five states a decade ago—but this program lost congressional matching money and had to drastically reduce programs. There are some workshops linked to the sales of textbooks or connected to constitutional studies, but in-service or experienced-teacher short courses on American politics are few and far between.

Teaching Guidelines

Instructional guidelines provided directly to teachers can go a long way toward the improvement of education about Congress. The support material should include a carefully developed rationale and a framework for teaching about

Congress, including substantive summaries by scholars, outlines for units of study, case studies by civics specialists, and an annotated list of recommended resources. The guidelines should be prepared by a team of congressional scholars and teacher educators to meet the substantive requirements discussed earlier, as well as the practical requirements of schooling. Then they should be reviewed by scholars and teachers. Selected recent topics and instructional approaches for teaching about Congress combined with interesting case studies and pro-con summaries for issue discussions would be very helpful to teachers. Instructional cues could assist teachers in organizing congressional lessons not only for civics and government classes but also for history, law, economics, and general social studies classes. Such guidelines could be disseminated by cosponsoring professional organizations, demonstrated in proposed experienced-teacher short courses, and made available to all teachers whose courses have civics objectives.

Supplemental Media on Congress

Changing communications may help to open secondary school classrooms to multiple viewpoints and debate while offering good opportunities for students to view Congress live. Several small publishing houses now turn out useful supplemental print materials on opposing viewpoints on public issues.[3] However, for secondary school students of the late 1990s, the video screen is the main source of news and entertainment. At least 99 percent of American households have television; two-thirds have two, three, or more sets; and about 54 percent of children in the United States have a TV in their bedroom (Media Dynamics, 1996). Besides the many hours they spend on video games and video movies, many young people are also using the Internet. Electronic mass communications are pervasive and have a powerful attraction for young people. Their educational potential should not be overlooked in civic education. It is of extraordinary importance that students learn about the range and quality of the information they can obtain about Congress from television and the Internet. It is even more important that they comprehend the necessity of being critical and analytical regarding the reliability of these vast resources (Hepburn, 1998). Study of the effects of electronic media on, for example, Congress and on the national viewing public should be included. Likewise, it is essential that educators learn about the great teaching potential of visual-oral media that can, for instance, take the viewer to the floor of the Senate or the House and into committee hearings where the diversity and drama of politics can be witnessed.

For the study of Congress, educators and students are fortunate to have an established sight-and-sound record of each house at work on the cable channels C-SPAN I (House of Representatives) and C-SPAN II (Senate). The House, in 1979, and then the Senate, in 1986, agreed to install cameras for televised coverage of their sessions to increase their public visibility (Frantzich and Sullivan, 1996). Though Congress, compared to the president, still continues to get less overall media coverage, more information about Congress is appearing in the news because C-SPAN is heavily used by the press. A direct benefit to teachers is that they can tape any portion of a C-SPAN broadcast for use in the classroom without copyright concerns. Seeing and hearing committee and floor debate has great potential to make the process come alive *if* the action is recorded and used with prudence. Brief tape segments should be interspersed with explanation, questions, and discussion. Portions of lively exchanges among members of Congress can show current issues, partisan differences, cross-party alliances, formal procedures, heated disagreement, "special orders" broadsides, and other types of congressional activity. In our experience, students will watch the debate intently if a clear context is set *before* using the video and if the segment is short enough to allow time for questions and discussion. Tapes of committee or floor sessions must be used with care. A long uninterpolated tape of the House or Senate can be as eye-glazing as the worst textbook.

An election-focused program that involves use of the news media offers promise for generating more interest in congressional elections. Kids Voting engages students in learning from the news about election issues and the election process in the weeks preceding an election. Students then go to the polls with their parents and cast their own ballots in a separate canvass. The program, organized by Kids Voting USA in schools all across the country, requires cooperative efforts by teachers and the school system, the local news media, and families throughout the community. The program tested with various grades and ages has been found to increase student use of news media and the discussion of public affairs both in school and at home. Studies have shown that students not only gain in political awareness but, by accompanying their parents to the polls, help to increase voter turnout (McDevitt and Chaffee, 1998; McLeod, Eveland, and Horowitz, 1998; Simon and Merrill, 1998). One effect is a kind of reverse political influence, from child to parent, which some researchers view as "second chance political socialization" (McDevitt and Chaffee, 1998). Such election-based learning activities may be an effective means to heighten student and parent interest in Congress every two years.

Computer-accessible resources on the Internet can complement reading and video. For example, C-SPAN has established a Congress section on its website that provides the opportunity to submit questions about Congress. Interesting and concise answers are given by a congressional expert and collected on the website for educational purposes. The topics range across procedural, definitional, historical, issue, and personal background questions. Obviously an instructor can select the most interesting and appropriate topics to utilize with students.

CongressLink, a new website sponsored by the Dirksen Congressional Center, will assist schoolteachers in learning and teaching about Congress. Not only does it provide guides to Congress, discussions by experts, student activities, and an online resource center with materials from at least two archival collections, but it also has contact with "experts online"—scholars, members of Congress, and other practitioners with whom teachers and students can discuss Congress. Through this site, learners can connect with a number of other websites sponsored by government agencies and educational institutions to trace the progress of a particular bill in committee or to obtain current or past data on Congress and other government institutions. (A list of several websites can be found at the end of this chapter.)

Summary

While it seems unlikely that deficient congressional studies in secondary schools can be improved radically or immediately by a quick change of the curriculum or textbooks, gradual change can begin now by (1) initiating more postemployment congressional education courses for civic teachers; (2) developing instructional support materials, especially those using electronic media; and (3) providing substantively and methodologically sound guidelines for teachers.

To be able to reach out far and wide to improve civic education in American secondary schools will require a collaborative effort by professors and teachers. The three strategies proffered here to advance education about Congress should be conducted by a collaboration of congressional scholars, experienced teachers of government and civics, and teacher education specialists in civics.

Higher Education: Where Teachers, Journalists, and Degree-Bearing Citizens Should Learn About Congress

In all likelihood, by the time students reach college they have had one or more courses focusing on the American form of government. Collegiate coverage of the subject matter, therefore, will be at least partially a review but may also involve exposure to new materials and new ways of thinking about the genius of our political system and, of particular concern to this chapter, an enhanced appreciation of the role of the legislature. Mastery of a body of information is essential to understanding the ways in which the system operates, but learning facts and nothing more will not produce an awareness of the need for a vigorous Congress.

Since the opportunities for political scientists to teach about the Congress are limited, imparting an appreciation for and understanding of Congress to a broader audience requires enlisting the help of high school teachers and journalists. Public school teachers encounter a much larger segment of the population than do political scientists engaged in postsecondary education. Journalists also have a broader reach than political scientists, and the media may catch its audience when it is more concerned about the consequences of political decisions, since it can inform the public about Congress long after voters have completed their formal education. The effectiveness of both allies in promoting an understanding of Congress depends in no small measure on the information they acquire while in college. To the extent that teachers and journalists acquire a more realistic and less hostile perspective on the legislature, those with whom they interact are also likelier to acquire a more sophisticated awareness.

This section on higher education as a setting for reaching undergraduates generally, and future teachers and journalists more specifically, concentrates on three potential problems: time, training, and orientation. Because it is the most frequent point of contact for undergraduates, we pay special attention to the introductory American politics course. Within each section, we set out current problems and, where available, suggest potential solutions. The constraints on the time available for the study of Congress and the preparation of those who teach the introductory course currently seem to be largely intractable problems, so these sections are heavily skewed toward identifying those problems. The orientation section, however, includes a more extended discussion of possible solutions along with a review of present difficulties.

Time

An introduction to American government course is standard in most college and university curricula, although mandatory study of the American political scene is probably more likely at state-supported institutions than at private ones. Public colleges in Texas, for example, require a year's study of state and national government, while the Georgia constitution mandates that graduates of the state-supported system demonstrate knowledge of the federal and state constitutions. The one course that provides presumptive evidence on both counts is Introductory American Government.

Study of Congress is but one of the many components of the collegiate survey courses in which students are most likely to be exposed to American politics in a systematic fashion. If the time given topics in a collegiate American government class is divided roughly evenly across chapters in the text, Congress receives no more than a week's attention. Two or three lecture periods devoted to the national legislature may be the norm in a one-semester or one-quarter American government course. Classes taught by instructors who specialize in legislative politics are likely to spend a few additional days on Congress and to refer to Congress in discussions of other topics such as elections, interest groups, and the executive branch; courses taught by instructors with other interests may devote as little as a single day to Congress. In Texas public institutions or other schools that devote a year to American politics, Congress and the state legislature may receive more in-depth coverage. Given the breadth of the curriculum of American government classes in both high school and college, the instructor has little time to offer information and activities designed to counter negative conceptions about Congress and its members.

Replacing lectures with student-centered interactive activities would probably lead to a more sophisticated appreciation of the untidy, deliberative processes of democracy. The National Budget Simulation, for example, presents short and long versions of a game in which the student decides priorities in the federal budget by increasing and decreasing percentages in major categories, such as defense and medicare.[4] Time pressures, however, make inclusion of such activities difficult, especially when teaching takes place in lecture sections of several hundred students. Before students can effectively play the role of a member of Congress wrestling with budgetary trade-offs, they must know something about the functions of the programs to which they are making allocations. And though the budget simulation game provides a taste of the problems of budget balancing, it may do little to provide an awareness of the negotiating that takes place in committees and on the floor and how these activities interact with the demands of constituents, interest groups, and the administration. Devoting too much time to one simulation may shortchange other objectives.

Most universities and some colleges offer a course devoted to the study of Congress or to legislatures more generally. Students who take such a class should acquire the kind of sophisticated appreciation for Congress and its contribution to the political system that we encourage. We suspect, however, that rarely if ever is such a course required, so only a tiny fraction of the college-educated public, high school teachers, and journalists have studied the legislature extensively.

Training

Students taught by instructors who do research on Congress or other legislative bodies probably have a more nuanced classroom experience than do those whose teachers have little interest in legislative politics. Because many graduate students earn their daily bread by serving as teaching assistants in sections of large American politics classes, it is often assumed that any political scientist can teach the basics of the U.S. political system. Consequently many American government courses are taught by instructors whose primary interest is not the American political system and who have no specialized knowledge about Congress. In community and junior colleges and some small four-year institutions, those who teach about American politics are not political scientists but instead have been trained as historians, sociologists, or geographers. The easiest course of action for instructors with little expertise in Congress may be to propagate stereotypes.

While legislative specialists are the best prepared to teach about Congress, they may fail to provide an awareness of the strengths of the national legislature, but for a different reason. The risk is that they become so engrossed in their own research or in the latest refinements in the scholarly literature that they do not meet the needs of students. Some texts lapse into this pattern and go deeply into findings of the incumbency research that has attracted the efforts of many fine congressional experts. Scholars are immersed in the correlates of incumbency success, the extent to which marginality has declined, and variations in the impact of the retirement slump and the sophomore surge, topics that college students find less captivating than do participants on a panel exploring these issues at an APSA meeting.

If there are gaps in the training of some college American government instructors, the college preparation of high school teachers in government and civics courses is even spottier. Secondary school teachers usually take minimal political science course work. Pedagogical courses in many smaller colleges offering teacher certification may be generalized to all or a cluster of subject areas. However, with a smaller faculty there may be more communication by professors across the disciplines and more opportunity to unify subject matter with instructional training. In larger institutions, it usually falls to the students to relate the substance of the subject to instructional skills.

Most social studies teacher candidates seek broad field certification that will allow them to teach two or three subjects and thus better compete in the unpredictable job market. In our state university, a bachelor's degree in social science education requires sixty-five quarter hours of social science and history, including a minimum of fifteen hours of political science. Students who obtain specialized political science certification must have twenty-five hours of political science, but neither certification requires a legislative politics course.

In our experience, the greatest promise for enhancing the political science education of teachers comes in special postgraduate courses (such as the Taft Seminars, the Dirksen Center's Congress in the Classroom, and National Issues Forums) offered to faculty currently teaching government, civics, or law. Educators seeking to improve their teaching skills come to these classes more interested in learning about American government than are most undergraduates. Specially designed classes for government/civics teachers usually bring together political scientists, social studies education specialists, and practitioners from politics and government. In these courses teachers can become better acquainted with political science and education faculty and improve communications in both directions, benefiting political science education at both levels.

Journalists who write about Congress, like public school teachers, may have had a course on the subject but probably have taken nothing beyond the introductory class in American politics. Unlike teachers, however, journalists acquire much of their information about the legislature on the job; how they integrate this additional knowledge may depend on the kinds of courses they took in college. The inadequacy of the training received is shown in an analysis of the leading programs in mass communications and journalism by Roberts and Eksterowicz (1996), who concluded that journalism students can graduate without a working knowledge of political science, government, or political behavior. To correct this problem, journalism programs should require students majoring in news writing, reporting, editing, and related fields to obtain a solid grounding in American politics.

Orientation

Unlike earlier teaching materials designed to socialize students to become citizens who trusted and admired their leaders, neither the authors of today's college textbooks nor those who teach from them see their primary function as developing support for Congress or other governmental institutions. Beginning with the Vietnam War, many instructors believed they had an obligation to unmask the abuses of government. Teachers who pointed out the foibles of political leaders and inconsistencies between American ideals and actual governmental practices were often popular with students.

Textbooks that carefully avoid becoming cheerleaders for the government, its leaders, and their policies have concentrated on imparting facts. A review of a sampling of leading collegiate texts used to teach American politics reveals that they contain a wealth of information about members of Congress and the activities of the institution.[5] Texts invariably provide basic constitutional information on the requirements for serving in each chamber and the responsibilities assigned the legislature in Article 1, and explain how a bill becomes a law. Popular textbooks generally contain solid information on the background characteristics of members of Congress, congressional elections and the advantages of incumbency, and the workings of the committee system. Although the level of detail varies, a student reading any of these texts will gain extensive information about the national legislature but may not acquire a realistic feel for the untidy nature of its policymaking process. Among our concerns is whether factually accurate and comprehensive information about Congress can offset the negative stereotypes that students bring to the classroom.

Texts, like teachers, face the problem of too much information for the time available; they often focus not on activities at which Congress excels but on activities to which the legislature is less well adapted. For example, Congress, with its hundreds of members and relatively weak leaders, will not score well if one is assessing efficiency, especially compared with the president, who entertains alternatives, sorts through them out of public view, and therefore appears to take decisive action. On the other hand, if one values representativeness, then the varied backgrounds of the members and their willingness to push the concerns of their constituents make the legislature look better than the executive and judicial branches. Despite the predominance of middle-aged, white males, Congress includes growing numbers of women along with representatives of ethnic and racial groups and members with diverse religious beliefs and varied vocational experiences. Rather than noting the extent of diversity in Congress and its success in providing substantive representation, texts more often criticize the body as a distorted mirror that fails to represent proportionally all elements of society.

The range of backgrounds and perspectives, though perhaps not perfect, makes attainment of consensus problematic when coupled with electorally induced policy responsiveness. In the absence of consensus, congressional leaders are usually too weak to impose policy positions. Being representative of the nation's varied interests might be portrayed as a congressional strength, but it is more often seen as an obstacle to quick responsiveness to presidential requests or even to crises. There is, as Fenno (1977) observed, a trade-off between representativeness and efficiency: "Congress is, and always will be for better or worse our slow institution" (p. 263). Having learned the generalization in college, journalists and, we suspect, teachers often emphasize the lack of speed rather than the representative and deliberative strengths of legislative decisionmaking; Congress's reputation suffers as a result.

Oversight of the executive branch is another congressional responsibility, and one it has carried out well at times, as in the Watergate and MacArthur hearings. Although most Americans become aware of Congress's oversight activities only when major scandals are being unveiled, the balance between the legislative and executive branches is determined in part by the vigor with which Congress carries out these responsibilities. This topic, which takes on greater significance in the course of the prolonged effort to balance the budget, often gets short shrift in texts, although there are exceptions (see, for example, Ginsberg, Lowi, and Weir, 1997; Welch et al., 1996).

Managing conflict through bargaining and compromise is another task for which Congress has a talent. Many students, like the rebels who sought to topple Speaker Newt Gingrich in 1997, see compromise not as a critical component of successful democratic policymaking in a weak party system but as a betrayal of principles (cf. Hibbing and Theiss-Morse, 1997). There may be too little awareness in texts that for our system to succeed, especially under the divided control that has characterized American politics during the last third of the twentieth century, legislative leaders must work to find a widely acceptable middle ground.

To comprehend the deliberateness of congressional activity requires understanding not just the design of Congress but also the competing demands placed on its members. Do students acquire a sense of the competition between constituents, the party, the member's conscience, interest groups, and the White House? Certainly some texts capture this tension. A particularly good job is done in the opening passage of the Congress chapter in *American Government* by Welch and her colleagues (1996), which shows the crushing forces bearing down on Representative Marjorie Margolis Mezvinsky (D-PA) as she cast the decisive vote for the 1993 Clinton economic plan despite awareness that her action would be viewed as betrayal in her traditionally Republican district. Although the vote and Mezvinsky's subsequent defeat at the polls provided dramatic material for this text, every day in many ways members of Congress must deal with conflicting demands. There are excellent treatments of the ways in which representatives try to chart a course through the competing currents, such as John Kingdon's *Congressmen's Voting Decisions* (1989), but not much of this material makes its way into introductory texts.

As noted earlier, texts regularly detail congressional powers but may fail to explore fully legislative-executive relations. It is at this intersection that authors could explain the differences in the constitutional roles assigned the two institutions and underscore the advantages of an independent legislature. Texts could explain that when Congress does not quickly accede to presidential requests, it may not be because the legislature is "playing politics" or intruding on the prerogatives of the chief executive; rather, it may be because legislative leaders see problems with the president's initiatives, or because the bulk of the legislators' constituents oppose what the president wants. Not surprisingly, in light of George Edwards's (1980) extensive work on the presidency and his research into the correlates of presidential success with Congress, Edwards, Wattenberg, and Lineberry (1996) gives this topic serious attention.

Texts invariably explain how a bill becomes a law, and most have a diagram identifying the points at which approval must be secured. There are two potential problems here: The coverage does not go beyond materials presented in high school, and the treatment gives insufficient attention to politics. Although repetition has its virtues, if the presentation lacks interesting new details, many students will gloss over the diagram and discussion or have a flashback to the Saturday morning cartoon presentation of "I'm Just a Bill on Capitol Hill." To the extent that using an example makes the process more meaningful, then among the more successful presentations of the steps to enacting legislation are Welch et al. (1996), who focus on the minimum-wage bill to illustrate the various stages in the process, and O'Connor and Sabato (1997), who use the 1990 amendments to the Clean Air Act as an example. O'Connor and Sabato go so far as to contrast the "textbook" version with what they label "How a Bill Really Becomes a Law."

Even textbook and classroom presentations sensitive to the subtleties of the legislative role may not fully correct the orientation problem. For example, a hypercritical approach toward Congress and the government in general has become common in the fourth estate, since uncovering a scandal involving public officials seems to be the surest way to win a Pulitzer Prize. In a Freedom Forum national survey (Kees and Phillips, 1994), 72 percent of the public complained that journalists underestimate their news interest and assume they want stories about scandals instead of stories about policy issues. Most journalists (51 percent) and two-thirds of the politicians agreed with that appraisal. It will not be easy to convince journalists to concentrate on providing explanations when recognition and financial rewards go primarily to those who uncover malfeasance.

Another factor in choosing what news to report is the commercial motive of mass media organizations. In response to a question about whether top managers of the news media are more interested in selling newspapers or increasing viewership than in telling the public what it needs to know, 79 percent of the public and 82 percent of the politicians, but only 27 percent of the journalists, perceived an overemphasis on the bottom line (Kees and Phillips, 1994). The suggestion here that journalists do not perceive a problem in the media's orientation will make it doubly difficult, if indeed a conflict exists, to bring about change.

Conclusions

Future members of Congress, future journalists, and future voices of the American public sit in the same classes in secondary schools, and later some have another dose of American politics course work in college. For most voters, journalists, and teachers, these courses provide the last opportunities to learn about the realities of the U.S. democracy, a political process that is often messy, inefficient, and filled with conflict. If well conceived and well communicated, these classes can create a critical linkage between citizens and their government. Attitudes about Congress hinge on the degree to which realistic expectations about the institution are imparted, and that, in turn, depends on whether students come away with an understanding of how government works and an awareness that not all public officials are crooks. If done skillfully, political education at the secondary and collegiate levels can provide an antidote to the spreading cynicism about American government.

An appropriately tailored curriculum conveyed by talented instructors might leave more Americans with views similar to those of George Reedy, who served as President Lyndon Johnson's press secretary. Reedy (1986) comments on the excitement felt by those who know the Congress, and specifically the Senate.

> This, in my mind, is the most fascinating of all governmental institutions. It has the capacity to discriminate between winds of social change and temporary gusts that will leave no lasting impression. When there is a genuine emergency, it can act with bewildering speed. But there are other times when it can dawdle with a frustrating indifference to the urgings of partisans. Above all, it is a purely political organism that reflects, with a high degree of verisimilitude, the political realities of democracy in the United States. It is our most representative institution. (p. 2)

Why do so few Americans feel this kind of excitement about the legislative branch? Several of the themes in our chapter offer possible explanations. Most voters have engaged in little if any systematic study of Congress. Voters' perspectives are largely shaped by what they hear or see in the media, which often emphasize the shortcomings of the institution to the near exclusion of its strengths. Key to enhancing Americans' understanding of their national legislature is a different kind of information base.

Research by Hibbing and Theiss-Morse (1995) suggests that learning facts alone will not produce more positive attitudes toward Congress. We hesitate, however, to conclude that education cannot improve assessments of the national legislature. It would not be surprising to find education associated with more negative attitudes if the information conveyed in American government courses is highly critical of the institution and propagates unflattering stereotypes. An instructor who concentrates on criticizing the political system and Congress and fails to point up their strengths provides additional fuel for cynicism, so that the more one learns about American politics, the more alienated one becomes. Before concluding that education undermines support for Congress, one would want to know whether those who have been through a course that emphasizes the institution's strengths and shows how congressional debate and compromise promote the deliberative process by giving voice to diverse perspectives emerge more jaded.

Texts and teachers provide a multitude of facts but too often fail to convey an understanding of the politics. Instruction about Congress needs to impart an awareness of the role of the institution in shaping public policy and of the forces that impinge on that process. Much of what political scientists have learned about the clash of interests—mediated by responsiveness to constituency interests, partisan demands, concern about sources of campaign finance, and the constraints of the budget—that influence policymaking is not getting through to students. Young Americans do not have an adequate understanding of the role of the national legislature and the way it works. Insufficiently educated teachers and journalists, the lack of appropriate instructional materials and approaches, and a failure to examine the argumentation and controversy related to public policy decisions all contribute to deficiencies in public understanding and low levels of trust of Congress.

References

Beale, Howard K. 1936. *Are American Teachers Free? An Analysis of Restraints upon the Freedom of Teaching in American Schools.* New York: Scribner's.

Bennett, Stephen E. 1997. "Why Young Americans Hate Politics, and What We Should Do About It." *PS: Political Science and Politics* 30(1): 47–53.

Cooperative Institutional Research Program, American Council on Education. 1996. *The American Freshman: National Norms for 1996.* Los Angeles: University of California at Los Angeles.

_____. 1997. *The American Freshman: National Norms for 1997.* Los Angeles: University of California at Los Angeles. Available at: http://www.gseis.ucla.edu/heri/press97.html. Accessed January 14, 1998.

Cussler, Clive. 1993. *Sahara.* New York: Pocket Books.

Dye, Thomas, and Harmon Zeigler. 1996. *Irony of Democracy.* Belmont, CA: Wadsworth.

Edwards, George. 1980. *Presidential Influence in Congress.* San Francisco: Freeman.

Edwards, George, Martin Wattenberg, and Robert L. Lineberry. 1996. *Government in America.* New York: HarperCollins.

Fenno, Richard F., Jr. 1977. "Strengthening a Congressional Strength." In *Congress Reconsidered,* 1st ed., ed. Lawrence C. Dodd and Bruce I. Oppenheimer (pp. 261–268). New York: Praeger.

Frantzich, Stephen, and John Sullivan. 1996. *The C-SPAN Revolution.* Norman: University of Oklahoma Press.

Ginsberg, Benjamin, Theodore J. Lowi, and Margaret Weir. 1997. *We the People*. New York: Norton.

Hepburn, Mary A. 1983. "Can Schools, Teachers, and Administrators Make a Difference? The Research Evidence." In *Democratic Education in Schools and Classrooms*, bulletin 70, ed. Mary A. Hepburn (pp. 5–29). Washington, DC: National Council for the Social Studies.

_____. 1998. "The Power of the Electronic Media in the Socialization of Young Americans." *The Social Studies* 89(2): 71–76.

Hibbing, John R., and Elizabeth Theiss-Morse. 1995. *Congress as Public Enemy: Public Attitudes Toward American Political Institutions*. Cambridge: Cambridge University Press.

_____. 1996. "Civics Is Not Enough: Teaching Barbarics in K–12." *PS: Political Science and Politics* 29(1): 57–62.

_____. 1997. "What the Public Dislikes About Congress." In *Congress Reconsidered*, 6th ed., ed. Lawrence C. Dodd and Bruce I. Oppenheimer (pp. 61–80). Washington, DC: Congressional Quarterly Press.

Horatio Alger Association. 1996. "How Teenagers See Things." Report of an NFO Research study (April 1996). *Parade*, August 18, pp. 4–5.

Kees, Beverly, and Bill Phillips. 1994. *Nothing Sacred: Journalism, Politics, and Public Trust in a Tell-All Age*. Nashville, TN: Freedom Forum First Amendment Center.

Kingdon, John. 1989. *Congressmen's Voting Decisions*. 3rd ed. Ann Arbor: University of Michigan Press.

Matthews, Donald R. 1960. *U.S. Senators and Their World*. New York: Vintage.

McAneny, Leslie. 1997. "Pharmacists Again Most Trusted; Police, Federal Lawmakers' Images Improve." Gallup Poll Release, January 3. Available at http://-www.gallup.com/poll/releases.

McDevitt, Michael, and Steven Chaffee. 1998. "Second Chance Political Socialization: Trickle-Up Effects of Children on Parents." In *Engaging the Public: How Government and the Media Can Reinvigorate American Democracy*, ed. Thomas J. Johnson, Carol E. Hays, and Scott P. Hays (pp. 57–66). Lanham, MD: Rowman & Littlefield.

McLeod, Jack M., William P. Eveland Jr., and Edward M. Horowitz. 1998. "Going Beyond Adults and Voter Turnout: Evaluating a Socialization Program Involving Schools, Family, and Media." In *Engaging the Public: How Government and the Media Can Reinvigorate American Democracy*, ed. Thomas J. Johnson, Carol E. Hays, and Scott P. Hays (pp. 195–205). Lanham, MD: Rowman & Littlefield.

Media Dynamics. 1996. *TV Dimensions 1996*. New York: Media Dynamics.

Merelman, Richard M. 1996. "Symbols as Substance in National Civics Standards." *PS: Political Science and Politics* 29(1): 53–57.

Morin, Richard, and Dan Balz. 1996. "Americans Losing Trust in Each Other and Institutions." *Washington Post*, January 28, p. A1.

National Assessment of Educational Progress. 1978. *Changes in Political Knowledge and Attitudes, 1969–1976*. Washington, DC: National Center for Education Statistics.

National Association of Secondary School Principals. 1984. *The Mood of American Youth*. Reston, VA: NASSP.

Niemi, Richard. 1995. "Survey of Social Studies Coordinators in Fifty States." Unpublished report to the American Political Science Association.

Niemi, Richard G., and Jane Junn. 1998. *Civic Education: What Makes Students Learn.* New Haven, CT: Yale University Press.

O'Connor, Karen, and Larry J. Sabato. 1997. *American Government: Continuity and Change.* Boston: Allyn and Bacon.

Paine, Albert Bigelow. 1912. *Mark Twain: A Biography: The Personal and Literary Life of Samuel Langhorne Clemens.* New York: Harper and Brothers.

Parker, Glenn R. 1977. "Some Themes in Congressional Popularity." *American Journal of Political Science* 21 (February): 93–109.

Reedy, George E. 1986. *The U.S. Senate.* New York: Crown.

Roberts, Robert N., and Anthony J. Eksterowicz. 1996. "Local News, Presidential Campaigns, and Citizenship Education: A Reform Proposal." *PS: Political Science and Politics* 29(1): 66–72.

Simon, James, and Bruce D. Merrill. 1998. "Political Socialization in the Classroom Revisited: The Kids Voting Program." *Social Science Journal* 35(1): 29–42.

Welch, Susan, John Gruhl, Michael Steinman, John Comer, and Susan M. Rigdon. 1996. *American Government.* Minneapolis: West.

INTERNET RESOURCES

Center for Responsive Politics

   http://www.crp.org

CongressLink

   http://www.congresslink.org

C-SPAN in the Classroom

   http://www.c-span.org/classroom

Gallup Poll

   http://www.gallup.com/poll/index

Project Vote Smart

   http://www.vote-smart.org

Teaching Political Science (American Political Science Association)

   http://www.apsanet.org/teaching

Thomas—U.S. Congress on the Internet
   http://thomas.loc.gov

NOTES

1. The Center for Civic Education, a private nonprofit organization in Calabasas, California, prepared the National Standards for Civics and Government and has distributed them through several national organizations.

2. Reviewed were the chapters on Congress in James MacGregor Burns, J. W. Peltason, Thomas E. Cronin, and David B. Magleby, *Government by the People,* 15th ed. (Englewood Cliffs, NJ: Prentice-Hall, 1993); William A. McClenaghan, *Magruder's American*

Government (Needham, MA: Prentice-Hall, 1997); Richard C. Remy, *United States Government: Democracy in Action* (Lake Forest, IL: Glencoe, 1993); and Mary Jane Turner, Kenneth Switzer, and Charlotte Redden, *American Government: Principles and Practices* (Columbus, OH: Merrill Publishing, 1991).

3. An example of educational print materials on public issues is Greenhaven Press's *Opposing Viewpoints* books, which contain differing opinions on social, environmental, and technological questions, many of which become congressional issues. Other publications (for example, see *Update on Law-Related Education* [Chicago: American Bar Association, Fall 1997]) use an examination of a public controversy to activate information gathering and evaluation of the pros and cons of an issue. "Academic controversy" is the term used by David Johnson and Roger Johnson, professors at the University of Minnesota, to describe an instructional approach that uses intellectual conflict to increase student research, problem solving, critical review, and decision thinking to promote higher achievement; David W. Johnson and Roger T. Johnson, *Creative Controversy: Intellectual Challenge in the Classroom,* 3rd ed. (Edina, MN: Interaction Book Co., 1995). The teaching technique they propose holds promise for immersing students in the study of congressional decisions using news and opinions from current publications.

4. The National Budget simulation is available at: http://garnet.berkeley.edu:3333/budget.html or http://violet.berkeley.edu:6997/budget.html.

5. Included in this survey were the chapter(s) on Congress in Burns, Peltason, Cronin, and Magleby, *Government by the People;* Thomas Dye and Harmon Zeigler, *Irony of Democracy* (Belmont, CA: Wadsworth, 1996); George Edwards, Martin Wattenberg, and Robert L. Lineberry, *Government in America* (New York: HarperCollins, 1996); Benjamin Ginsberg, Theodore J. Lowi, and Margaret Weir, *We the People* (New York: Norton, 1997); Kenneth Janda, Jeffrey Berry, and Jerry Goldman, *The Challenge of Democracy* (Boston: Houghton Mifflin, 1997); Karen O'Connor and Larry J. Sabato, *American Government: Continuity and Change* (Boston: Allyn and Bacon, 1997); Thomas Patterson, *The American Democracy* (New York: McGraw-Hill, 1996); Susan Welch, John Gruhl, Michael Steinman, John Comer, and Susan M. Rigdon, *American Government* (Minneapolis: West, 1996); and James Q. Wilson and John J. DiIulio Jr., *American Government: Institutions and Policies* (Lexington, MA: Heath, 1995). We reviewed only the chapters on Congress so would not have picked up on coverage in other chapters that mentioned Congress, such as those on the presidency or interest groups.

7

Performance and Expectations in American Politics

The Problem of Distrust in Congress

JOSEPH COOPER

Despite the large amount of attention given to distrust in Congress over the past few decades, its character, causes, and consequences continue to puzzle and confuse us. As noted in the first chapter of this volume, the problem of distrust in Congress involves a host of conflicting facts and issues that defy easy resolution. It should not be surprising, then, that the question of distrust in Congress is treated in very different terms, both factually and normatively, by different observers of American politics. Many see trust in Congress as alarmingly low and in need of being substantially heightened (Craig, 1993, 1996). Others see distrust in Congress as in accord with traditional patterns of attitude in the United States and reflective of anti-authority modes of thought that have long characterized political culture in this country (Huntington, 1981). For many of these observers, distrust does not threaten but rather contributes to the workings of American democracy (Sniderman, 1993).

The aim of this concluding chapter is to provide an overview of the problem of distrust in Congress by analyzing the character, causes, and consequences of distrust in a comprehensive fashion. In so doing, I rely heavily on the contributions of the authors of the preceding chapters as well as other work. However, I also impose an analytical framework, of my own construction, that will lead us to explanations and conclusions not present in the preceding chapters, or even suggested by them.

Framing Analysis

We may begin by identifying the character or contours of distrust in the modern Congress. Though we have no polling data on the state of trust until the 1930s, and no consistent and comprehensive data until the 1960s, it is undeniable that distrust in Congress has been a feature of every era of American history and is far from a new phenomenon (Kimball and Patterson, 1997). Nonetheless, it is clear that cynicism regarding the representativeness, competence, and honesty of Congress and its members has dramatically increased since the mid-1960s. Whether the mid-1960s represented an unusual high point in trust we cannot know for certain. What we do know is accurately presented in the chapters by Bill Bradley, John Hibbing, David Shribman, and myself and is documented more fully in the Appendix. Trust in government generally, and by all indications in Congress as well, fell substantially in the period from 1966 to 1974, following massive U.S. involvement in Vietnam and the Watergate scandals, recovered somewhat in the mid-1980s, declined again to the low levels of the 1970s in the 1990s, and seems stable at these levels.

This pattern of increased distrust applies across a broad cross-section of American institutions. Heightened cynicism has been a general phenomenon since the mid-1960s. As David Shribman and John Hibbing document in their chapters, trust in the presidency and the Supreme Court has also declined, though the Court still enjoys significantly higher levels of confidence than either the Congress or the presidency. Moreover, as Shribman and Hibbing also show, the decline in trust in our foremost national political institutions is associated with a substantial decline of trust in societal institutions and professions generally. Though this decline includes all levels of government, it has been especially marked in the case of the federal government (Blendon et al., 1997). Whereas in the 1960s the great majority of the people believed that the federal government was attentive to their interests and effective in performing its duties, in the 1990s the great majority of people see the federal government as neither representative nor effective. Rather, they see it as unresponsive to the needs or ordinary people, controlled by special interests, and incompetent and wasteful in the performance of its tasks (Orren, 1997). Yet at the same time allegiance to the system of government established by the Constitution remains high. Large majorities of Americans affirm that our system of government is the best possible system and that they are proud to live under it (Hunter and Bowman, 1996).

The Layers of Trust

All this testifies not only to the broad relationships that exist between major political institutions and between these institutions and other sectors of society, but also to the multidimensional character of trust itself. As suggested in the first chapter of this volume, political trust is clearly not a flat, homogeneous entity, but something that is layered and involves different forms or types of trust at different levels of governance (Easton, 1965). Faith or belief in the ability of government to produce policy outcomes that meet the needs of its citizens, faith or belief that the actual operations of governmental decisionmaking conform to and serve basic democratic decisionmaking values and goals, and faith or belief in the legitimacy of the overall framework of government are all aspects or dimensions of public trust. Thus, the analysis of distrust must be sensitive both to the different character of distrust at the policy, governmental, and system levels and to the patterns of transition from lower to higher levels of distrust.

The existence of different forms or types of trust has relevance for the analysis of major institutional components of the political system, such as the Congress, as well as for the analysis of the system as a whole. However, to suggest that different levels or dimensions of trust exist is not to suggest that trust cannot be treated in a holistic fashion across dimensions. Thus, throughout this chapter I shall treat distrust in Congress as a general phenomenon but be concerned with how various forms or types of trust define the contours of distrust in Congress and, through Congress, shape the contours of distrust in the political system as a whole. Nor do I wish to suggest that the relationships between dimensions are structured in a purely linear and rigidly hierarchical fashion. Though it is valid and useful to see the transition from distrust at the policy level to distrust at the governmental level to distrust at the system level as steps in a "ladder of alienation," the process of transition is not mechanistic and does not automatically advance or regress simply because distrust has risen or fallen at a lower level.

There are, of course, broad and important continuities in the transitions from one level or dimension of trust to another in the case of the political system as a whole and Congress. Otherwise, our metaphor of a "ladder of alienation" would have no validity whatsoever. For example, the legitimacy of a political system is called into question only when faith in the fairness and integrity of governmental decisionmaking, as well as its capability or competence as a policymaker, is lost. When this occurs, alienation at the lower levels has become so serious that it can no longer be absorbed by focusing blame on particular aspects of policy, process, or officialdom. Similarly, I will argue later in this chapter that there are strong ties between distrust in the ability of government to produce and implement policies that successfully address citizen demands and distrust in governmental decisionmaking processes and decisionmakers, and that the character and determinants of these ties can be used to explain why distrust in Congress both persists and varies over time.

Nonetheless, there are discontinuities as well as continuities in the transitions from one level or dimension of distrust to another. This can readily be seen in the polling data on trust that have been gathered over the past half-century. For example, in the case of the political system, policy satisfaction since the 1960s, as measured by congressional and presidential job approval, has been highly volatile (Gallup, 1998). Yet trust at the governmental level, as measured by various indicators of belief in the representativeness and integrity of governmental processes and officials, declined substantially after 1968 and has remained low with far less variation (Bowman and Ladd, 1994; Orren, 1997). Conversely, in the decade preceding the mid-1960s trust at the governmental level appears to have been high, even when levels of congressional job approval were low (Davidson, Kovenock, and O'Leary, 1966; Lipset and Schneider, 1987).

In sum, trust at the governmental level is to some significant degree independently determined and not rigidly or mechanistically responsive to the state of policy satisfaction. Similarly, trust at the system level clearly is not necessarily undermined by distrust at lower levels, though, as the Civil War illustrates, under the right conditions it can be overcome by distrust at these levels. We shall therefore throughout this chapter be concerned with understanding the continuities and discontinuities that characterize the transitions between levels or dimensions of distrust and their significance.

Congress as the Fulcrum of Distrust

How, then, do the contours of distrust in Congress figure in the more general pattern? The answer hinges on the relationship between levels or dimensions of trust in the political system as a whole and in its major institutional components. What we have in the case of the political system in the 1990s are varying levels of distrust at the policy level combined with high levels of distrust at the governmental level and high levels of trust at the systemic level (Hunter and Bowman, 1996; Gallup, 1998; Pew, 1998). In the case of Congress, similar patterns of attitude characterize public assessment of its policy outputs, the representative quality of its decisionmaking and decisionmakers, and the legitimacy of its constitutional role as lawmaker (Hibbing and Theiss-Morse, 1995). This is no accident. The contours of trust in the system as a whole are shaped by the contours of trust in its major institutional components. And in this regard what must be understood is the crucial role that distrust in Congress plays in determining the character of distrust in the American political system. Congress is not only a component in the overall pattern, but a key component. Whatever the dissatisfaction with presidential leadership or the disdain for the ineffectiveness of the federal government, the fulcrum of distrust in American democracy is dissatisfaction with the Congress. This is as it should be. The Constitution establishes Congress as the primary arena in which the system's need to base action on high levels of consent is to be engaged and satisfied. Citizens therefore justifiably hold Congress largely, if not primarily, accountable for the representativeness and effectiveness of governmental decisionmaking, and particularly so in domestic policy. Ironically enough, then, the scope and intensity of distrust in Congress provide dramatic evidence not only of weakness but also of strength. Distrust is the tribute that perceived failure to live up to core values and beliefs pays to the continuing hold of these values and beliefs (Huntington, 1981).

However, it is also true that the relations between trust in the political system and trust in its major institutional components are complex, not simple. Even more than in the case of the different levels or dimensions of trust, these relationships are conditioned by factors we do not fully understand. Thus, the fact that distrust in the representativeness and integrity of Congress can and does co-exist with trust in the basic framework of constitutional government is not sub-ject to any simple and uniform conclusions. Continuing belief in the legitimacy of the system sustains and supports the continuing operation of the Congress. Nonetheless, it remains true, given the pivotal role of Congress in American democracy, that high and persistent levels of distrust in the representativeness and integrity of Congress may threaten the legitimacy of the system as a whole.

One final characteristic of the present situation thus needs to be highlighted. We have known for several decades that citizens consistently rate the perfor-mance of Congress as a whole lower than the performance of their own mem-bers (Bowman and Ladd, 1994). Diana Mutz and Greg Flemming extend the sig-nificance of this finding by suggesting that the linchpin of distrust in Congress is distrust of members other than one's own member. Given this finding, what also should be noted is that distrust of the individual member has deepened in recent decades. Most respondents now doubt the fundamental honesty of mem-bers (Gallup, 1998). These attitudes in themselves are not new. Still, such atti-tudes have now been rationalized and generalized in a way that is new. The pro-fessionalization of service in Congress during the twentieth century has combined with increased distrust since the 1960s to produce a mode of charac-terizing members of Congress that casts their identity in institutional terms rather than in terms of their individual characters. Seen through this new lens, members are viewed as constituting a distinct "political class" intent, like any special interest, on exploiting its power for its personal benefit (Will, 1992). The basic claim is that the current system of politics produces members who are not only professional politicians but corrupt individuals because that is part and parcel of being a professional politician. It follows, of course, that if the mem-bers are corrupt, so, too, must be decisionmaking in the body as a whole since it is no more than an aggregation of professional and hence corrupt politicians (Gross, 1996).

The Endemic Character of Distrust

In seeking to analyze the causes and consequences of distrust in Congress, I will, for purposes of tractability, equate the political system with the federal govern-ment and view Congress as a component of the political system delimited in this fashion. With this limitation understood, we may begin by taking our cue from the fact that cynicism toward Congress has always been present in American pol-itics. If distrust in Congress is an endemic feature of American politics, asking why this is so will uncover the factors that nurture and sustain it over time. Once we understand the factors that cause distrust in Congress to be persistent, we will have a basis in subsequent sections of this chapter for analyzing why it varies in strength and, combining both forms of analysis, for assessing the dangers it now poses.

Performance and Expectations

Students of modern American democracy often seek to explain variations in trust by focusing on gaps between performance and expectations (Craig, 1993; Orren, 1997). Simply put, performance pertains to the ability of government to respond to citizen needs and demands with policies that do in fact relieve distress and alleviate problems. Expectations pertain to the standards applied to judge performance. This approach is a useful one, and one we shall apply to analyzing trust. To do so, however, we must first explore the factors that determine performance and expectations in the American political system.

With regard to performance, the American political system is designed to make the balance all democracies must strike between consent and action a very demanding one (Cooper, 1975). The process of transforming shared electoral goals or interests into legislative majorities capable of enacting major policy change is one that is full of barriers. This is true for reasons that extend beyond the effects of formal divisions of power among the House, the Senate, and the presidency. Each of these entities is also based on a different constituency principle. Elections to choose congressmen, senators, and presidents thus channel different configurations of views and interests into the legislative process and confer varying degrees of advantage on them at different stages of that process. In a diverse nation, such as the United States, the result is to complicate the problem of building coalitions powerful enough to traverse all the veto points involved in the legislative process and to intensify the need to accommodate differences in order to aggregate the support needed to win. In sum, the result of diverse patterns of interests, different constituency principles, checks and balances, and the leverage that legislative rules directly or indirectly give to minorities is, as Madison foresaw in a far simpler world, to make the passage of major legislation a very difficult proposition.

With regard to expectations, standards of judgment are not defined purely and simply in terms of technical effectiveness or efficiency in relating means to ends (Cooper, 1981). It is not enough that the ends to be served by government pertain to areas in which citizens see serious threats to or impingements on their welfare. Rather, the ends must also be consistent with shared values and beliefs regarding the proper role of government as an agent of society in promoting the general welfare. Nor is it enough that the means be efficient and effective in relation to the ends in some abstract or objective sense. Rather, the identification of governmental policy goals and the fitting of means to these goals must be responsive to values and beliefs regarding the representativeness and integrity of the decisionmaking process. It is both the genius and the bane of democratic government that neither the ends the government should pursue nor the fit between ends and means in highly discretionary areas of policy is regarded as subject to "objective" determination by some group of experts or class of notables, but rather is seen as subject to determination by the whole body of citizens through the institutions and procedures of democratic government.

Thus, despite the fact that performance ultimately must be capable of sustaining and renewing expectations, gaps necessarily exist between the character of performance and the character of expectations. Expectations are in essence aspirations, based on values and limited only by fragile estimates of the constraints that empirical reality and human nature impose on their realization. In contrast, performance is always captive to the actual operation of these constraints, whether correctly estimated or not. As a result, performance and expectations inevitably clash, at least in the short run. When they do, trust at all levels of what we have called the ladder of alienation is endangered and may, when the clash is sufficiently severe, be vitiated. Given the character of performance and expectations as determinants of dissatisfaction, it becomes clear why the problem of trust in the federal government generally and in Congress specifically is an endemic one. Distrust is not rooted simply in the dissatisfactions that arise as the constraints on action inherent in the American political system block or dilute policy response to citizen demands. Nor is it rooted simply in human frailties, as manifested in various forms of official malfeasance or dereliction, though these have an impact in every age. Rather, the persistence and depth of distrust are tied to a more basic and encompassing cause—the character of aspirations or expectations in American democracy.

Foundations of Distrust: Members and Constituents

One defining feature of core democratic values and beliefs in the United States is that they are very demanding. Levels of expectation are high, and they inevitably breed dissatisfaction with outcomes and suspicion of politicians (Huntington, 1981). Substantively, citizens are encouraged to believe that government exists to protect their liberty and promote the general welfare. Yet capability for performance is constrained in very demanding ways, and widespread pressure for major policy change often frustrated. Procedurally, citizens are encouraged to believe that their views and interests will matter, that conflict will be resolved in a manner that is in accord with the canons of representative government, and that results will not be corrupted by the power of special interests or self-serving officials. Yet the political system is too large for citizens not to feel remote and ineffectual, the processes of accommodation and aggregation too intense and removed for citizens not to feel deceived, and standards regarding service to the public interest too vulnerable to conflicting interpretation and the corrosive realities of self-interest not to breed suspicion. Nonetheless, the reasons distrust in Congress is endemic do not lie simply in the high levels of aspiration or expectation that core democratic values and beliefs inspire. The continuing presence of distrust derives as much, if not more, from the ambiguous and conflicting nature of these values and beliefs as standards for judging behavior and decisionmaking at both the electoral and legislative stages of decisionmaking. In short, core democratic values and beliefs contain a variety of inner tensions that are impossible to resolve and continually generate distrust.

If we turn first to the relation between members and constituents, democratic values and beliefs are not blind to the lures and distortions of personal ambition. Here as elsewhere, one of the prime strategies they embody and apply is to tie self-interest to public purpose through reliance on the principle of election. Yet, despite the strength of elections in ensuring overall accountability and responsiveness, they are necessarily a very blunt instrument for reconciling the conflicting and ambiguous conceptions of representation that core democratic values and beliefs in the United States involve.

Perhaps the most basic contradiction pertains to the manner in which democratic conceptions of representation sanction behavior both as delegate and trustee. Members are expected to bow to and to lead constituent opinion. They are expected to represent what divides their constituencies from other constituencies and what unites them; to serve the immediate and particularistic interests of their constituents and their broader, long-run interests (Parker and Barrilleaux, 1996). In addition, both the realities and needs of democratic politics require that the representative process be seen as a dynamic process of interaction between members and constituents, not a static, mechanical regimen of external control (Fenno, 1978). Yet the leeway such interaction provides members to shape as well as understand constituency opinion also provides them with opportunities for self-promotion that can turn the relation between members and constituents into a manipulative rather than a representative one (Mayhew, 1974). Finally, in enjoining and sanctioning compromise as an essential ingredient of majority building, democratic values and beliefs undermine as well as promote their goals. The realities of coalition formation can require members to avoid issues that will destroy the aggregation of support on a host of other issues and to temper differences among supporters by presenting different faces to different groups. Once again, such behavior is unavoidable, and not necessarily dysfunctional, but is not acceptable in any unlimited fashion (Arnold, 1993).

All this is not to argue that democratic values and beliefs provide no standards of judgment. Democratic conceptions of representation cannot countenance corruption, cynical and systematic manipulation of constituents, or even abject catering to their views (Thompson, 1995). Nonetheless, in less than extreme cases, judging the quality of representation remains problematic. No formulas are provided that can be applied to resolve the contradictions and ambiguities in any precise and objective fashion. Rather, these ambiguities and contradictions permit varying types of responsive and responsible performance among members, varying modes of being legislators, not demagogues, in line with different views of legislative duties and different political circumstances. My point, then, is not that members do not vary in their integrity and responsibility, but that these qualities are difficult to judge precisely and objectively, except in cases of gross corruption or uncommon courage and honesty. Instead, they become matters that are politicized as members and challengers contest to define the perceptions and judgments that constituents will rely on to assess reality. All this is an inevitable result of the bluntness of electoral control and the fact that both policy choices and the imperatives of responsibility and integrity escape scientific or objective determination.

The fact that democratic values and beliefs contain no definitive formulas for resolving the tensions they involve is, of course, no accident. These tensions reflect complex and valid needs, and the conflicts that result must be balanced, not eliminated. Yet, given the underlying premises of democratic values and beliefs, the only legitimate mechanisms for doing so are the processes of democratic politics. Indeed, the basic faith of democratic government is that, with all its warts, reliance on popular judgment and elections in choosing political leaders and policies is the form of government most likely to serve the public interest and secure justice. Nonetheless, the impacts of the ambiguities and contradictions of democratic values and beliefs on actual practice make members very open to charges of hypocrisy and self-seeking (Ladd, 1990). The tensions involved in the roles of members are obscured by the glaring light of broadly defined and demanding expectations, with the result that the ambiguities and contradictions these expectations involve readily lend themselves to negative judgments of whatever balances members strike. This is especially so to the degree that citizens are dissatisfied with policy results. As disappointment intensifies, suspicions that the results derive from the self-serving and even corrupt character of politicians easily come to the surface. Moreover, as Diana Mutz and Greg Flemming cogently demonstrate, these tendencies are confirmed and amplified by even a few examples of egregious self-serving or outright corruption. Such evidence is easily generalized to the whole body of members, given the lack of familiarity and contact that constituents have with members who are not their representatives. The character of relations between members and constituents thus becomes a source of distrust because barriers to performance combine with extremely high and internally contradictory expectations to undercut faith in the responsibility and integrity of politicians.

Foundations of Distrust: The Workings of the Legislative Process

A similar scenario of causes and effects pertains to the workings of the legislative process. Here, too, ambiguities and contradictions in democratic values and beliefs undermine trust. For all the reasons discussed earlier, the workings of the legislative process involve obstruction and conflict as well as compromise and agreement. Yet both action and inaction are sanctioned directly or indirectly by core democratic values and beliefs, which prize action only when based on high levels of consent. As a result, the question of where the balances between controversy and agreement, compromise and obstruction, majority will and minority rights, should be struck remains highly contestable. Under these circumstances, the case for tolerating inaction on the basis of the need for accommodation and agreement is always a difficult one to make to a frustrated majority, and even less persuasive, both logically and practically, when the responsibilities of the government are broad and the penalties of inaction are substantial. Nonetheless, in the twentieth century, as in the eighteenth, core democratic values and beliefs provide no clear and definitive standards for balancing the conflicting needs of consent and action. They simply insist on their combined presence.

A related and reinforcing source of distrust derives from the problems of distinguishing what serves to advance the general welfare, and is therefore good and wise public policy, from what does not serve to advance the general welfare, and is therefore bad and unwise public policy. Such distinctions, whether substantively or procedurally based, are critically involved in citizen assessments at all rungs of what we have called the "ladder of alienation." As theorists as different as Aristotle, Augustine, and Madison have understood, without broad and meaningful conceptions of justice and the public interest to constrain and guide the use of its coercive power, the state is indistinguishable from a band of robbers. Though it would be naive to ignore the "struggle for advantage" or "divide up the pie" components of American politics, it is equally true that to see our politics as essentially exploitive provides no basis for understanding the overall sense of legitimacy, peaceful reconciliation of conflict, and orderly transfer of power that distinguish American democracy from more troubled regimes.

It is a mistake, then, though a fashionable one, to dismiss concern for the public interest on the part of citizens or elected officials as mere rhetoric. To do so is to miss its importance for trust and the long-run viability of democratic order. Yet standards for making judgments regarding the public interest are necessarily imprecise and inconclusive. The identification of policy that serves the general welfare cannot be tied simply and purely to the identification of some clear and homogeneous will of the people. Though democracy rests on consent and depends on shared values and compatible interests to provide a basis for accommodation and agreement, differences in views and interests are not only inescapable but the basic building blocks of democratic politics. If there were no differences over policy, there would be no need for politics. If it were assumed that some views and interests are necessarily right and others necessarily wrong, there would be no need for democratic politics. And finally, if all differences were fully reconcilable through democratic politics, there would be no need to balance consent and action, to establish institutional parameters both for majority rule and minority rights. In short, the will of the people does not so much direct the process of decisionmaking as emerge from it, and its character cannot be confirmed by immediate majorities, but only by subsequent consensus on policies that are initially highly controversial (Macmahon, 1948).

It is equally true that standards for judging the public interest cannot be based on distinguishing the partial from the diffuse or universal. Though the values and interests we broadly share as citizens in matters such as defense, clean air, or consumer benefits have more influence in the legislative process than those who view American politics as a struggle for group or individual advantage acknowledge, they provide neither a definitive nor a comprehensive basis for identifying the public interest. Judgments that equate the general welfare with universal interests remain open to challenge on the ground that intensity must count as well as number (Lindblom, 1965). Moreover, the values and interests that all citizens share usually can only be advanced by serving partial or particular values and interests. This is clearly true of partial interests that encompass wide segments of the population—the aged, the poor, labor, business, or certain minorities. But it applies as well to narrowly defined or highly particularistic interests. For example, though water and highway project programs are of direct benefit to particular constituencies, they can and must be capable of being justified in terms of some broader conception of general benefits to the nation through resource or infrastructure development (Maass, 1970). Conversely, even when policy is directed at providing equal or universal benefits to all, as in defense or environmental policy, there are always particularistic distributions of benefits and costs involved as well. There is, for example, inevitably both a politics of defense policy in terms of strategies and weapons and a politics of defense contracts in terms of the distribution of projects to constituencies.

Thus, once again, core democratic values and beliefs involve significant ambiguities and contradictions. They enjoin balancing consent and action, controversy and agreement. They direct that policy be in the public interest but recognize that this can include both deference and service to partial and even highly particularistic interests. In short, at the legislative stage, as at the electoral stage, these values and beliefs create significant tensions but provide little guidance on how to resolve them. Nor can they. Once again, resolution is and must be left to the processes of democratic politics. Nonetheless, at the legislative stage as at the electoral stage, these tensions serve as ready engines of distrust.

John Hibbing's insight that the American people subscribe to democratic ideals while rejecting the processes of controversy and compromise their practice necessarily involve thus becomes quite understandable. The conflict, compromise, and halting action that American politics typically entails in major areas of lawmaking are hard to reconcile with the notion that public policy is to serve the public welfare and to implement the public will. Rather, as at the electoral level, the compromising of positions and the strategic play of legislative politics can readily be seen as the machinations of self-serving and hypocritical politicians. In areas of policy in which large groups of citizens feel severe distress and can easily believe that the policy action they desire would promote liberty and/or equality in clear and important ways, and hence is in the public interest, inaction or limited action can readily be attributed to the power of special or selfish interests. The same is true in areas in which there is wide public agreement on a broad public policy goal but an underlying welter of disagreement on the appropriate means to realize that goal. Ironically enough, similar results can flow from action when it does occur. The compatibility of core democratic values and beliefs with action in support of partial interests, their plasticity in rationalizing them, and the role that the exchange of various forms of particularistic benefits plays both in distributive and nondistributive areas of politics confirm and foster the belief that politics is nothing more than a bunch of greedy private interests seeking to divide up a pie of benefits at public expense. Finally, as Roger Davidson points out, both the openness of the lawmaking process and its organizational complexity encourage those frustrated with policy outcomes to see results as tied to a conspiracy among special interests that find a hospitable home in the labyrinths of legislative structure.

In sum, then, given the demanding and conflicting character of democratic values and beliefs, higher levels of distrust than mere policy alienation are unavoidable. Distrust inevitably encompasses the basic fairness and integrity of the decisionmaking processes themselves, and even promotes suspicion of the basic framework of government. To argue this is not to deny that the leeway that core democratic values and beliefs allow to serving partial or particularistic interests is not subject to abuse. The American political system, as noted earlier, is not designed to ignore or suppress the self-interest of its citizens. As Madison realized, this would not only be impossible in any form of representative government but also counterproductive to its desire to base government on consent and promote the liberty and equality of all its citizens. After all, both the identification of the sources of distress the government should act against and the construction of majorities around concrete policy solutions must be fueled in large part by the assertion and reconciliation of demands based on self-interest.

Still, if the intent of the Framers was not to ignore or suppress self-interest, it was also not their intent to give it free rein. It was rather to harness self-interest to the achievement of policy that serves the general interest or welfare. And in the Madisonian framework, this is accomplished both by forcing different interests and views to find common ground at both the electoral and legislative stages of government and by seeking to establish a deliberative process at the legislative stage that will subject the satisfaction of interests, both broad and narrow, to the discipline of shared conceptions of what our common values and interests justify and require. Nonetheless, ideals and aspirations are one thing and realities another. Democratic government is always a work in progress with no guarantees of success and no easy formulas to direct or confirm results. Hence, trust is fragile as well, and distrust an unavoidable companion in a politics that seeks both to base itself on and to transcend self-interest.

The Ebb and Flow of Distrust

We may conclude that distrust in Congress specifically and in the federal government generally is endemic to the American political system. Moreover, the point applies not simply to the policy level, where the barriers to action might be expected to produce dissatisfaction, but also to the governmental level, for the reasons discussed earlier. However, trust at the policy and governmental levels also varies over time. We will ultimately wish to address the consequences of such variation. But we must first deal with its causes, especially as they pertain to trust at the governmental level—to trust in the quality or character of governmental decisionmaking processes and decisionmakers.

The Cyclic Character of Distrust

As noted earlier, trust in the representativeness, wisdom, and integrity of the federal government and Congress was relatively high in the mid-1960s and has declined substantially in recent decades. Such variation is not unique to the latter part of the twentieth century but rather provides as defining a feature of distrust as its persistence. Though we lack modern polling data, we can presume that distrust at the governmental level must also have been very high in several previous periods of our history. Take, for example, the late 1790s, when Hamiltonian economic policies and the Alien and Sedition Acts convinced the Jeffersonians that the Federalists were committed neither to the welfare of the people nor to representative government. Similarly, whatever the character of distrust today, the situation in the late 1850s must have been worse. For the only time in our history distrust grew to such proportions as to cause close to half the nation to reject the basic framework of government. Finally, one may cite the last several decades of the nineteenth century and the 1930s as periods when politics was characterized by high degrees of distrust across several levels or dimensions of trust. In the former case, rapid economic, cultural, technological, and social change created a new and very different America with a far more difficult set of domestic economic and social problems and a far broader involvement in the world. The result was not only an expansion in the character and complexity of the political agenda but also substantial farmer and labor unrest, a variety of reform movements and third parties, and some very dramatic instances of violence. In the latter case, the arrival of the Great Depression created immense unemployment and unrest. Absent successful policies to relieve the distress and dangers of the Depression, alienation overflowed the bounds of policy dissatisfaction, encompassed the governmental level, and threatened to spill over to the political system itself. Moreover, the actions Roosevelt took to relieve this stress made him a hated, not a revered figure to many Americans. Much of American business and a large portion of middle-class Protestant America strongly believed that he had permanently undermined individual liberty and enterprise in the United States.

However, there have also been periods of our history when the degree of distrust at the governmental level may be presumed to have been quite low. The decades between what the Jeffersonians called the "Revolution of 1800" and the late 1840s, when slavery emerged as a continuing, not episodic, destabilizing issue, appear largely to be characterized by low levels of rancor. With the exception of a brief period around the War of 1812, the first quarter of the eighteenth century was marked by the disappearance of old grounds of conflict between the Federalists and Jeffersonians and the emergence of a new politics of national expansion and development that has been described by historians as an "era of good feeling." Though the decade that followed saw the rise of Jacksonian democracy and intense conflict over the tariff, bank, and internal improvements in the 1830s, by the end of Jackson's presidency in 1837 the role of the federal government as an agent of national development had been capped in all these areas and a new version of Jeffersonian faith in limited government had emerged triumphant. Similarly, the achievements of the Progressive movement and the First World War ushered in a decade and a half in which even discord over policy was muted, and the achievements of the New Deal and the Second World War led to several decades in which the role of government and America's international role became matters of broad and deep consensus.

Without postulating any exact degree of regularity in periodicity or swing, or any exact equivalence in amounts of trust at the policy and governmental levels, variations in distrust at these levels nonetheless appear to be cyclic in character and interrelated (Dodd, 1994; Uslaner, 1993). Both forms of distrust appear to have waxed and waned in rough correlation with one another over the course of our history. If we may for purposes of analysis "stylize" these cycles, a distinction between short-run and long-run effects can be drawn that is quite instructive in explaining variations in distrust.

Short-Run and Long-Run Effects

In the short run, disappointment with major policy outcomes and politicians is unavoidable. When policy response to major sources of citizen demand are delayed, citizens who desire governmental action and are quite prone to see it as essential to the general welfare become aggrieved, and for all the reasons previously identified, their dissatisfaction easily leaps beyond the level of policy. Given the high level of expectations and the tensions core democratic values and beliefs involve, alienation intensifies and blame is readily assigned to the failings of key governmental processes and personnel. Yet even when action does occur, it does not necessarily relieve alienation in any quick or automatic fashion. Rather, positive action normally produces negative feelings for both advocates and opponents (Durr, Gilmour, and Wolbrecht, 1997). The compromises inevitably involved in passing major legislation lead advocates to see the action as impaired or flawed, whereas opponents are distressed that the legislation passed. The more critical the problem, the stronger the character of policy change, and the deeper the divisions over it, the more intense the dissatisfaction will be, particularly among opponents, and the greater the likelihood that the cognitive and normative factors discussed above will lead policy discontent to ignite higher levels of alienation. Hence, as noted earlier, even what is regarded by most of the public at the time as successful performance—for example, the programs of the New Deal—can be a source of alienation and distrust when policy change clashes seriously with the beliefs of a substantial part of the public about the role of government, the character of the general welfare, and desirable policy goals (Bennett and Bennett, 1996).

Yet this is just the kind of policy change by which the performance of the American political system and expectations regarding it are ultimately tested and vindicated. What becomes critical are the long-run results. Major policy changes must be capable of being transformed over time into matters of broad agreement, both because they do in fact relieve problems and because they can be accepted by the public as proper and appropriate governmental responses. In this process, the potential for diminishing the gap that separates performance and expectations through social learning becomes crucial (Dodd, 1994). Over time it is a seamless web of changes in empirical effects and changes in ways of viewing problems and results that accounts for the relief of citizen distress, not simply the "brute" empirical effects per se. Thus, every age must supply its own formulation of the proper role of government vis-à-vis society, and do so in a way that it can see as appropriate in terms of its understanding of what the impacts of major patterns of change have been, and what core democratic values and beliefs require and permit (Dodd, 1993, 1997). This enterprise, in turn, requires rethinking the proper relation between public and private, and hence also defining new standards or parameters for circumscribing conflict and legitimating results in terms of broad conceptions of the public interest or general welfare. In a similar fashion, every age must supply its own formulation of the proper role of the United States in the world. And this enterprise requires rethinking the relationship between domestic security and prosperity and international threats and dependencies.

In sum, to manage and control distrust at both the policy and governmental levels over time, broad "public philosophies" that discipline and harness interest-group demands to the general welfare and protect the security and prosperity of the United States from international infringement must emerge and become widely accepted (Beer, 1978). Such philosophies do not end conflict, and they do not immediately become matters of consensus. But they do frame the definition of problems and solutions regarding the needs of the public interest or general welfare, and they inspire the creation of new paradigms for policymaking in specific areas of policy. In so doing, they leaven the ability of democratic politics to respond successfully to the challenges of change in particular periods. Such success, in turn, results in the addition of new layers of consensus about the role of government and the public interest, and these serve to remove the weight of past divisions and to facilitate processes of accommodation in the existing era. Moreover, although their relevance and power atrophy as new patterns of social and economic change transform the context of politics, public philosophies that succeed in dominating the politics of an era also parametize the issues and controversies of the succeeding era.

The New Deal provides a good example. On the domestic side, the New Deal evolved a new public philosophy that redefined the role and responsibilities of the federal government. This new philosophy or outlook saw national politics as an arena in which the public interest was far more likely to prevail over special interests than state politics, and it regarded national effort, rather than state or private effort alone, as essential to satisfying the needs of the public interest. To meet the challenges of its era, the New Deal therefore accorded the federal government new responsibilities for promoting the economic health of the nation and for strengthening various sectors of society that had been seriously disadvantaged by the industrialization of the United States and its increased involvement in the world economy. In addition, the emergence of a changed outlook on problems and policy directions in domestic affairs was conjoined more closely than in other eras with the definition of a broad, new organizing perspective in international affairs, centered on the need for U.S. involvement and leadership in preserving the peace of the world. As suggested, these broad public philosophies inspired discrete paradigms for policymaking—from agricultural parity to a safety net for economic deprivation to collective bargaining to containment—which defined the premises and contours of policymaking in a variety of specific areas of policy. If the dominance of the New Deal public philosophy has weakened in recent decades and many of its premises and policy paradigms reexamined or even displaced, the commitments that underlay them with respect to the broad responsibilities of the federal government and the concrete results of these commitments are irreversible in a wide range of policy areas and continue to frame the policy conflict of the contemporary era (Mayer, 1992).

Thus, whatever the character of immediate response, it is the long-run effects, not the short-run effects, that are critical. For reasons that have been discussed, the story of American politics is typically not one of quick and profound response to threats or impingements on the lives of citizens. Rather, American politics has been characterized by long periods in which incremental policy change, discrete or isolated major policy change, and stalemate vary in their proportions but exhaust the nature of outcomes, punctuated by brief periods of major policy change that is programmatic in scope (Brady, 1988). This basic pattern reflects the rise of particular public philosophies to positions of dominance in determining the policy orientations of an age and then their decay as new problems arise, reveal the inadequacies of existing paradigms, and spark increasing amounts of dissatisfaction and distrust. With one glaring exception, such cycles in the past have been continuous and marked by the emergence of a series of dominant public philosophies and a continuing renewal of consensus, even though the broad visions of the proper role of government and the needs of the general welfare that sustain the process of cycling evolve and change (Uslaner, 1993).

As a result, trust in the basic framework of government has remained strong. Though trust at lower levels has ebbed and flowed, the divisions of one age have not been visited into the future so as to complicate and deepen bases of division to anywhere near the degree that they have in countries in Western Europe or Central America. Rather, questions have been settled and conflict circumscribed through the recrafting and reemergence of dominant public philosophies and discrete policy paradigms that renew agreement on what core values and beliefs entail (Morone, 1990). What appears critical, then, is that every age continue to find a pattern of responding to the problems of its era that has the capacity to renew and sustain a moving consensus on the essential parameters of the general welfare (Macmahon, 1948). But such patterns of response are themselves the prisoners of time because change is constant. As new problems emerge and replace familiar ones, old certainties begin to be questioned, old formulas lose their instructive power, and limited capabilities for response combine with high and ambiguous expectations to generate increased conflict, dissatisfaction, and distrust (Dodd, 1994). Every age is thus a time of testing for democratic government in the United States, and every age must be an age of redefinition and renewal if the "experiment in free government" begun in 1789 is to continue.

The Determinants and Consequences of Distrust in the 1990s

All this suggests a framework for answering the question of why trust in the federal government and Congress has been so low in recent decades. We may presume that the same factors that cause distrust to ebb and flow in all eras are key to explaining its state in any particular era. If so, the concrete aspects of the contextual conditions, which give shape and substance to these factors, must always be identified to give flesh to analysis. This is especially true for the contemporary era. The pace of change in multiple sectors of social life has been more rapid than in most, if not all, previous eras and has profoundly affected the context of politics. The consequences for trust have been extremely negative. The factors endemic to American politics that foster distrust have been substantially strengthened, and the factors that promote cycling have been substantially weakened.

Performance and Expectations in Recent Decades

In examining the impacts of the current context of politics, we shall focus our attention once again on the character of the interaction between performance and expectations and analyze the consequences for trust at both the policy and governmental levels. In terms of performance, it has become even more difficult than in the past to put policy coalitions together that are strong enough to produce more than limited and halting responses to citizen needs and demands. The underlying causes are highly related, of course, to the patterns of cultural, social, economic, and technological change that have prevailed in recent decades. These patterns of change have had decisive impacts on the character and conduct of politics. They have multiplied the grounds of conflict, reshaped the nature of organization and communication, and redefined the constraints that govern coalition building (Dodd, 1993; Neustadt, 1997).

One result has been that the American people themselves have become increasingly divided in their policy desires. In part, this is attributable simply to the manner in which patterns of change have transformed the policy agenda. New forms of cultural or value conflict over questions of race, gender, religion, and family life have added a new dimension of conflict to the traditional social and economic issues of the past and sparked the emergence of strong, new, cross-cutting issue divisions (Hunter and Bowman, 1996). At the same time, as the society has grown and entered a postindustrial and globalized era, new problems have emerged and old problems have been redefined. In contrast to the 1960s, American politics is now a politics of trade expansion, clean air, school vouchers, and patient rights as well as a politics in which issues like social security, medicare, welfare, tax policy, and government regulation of industry have reappeared in altered and difficult forms (Brady and Volden, 1998). In part, however, present levels of policy division also derive from the aggregate consequences of changes in the policy agenda. An inevitable concomitant has been decay in the relevance and hold of the public philosophy and policy paradigms that ordered and legitimated the politics of mid-twentieth-century America. Yet, the changes in the policy agenda of modern politics have not been able to generate any new public philosophy of comparable appeal and power. This failure is both cause and effect of low levels of trust, and we shall return to it shortly. Our point here is that, in the absence of a comprehensive and powerful public philosophy regarding the proper relationship of government to society, it becomes difficult to rationalize the relationship between policy proposals and the general welfare in ways that provide general standards for judgment and consistent benchmarks for organizing opinion (Dionne, 1991).

A second result has been an explosion in the number of interests represented in Washington and the emergence of a new and distinctive form of party politics (Aldrich and Niemi, 1996). Because of the cost of campaigns, the declining significance of party identification, and the role of the media in modern elections, candidates and interest groups operate far more independently than in the past. At the same time, continued, broad federal involvement in an increasingly complex society and a substantial rise in the salience of national policy concerns have combined to heighten ideological orientations toward politics, multiply the number of interest groups, and increase the intensity of commitment to them. As a consequence, party control of the policy agenda has diminished, rigidity within and between the parties has increased, and the scope of single-issue politics has expanded. The party politics of recent decades is thus not comparable to either weak party or strong party eras of the past. The irony is that in an era in which party voting in the Congress has risen in response to greater ideological coherence in each party, this coherence has reduced the ability of party leaders to control issues and accommodate differences, while simultaneously increasing the vulnerability of individual members to defeat by easily aggrieved and highly demanding interest groups.

A third result has been divided government, or its functional equivalent when government is ostensibly unified. It is not surprising that the range and complexity of issue division in modern American politics, when funneled through the constituency principles that define the House, the Senate, and the presidency, have made divided rather than unified government the modal pattern since the late 1960s. Nor is it surprising that in those isolated moments of unified government the president has usually been at war with his own party (Jones, 1995). Although it may be true that divided government is no stranger to major policy change, and unified government no stranger to stalemate, it is nonetheless true that in partisan and ideological eras of politics, the supermajorities divided government often requires for success are far more difficult to assemble than in more bipartisan eras. As a result, presidents and party leaders in Congress face harsh choices between a politics of obstruction that revolves around political maneuver and a politics of action that is both more alienating and less capable of confronting issues than has been true in the rest of the twentieth century and most of the nineteenth. Underlying patterns of politics since the early 1970s have thus made both divided government and unified government more ponderous, politicized, and captive to interest groups and single-issue politics (Brady and Volden, 1998).

In terms of expectations, what is critical is the ability to validate and sustain them. For reasons that include the limitations on performance but also go beyond them, doing so has become more difficult in recent decades, with the result that expectations provide a more fragile basis for maintaining trust than in the past. At the policy level, the fact that Americans now expect the federal government to take responsibility for the general welfare across a variety of broad areas, both domestic and international, has important consequences for trust. Whatever the support in recent decades for delegation of power to the states or for privatization, the clock cannot be turned back to the mid-1960s, let alone the 1930s (Bennett and Bennett, 1996). Expectations regarding the broader role of the federal government that were initiated by the New Deal have been confirmed and extended by all administrations through the early 1970s, and only trimmed, not vitiated, by succeeding administrations. The character of governmental performance thus has an even greater impact on levels of trust than before 1933, or even 1960, because expectations regarding its role are so much more extensive. Yet the complexity of the problems and the political constraints on passing effective programs make both the passage of programs and the realization of policy goals highly problematic. As a result, not only is discontent over substantive performance likely to be more comprehensive than in the past, but to the degree that it is not tempered by favorable economic conditions, it is also likely to be far more destructive of trust at both the policy and governmental levels.

The difficulties of sustaining expectations that are rooted in democratic ideals have also increased. As noted earlier, the expectations that serve as determinants of trust are not limited to matters of substantive performance. They also include expectations regarding the ties between representative government and government in the public interest. In this regard, the increased divisiveness of modern politics, the forms through which it manifests itself, and its policy consequences have powerfully strengthened the corrosive effects of the ambiguities and contradictions inherent in democratic ideals. Nonetheless, two other features of modern American politics must also be recognized for these effects to be fully appreciated. These features serve as cognitive filters that frame citizen assessment so as to foster the belief that decisionmaking processes are unrepresentative and captive to special interests, and decisionmakers self-serving and dishonest. Though the picture of politics these two features or filters present both reflects and distorts reality, the result in all cases is to exacerbate the degree to which citizens see democratic practice to be in conflict with democratic ideals.

The first is the role of the media in modern politics. The current impacts of the media in bolstering distrust are well documented and analyzed in the essays of Bill Bradley, David Shribman, and Diana Mutz and Greg Flemming. Though the character of politics in recent decades should not be blamed on the messenger, it is also true that the message framed by the messenger is far from neutral in its effects. Politics and politicians are covered in ways that highlight conflict and controversy, on the one hand, and personal ambition and ethical lapses, on the other. Such coverage, combined with the nationalization of the media, the prominence of TV news, and the frailties of human cognition, identified by Diana Mutz and Greg Flemming, has highly negative impacts on trust. The defining impression created is of Congress as a bunch of politicians squabbling over the distribution of benefits to special interests and jockeying for personal power while the needs of the country are ignored (Durr et al., 1997; Graber, 1993).

A second aspect of contemporary politics that has framed expectations regarding process and officials far more negatively than in the past concerns the role of money in politics. The emergence of a candidate-centered politics in which the media, and electronic media especially, dominate the processes of communication has dramatically increased the costs of campaigns, the amount of time politicians have to spend raising money, and the influence of the interest groups that play major roles in providing financial support. The problem is far more subtle than the outright buying of votes. Rather, it relates to the heightened importance of money in securing access and the distortions such advantages now entail both for the character of outcomes and for popular faith in the integrity of the processes of representative government. In the context of present laws regulating campaign finance, the result has been to create a vast number of situations in which conflicts of interest may be suspected or presumed and, in so doing, to provide a major focus of attention for a media predisposed to highlight controversy and corruption (Sorauf, 1992). Thus, as Bill Bradley argues so cogently, the main consequence of our current system of campaign finance has been to provide the public with persuasive evidence to confirm its worst suspicions and fears—that the political institutions of government are indeed captive to special interests, and their members self-serving, if not corrupt.

The contours of trust in recent decades can thus be understood in terms of the manner in which the context of modern politics has shaped the interaction between performance and expectations. In a context in which government is given broad responsibility for the general welfare, the problems that government is expected to solve have grown more numerous and complex, and the political capacity to address them has been subject to increased stress, it is not surprising that there have been failures in policy performance, that trust at the policy level has been volatile, and that the proper bounds and forms of governmental action have become matters of controversy in particular policy areas. Similarly, it is not surprising that trust at the governmental level would decline in an even more pronounced and stable way. In a context in which divisiveness, ideological rigidity, divided government, and single-interest politics prevail, the ambiguities and contradictions inherent in democracy ideals come to the forefront, and their corrosive effects are powerfully exacerbated by the role of the media and money in modern politics. Under these conditions, trust in the representativeness, wisdom, and integrity of governmental decisionmaking processes falls and remains at low levels, not simply because of dissatisfaction at the policy level, but even more because citizens are far more inclined than in the past to judge the practice of democratic politics harshly in terms of their understanding of democratic ideals.

The Consequences of Distrust

A number of consequences follow from the manner in which the context of modern politics in America constrains performance and shapes expectations so as to nurture distrust. In terms of immediate results, a politics that is far more negative, politicized, manipulative, and cynical emerges (Price, 1992; Uslaner, 1993). Whatever the endemic factors that lead citizens to see politicians as self-serving and hypocritical, these tendencies are reinforced and extended to a point where suspicion serves as a catalyst for the creation and broad acceptance of a view of politics that sees politicians as a corrupt political class. In such a context, politicians themselves confirm the claim by echoing the argument that politics corrupts government, attacking their own institutions, and presenting themselves to their constituents as outsiders. The same factors that produce this result, augmented by new technologies of polling and media advertising, also have broader, destructive effects on campaigns. The process of election becomes one in which the manipulation of images, negative appeals, and personal attacks gain more prominence and more resonance (McCubbins, 1992).

The process of legislating is also adversely affected. In his chapter, John Hibbing emphasizes the manner in which the expansion of complex and divisive policy arenas in recent decades has increased conflict and controversy and, in so doing, tapped the distaste for conflict present in the electorate and intensified distrust. All that is correct, but what is also true is that heightened suspicion and distrust in an age marked both by demanding expectations for performance and by extensive and confusing patterns of change transform the conduct of politics in highly detrimental ways. Whatever the difficulties democratic processes inevitably pose for motivating elected officials to confront issues and resolve differences, these difficulties are intensified by the forces that define modern politics and breed distrust. In a context in which the partisan politics of divided government makes supermajorities a vital necessity and candidate- and media-centered campaigns make interest groups more powerful and members more vulnerable, the legislative process becomes one in which normal tendencies to engage in gamesmanship, posturing, and credit-seeking are reinforced and extended. Politicians are increasingly motivated to pander to and manipulate the public, not to lead it.

What results is a form of politics that plays to democracy's weaknesses rather than its strengths. It is a politics that seeks legislation that looks good and appears to respond to intense public needs but avoids facing or resolving more demanding problems if there is political risk in addressing them or political advantage in stalemating them. It is a feel-good politics that rivets attention on second-tier issues identified in polls, laced by a politics of avoidance and blame on major issues. It is a politics in which public disgust with inaction is typically required to fuel the patterns of compromise needed for major policy change, and a politics in which the residue of such action is usually increased discontent within party ranks because compromise is seen as the triumph of expediency over principle. It is a politics in which the electorate's deep discontent and distrust lead it to vote for change uncorrupted by politics, but in which the electorate must be inevitably frustrated by the impact of the processes of democracy on the people it elects. It is a politics in which the electorate's lack of tolerance for the ambiguities and contradictions of democratic values is easily transformed into apathy, and at times anger, in its orientation to politics because the underlying conditions of politics heighten both gamesmanship and stalemate. And yet given its own ambivalence about process and divisions on policy, the electorate, as John Hibbing suggests, gets the policy results it deserves.

However, as we have argued, immediate or short-term results are exceeded in importance by long-run results. And here there has been a consequence of exceeding importance. The cyclic ebbing and flowing of distrust at both the policy and governmental levels appears to be frozen; the traditional rhythms of American politics appear to have been seriously disturbed and obstructed (Dionne, 1991; Uslaner, 1993). In sum, the short run has continued so long that it threatens to become the long-run result. What has happened in the past to renew American politics has not occurred. No new public philosophy that reinterprets the role of government in society so as to reestablish standards for public policy in the public interest and reorders political alignments in terms of this interpretation so as to limit the need for supermajorities has emerged to replace that of the New Deal (Greenberg, 1995; Mayer, 1992). Though portions of the Democratic Party from Johnson to Clinton and portions of the Republican Party from Goldwater to Gingrich have tried to define a new and dominant public philosophy, none of these efforts have succeeded. Results have been too haphazard and fragile to provide a generally applicable set of standards for distinguishing what serves the public interest as opposed to special interests or for defining a comprehensive set of policy paradigms whose broad goals and technical effectiveness are unquestioned by both leaders and ordinary citizens. Similarly, now that the cold war has ended, the nation is adrift in a world in which it has difficulty agreeing on what the problems are, let alone on the proper paradigms and policies. Conflict over domestic and international economic policy is thus intense and divisive between and within the parties. As a result, barriers to performance are even higher than they might otherwise be, and claims that policy is captive to special interests can universally be made. The New Deal vision of relying on the federal government to advance the general welfare and adjusting power relations to aid disadvantaged sectors of society becomes, in Ted Lowi's (1967) phrase, mere "interest group liberalism," but no equivalent philosophy or accompanying set of paradigms for orienting government to the economy has won acceptance. For reasons tied to the end of the cold war, a similar situation exists in international affairs.

A self-destructive cycle thus emerges in place of the traditional cycle that renews trust. As noted earlier, at the governmental level of trust the public is profoundly cynical about process and politicians, whereas at the policy level there is substantial instability in approval of the job performance of Congress and the president. The result is to make politicians fearful and timid. A climate of opinion, in which public attitudes toward politics are suffused with cynicism and public attitudes toward policy are highly ambivalent, instructs politicians that attempts to lead will not be rewarded and may be punished severely. Yet new public philosophies and sets of policy paradigms cannot be defined by fearful politicians. They require circumstances in which politicians have confidence in the common sense and forbearance of the public and are willing to lead it, not take their cues continually from polls, restrict their policy initiatives to what is safe and popular, and rely on media "spin" to escape criticism. In any era of profound change, new ideas and initiatives are needed, and these require political leeway, not only to encourage bravery but also to encourage and reward policy experimentation. In the end, then, the feelings of cynicism, apathy, and anger that distrust has engendered in the public in recent decades have undermined the very ability to relieve them. Politicians can reasonably conclude not to lead not simply because they want to preserve their jobs but also because they are not likely to succeed at either the legislative or electoral level. Yet in the absence of leadership, electoral verdicts are continually condemned to being negative and thereby become engines of distrust and frustration rather than of change and renewal.

Dangers and Remedies

We may conclude that American politics is now mired in a bog of distrust and self-destructive behavior for reasons that pertain both to the endemic character of distrust in the American political system and to the context of American politics in these last decades of the twentieth century. Two questions remain. How dangerous is this situation? Have we not witnessed and survived other eras in which distrust in government and officials was both low and prolonged? Second, even if we can conclude that current levels of trust are dangerously low, what, if anything, can be done to elevate them?

Dangers

To start, it must be conceded that we have no precise understanding of the dynamics of what we earlier called the ladder of alienation. The conditions under which alienation at the policy level becomes alienation at the governmental level, and alienation at this level becomes alienation at the systemic level, remain largely beyond our grasp. Our analysis of the cyclic character of distrust assumes a broad relationship between trust at the policy and governmental levels. So does our analysis of the determinants of distrust in recent decades. What is also clear, however, is that these levels are neither totally independent nor totally dependent on one another. As has been noted at several points in this chapter, popular assessments of the job performance of the president and Congress can vary widely without significantly affecting the amount of trust in governmental processes and officials, and the latter can remain low over an extended period of time without significantly affecting the amount of trust in the system as a whole. Given this fact, some important conclusions can be drawn.

The discontinuities that exist are quite fortunate for the stability of the system. The fact that higher levels of trust respond to socialization, historical memory, and other independent sources of determination to a greater degree than lower ones obstructs the ability of alienation to climb across levels. Nonetheless, the continuities or interdependencies that exist between the three levels of trust are powerful, even if not tightly connected in a linear fashion. Thus, while recognizing that distrust is endemic in American politics and that its impacts are not entirely negative, it remains true that distrust at the policy and governmental levels must always be managed because the potential for serious damage to the operation and preservation of democratic institutions is always present.

Though the amounts required vary among levels, maintaining certain minimal amounts of trust at all levels is necessary to permit the long-run unifying processes of American politics to operate successfully. As John Hibbing and Bill Bradley recognize, this is especially true with respect to trust at the governmental level. Given both the continuities and discontinuities that exist, faith in the representativeness, wisdom, and integrity of the processes and officials involved in governmental decisionmaking serves as the pivotal level of trust. Trust at this level both contains the alienation sparked by unsatisfactory policy outcomes and sustains the long-run dynamism of American politics by maintaining faith in the fairness and promise of basic democratic processes. Conversely, to the degree that it falters, declining trust at this level can endanger not only the dynamism but the very legitimacy of American democracy.

The persistence of low levels of trust at the governmental level should therefore not lightly be dismissed. It is no accident that the decline in the sense of citizen efficacy since the 1960s matches the decline in trust at the governmental level (Flanagan and Zingale, 1998). Similarly, while the invention and triumph of unifying public philosophies are required in every age to sustain trust, it is a process that also depends on trust, especially at the governmental and system levels. Trust, in short, is a cause as well as an effect. Although it may be analyzed as a product of the manner in which performance and expectations interact in the context of existing social and political forces, it is also true that the underlying characteristics of performance and expectations are affected by existing amounts of trust. As even those committed to the primacy of individual self-interest in politics have begun to recognize, realizing the potential benefits or gains of social cooperation depends on trust (Ostrom, 1990). Trust is, as Robert Putnam (1993) claims, a form of social capital that is vital to the success of democracies.

However, the reasons to be concerned about the persistence of low levels of trust at the governmental level since the 1960s relate to the concrete circumstances of modern American politics as well as to general patterns or relationships that apply in all contexts. It is true that we can find parallels with other periods, most notably the last decades of the nineteenth century. Nonetheless, our analysis of the context of modern politics strongly suggests that the endemic factors that cause distrust have been substantially strengthened and become more difficult to manage or reverse than at any period in our history, with the exception of the 1850s. Concomitantly, given the pace and scope of change, the difficulties of coming to terms with the new world that is emerging may well be more difficult than in the past. In all ages change makes the lenses we rely on to frame reality outmoded. And in all ages the ways in which these lenses should be modified and replaced do not become clear in an instant—rather, a process of adaptation that serves as the basis of social learning is required. Yet, as Larry Dodd (1997) argues persuasively, finding these new lenses and putting the old ones behind us will be far more difficult in a postindustrial age than in the past. For example, it can be argued that in the past trust could be restored by public philosophies and policy paradigms premised simply on reducing or expanding the scope of government domestically and treating the nation-state as the dominant actor internationally. In contrast, today, in the United States as in other nations, the challenges and complexity of economic, technological, and social change, combined with changing patterns of national identity, economic integration, and cultural conflict, make defining the role of the state vis-à-vis both domestic society and the international world a far more difficult problem to solve.

The result is that levels of trust at the policy and governmental levels that in the past were sufficient to allow the political system to redefine and renew itself may well now be inadequate, both because of the more demanding requirements of social learning and because the present context of politics restricts the leeway for innovation and experimentation on which social learning depends. We may be thankful that, despite all the difficulties, faith in democratic values and beliefs at more general and abstract levels remains strong enough in the United States to shield trust in the system from the effects of cynicism at lower levels. But the shield cannot be impregnable, and this is especially true in an era in which low levels of trust at the governmental level seem impervious to change, despite variations in support or approval at the policy level. The reemergence of third parties, reform movements, sporadic violence, and a substantial decline in the sense of citizen efficacy are strong symptoms of distress that should not be ignored.

One cannot but wonder about the current ability of the American political system to withstand a severe shock, most likely in the form of a worldwide depression or banking collapse, but also possibly in the form of some severe threat to national security involving atomic, chemical, or biological weapons. Admittedly, both types of shock seem quite remote at present, but no period of American history has escaped them, and they are rarely predictable. Yet even more dangerous than a shock too powerful for current levels of trust and legitimacy to absorb is the incremental erosion of representative government as a result of deepening cynicism about the fairness and integrity of governmental decisionmaking and recurrent patterns of intense anger and frustration with respect to performance. In this case, as in the case of a severe shock, Congress would necessarily be the focus of attack. But in the case of erosion, the danger is more subtle. It is that low levels of trust will slowly and silently, but nonetheless increasingly, lead to reductions in the role and power of Congress. Combined with the new technologies of campaigning and polling, the result could well be to transform representative government in the United States into a plebiscitary democracy led by the president and an administrative state controlled by his appointees. If that day comes, the irony will be that the forms and language of representative government will be preserved, but the demanding balance between consent and action, intended by the Framers, will pass from the scene.

Remedies

For all these reasons, we can conclude that the persistence of low levels of trust at the governmental level in recent decades is a valid cause for concern. Though diagnosis is far easier than prescription, our analysis provides some clear guidelines to apply in identifying strategies for enhancing trust.

The first is that strategies that do not recognize or cannot accommodate the tensions in core democratic values and beliefs are incapable of improving the situation and may in fact make things worse. Hence, approaches to political reform that are based on a moral distinction between citizen and professional legislators, or on a mechanistic conception of the role of the legislature, are likely to be not only ineffective but counterproductive. A second guideline derives from our argument that the prime problem in recent decades is not that politicians are corrupt or irresponsible, but that they are too fearful of their electorates to lead. If so, approaches need to be oriented to increasing the leeway politicians have to take risks in policymaking while still preserving accountability (King, 1997). A third and final guideline derives from the role that trust plays in creating leeway for politicians to lead and the role that expectations play in sustaining trust. If, as several essays in this volume have argued, popular beliefs regarding the representativeness and integrity of legislative decisionmaking now needlessly exaggerate the degree to which democratic practice is the enemy of democratic ideals, then redefining expectations regarding the processes of democracy in light of the tensions in democratic values and beliefs is essential. Conversely, if, as other essays in this volume argue, areas exist in which expectations are seriously undermined by forms of behavior that have no justifiable foundation in democratic ideals, then action also needs to be taken to bring practice into closer accord with expectations. In both cases, altering the cognitive maps in the minds of citizens by actions that sustain expectations provides a strategy for reigniting the traditional dynamism of American politics, despite the harsh constraints imposed by contextual factors in modern American politics.

These guidelines inform our judgment of what to avoid and what to try to achieve. In line with the focus and premises of this chapter, we shall apply them with particular emphasis on and concern for alleviating distrust in Congress. Perhaps the most familiar proposal in this regard is term limits. The case for term limits rests on the belief that action in the public interest will be enhanced if the legislature is composed of citizen legislators rather than professional politicians. This belief is a mirage, whether rationalized in terms of the superior virtue of citizen legislators, the capping of career ambitions, or the impact of turnover in unfreezing the power of entrenched interests. Citizen legislators are no more immune to all the conflicts in a representative's role than professional politicians and, as the present high rates of turnover in Congress demonstrate, no less captive to basic divisions in American society. Nor is the capping of career ambition likely to provide more benefits than costs. The abbreviated time horizons imposed by term limits make legislators less open to and less skilled in fashioning the creative compromises that deliberative democracy requires, threaten the recruitment of quality candidates, and introduce a set of incentives that are potentially even more corrupting than the desire to stay in office (King, 1997). In sum, then, the belief that politicians constitute a corrupt class whose role in politics needs to be reduced, if not eliminated, is a belief that both distorts reality and misunderstands the needs of democracy. In politics, as in all professions, there will inevitably be a bell curve distribution of character from scoundrels to saints. To premise action on any other assumption is to ensure adverse results.

Similar problems direct caution over proposals for increasing participatory forms of democracy (Citrin, 1996). Any proposal that would seek to enhance trust by involving citizens in decisionmaking in ways that seriously reduce or impair the power of Congress threatens to do far more harm than good. Government that acts in the public interest on the basis of citizen participation and consent is the defining ideal of American democracy. But as our discussion of the tensions in democratic values implies, the pursuit of this ideal involves balancing a number of conflicting ingredients—action and consent, deliberation and responsiveness, persuasion and compromise—not simply the testing of wills through majority voting. Moreover, enhancing direct democracy does not limit the power of entrenched interests; it only changes the ground rules of politics in favor of interest groups that are adept at arousing and exploiting those sweeping and momentary public passions that Madison and the Framers were so anxious to contain (Lee, 1997). All this is not to deny the possibility and value of finding ways to make government less remote to ordinary citizens. New and creative attempts to enhance citizen participation without enhancing the power of interest groups or injuring deliberation do exist (Fishkin, 1991). They are worth exploring in an age of technological revolution, but their reach and viability remain unclear.

Our guidelines, however, are positive as well as negative in their import. We have argued that citizen assessments of the workings of American democracy are critical for trust, and that prevailing perceptions of the representativeness and integrity of governmental decisionmaking can be altered in ways that bolster trust. If this is the case, then, several courses of action to reduce the gap between the realities of democratic practice and the demands of democratic ideals in the minds of citizens can be suggested.

First, as Bill Bradley argues, it is vital to do something about the problem of money in politics. There is no feature of the current political scene that is as corrosive to faith in the basic integrity of the system and officials than current practices with respect to campaign finance. This does not mean that there are any easy solutions, given the conflict between fair elections and free speech that regulating campaign finance inevitably involves and the inventiveness of professional practitioners. Different solutions provide different benefits and costs and vary in their amenability to manipulation by candidates, parties, and interest groups (Sorauf, 1992). Indeed, there is no area of American politics that better demonstrates how destructive the unanticipated consequences of reform can be than campaign finance. Nonetheless, action can be and needs to be taken to increase trust in politics and politicians. Certainly, tightening disclosure, taking additional action to bar foreign contributions, eliminating the subterfuges "soft money" permits, and improving enforcement are places to start. Beyond that, changes that reduce the costs of campaigns and limit spending should be explored with due regard for the need to balance conflicting "goods" and the impacts of reform on alternative patterns of political activity. Though campaign finance reform can serve only to reduce the problem, not eliminate it, there is no more important topic to address in sustaining the legitimacy and vitality of the American political system. Indeed, even if the American people refine their views of compromise and controversy so as to better understand their necessity and benefits, they can readily continue to believe in the rule of special interests given the present system of campaign finance.

Second, action needs to be taken to curtail the negative impacts of media reporting on Congress. The contemporary media equate objectivity with value neutrality in reporting the news. Their professional standards thus emphasize care in establishing the facts and the avoidance of opinion on the merits of policy or politicians. Equally important, they believe that these standards do in fact provide appropriate and effective guidelines for achieving objectivity. The public remains skeptical, however, primarily because it has serious doubts regarding the clarity of the line between facts and opinion in daily reporting. Be that as it may, there is another facet of the issue of media standards that both the public and the media have ignored and which is of far greater significance in institutional terms. It pertains not to bias in the presentation of policy issues or the actions of political leaders, but to bias in the presentation of democratic decisionmaking processes per se.

Even aside from the question of bias in reporting on policy or politicians, the media need to confront the harmful consequences of their belief in value neutrality as it pertains to the workings of democratic institutions. Here, even more than in the policy realm, they cannot simply assume that when they act "professionally" their regard for truth and overt antipathy to bias provide the best of all possible worlds. As a general proposition, objectivity is possible only within a framework of prior assumptions. Not to recognize this is to allow implicit value judgments and perceptions to control results in ways that threaten to make neutrality an illusion. This danger is even more pronounced when dealing with institutions. Here the media's penchant for the dramatic and the suspicion that has oriented its stance toward government since Watergate are inevitable sources of bias.

Thus, the issue is not whether the media should strive for objectivity. It is how to do so in a context in which commitments to democratic values set the parameters, not implicit assumptions about what makes an event "news" or whether government should be viewed with suspicion. The leaders of the media need to sponsor an extensive dialogue both inside and outside their ranks on how to improve the media's ability to tell the American people what is going on in government without needlessly undermining democratic values. If the media should not be mere cheerleaders for democratic government, neither should they indulge themselves in the cynicism that so easily proceeds from the gap between the ideal and the real. Rather, they must discipline their reporting with a recognition of the ambiguities and contradictions that democratic values and beliefs involve and serve as guides for balanced public understanding and judgment. In 1947 the Hutchins Commission concluded that the prime defect in press reporting on politics was that it did not report the context, and that is even more dangerously true today (Patterson, 1994).

However, we cannot rely entirely on media self-criticism and reform. The character of the media as a societal institution and corporate business in late-twentieth-century America imposes constraints that are very limiting and exacting (McCubbins, 1992). As Thomas Patterson (1994) suggests in the realm of presidential elections, politicians and political institutions need to be more attentive to presenting the nature and problems of democratic government to the public both through and independently of the media. If the media need to reexamine their practices and assumptions, so, too, does the Congress. For example, politicians who exploit distrust of the Congress as an institution for self-advancement ought to be subject to greater critique, if not scorn. In addition, as Roger Davidson suggests, the Congress needs to give far greater attention to how it presents and explains itself as an institution to the thousands of visitors who tour the Capitol. It needs to give greater attention to the role of its historical and other information offices in providing material to the public and public institutions, and particularly to how to use the Internet to tell the story of Congress as an institution.

It is true, of course, that there are dangers in encouraging Congress to pay greater attention to how it presents itself to the public. All facets of Congress are by nature unusually vulnerable to politicization to advance the interests of parties and members. Nonetheless, an institution that is incapable of setting limits on the degree to which the parts can exploit the whole is not an institution that can maintain its role or power over time, and this fact has special relevance for Congress in an age when both the informal norms and organizational mechanisms that support it as an institution are far weaker than in the past.

Finally, as a growing number of observers realize, we must subject the quality of civic education in the United States to a far more challenging process of review and improvement (Mann et al., 1996). If the persistence of distrust is a serious danger, and if addressing cognitive sources of distrust is a critical strategy in alleviating it, then the ways in which students are educated in schools and colleges about the workings of democracy must become a primary matter of both concern and action. As the chapter by Mary Hepburn and Charles Bullock suggests, the public's inability to understand and deal with the ambiguities and contradictions of democratic politics may be attributed more to defects in civic education than to defects in the media.

In the case of schools and universities, as in the case of the media, the problem is not that commitment to basic democratic values and beliefs is absent. These values and beliefs are affirmed in a variety of ways, both explicit and implicit. It is thus no accident that Americans remain strongly committed to democracy as a system of government. However, such commitment is broad and abstract. It does not speak to and cannot deal with the ambiguities and contradictions of democratic politics. These have to be dealt with at their own level if the successes and failures of American democracy are to be accurately assessed. In a large sense, that is the thrust of the argument made by both John Hibbing and Roger Davidson regarding the causes of distrust. Hibbing and Davidson argue that even though Americans venerate democracy as an ideal, they do not understand its practice, and hence they react negatively to the processes of conflict and compromise democratic politics necessarily involve. Not only is this argument correct; it directs us to ask why civic education in the United States produces such a result.

Once again, current positions on the issue of value neutrality do much to explain the outcome and to suggest the directions of constructive change. If anything, attachment to value neutrality in schools and universities has been stronger than in the media. This is not surprising. In schools and universities the strong appeal of treating facts and values separately rests not only on the veneration modern democratic values accord to individual conscience, but also on a philosophically sophisticated sense of the inability to settle value questions definitively on the basis of objective evidence. However, the intellectual climate of the twentieth century has sharpened and rigidified understanding and application of the fact-value distinction. For much of the twentieth century positivist views of the social sciences have been dominant. Such views direct that the social sciences should rigidly separate facts and values, treat values as tastes or preferences not subject to rational analysis or comparison, focus on the determination of facts, and confine the analysis of value questions to factual determinations of the most efficient relationships between means and ends. Moreover, the thrust of these assumptions and the problems of operationalizing them have led to an emphasis on the individual as the prime unit of analysis and the maximization of self-interest as the core analytical assumption.

Such an approach has characterized not only the study of economics but also the study of American politics since the 1950s. Whether couched in the broader and softer language of behaviorialism or the narrower and sharper language of rational choice, it has been particularly dominant in the study of Congress (Bessette, 1994; Maass, 1983). Politicians are largely viewed and treated as self-interested, particularly with respect to their careers, and as either captives or manipulators of their constituents. The legislative process is treated as a locus of conflict, either narrowly between interests or somewhat more broadly between parties that represent congeries of interests, and outcomes in this process are viewed as a struggle or game determined by the interests and power of the participants. In sum, those parts of Madison that speak to self-interest and conflict between interests are highlighted, and those parts that speak to the need to design political institutions to promote deliberation and the public interest are ignored. It is thus not surprising that whatever elements of disagreement or subtlety the professional literature does contain rarely surface in the textbooks used in the classroom.

As a result, the same general features that characterize media accounts characterize the accounts of political scientists. The consequences for trust, though unintended, are extremely harmful. If the media too often present Congress in ways that engender cynicism, and if the public distrusts politicians and lacks tolerance for controversy and compromise, in both cases the results are tied to the manner in which the present approach to the fact-value distinction in civic education turns the gap between democratic ideals and practice into an unbridgeable chasm. To put the point more concretely, if both the media and the public exhibit high amounts of distrust, both have been educated in classrooms and with textbooks that proclaim "government of, by, and for the people" to be the democratic ideal, while presenting democratic practice as self-interested conflict between interests, as an exploitive politics of "dividing up the pie" that rewards some interests at the expense of others.

The quest for advantage on the basis of self-interest is indeed an important part of American politics. But it is not the whole, and the consequences of presenting it as if it were are very destructive (Perrow, 1986). Once again, our assumptions and perceptions play a role in determining facts, and the facts we find have normative implications. If American politics was nothing but the pure and simple pursuit of narrow, selfish advantage without any leavening by deliberation and compromise on the basis of shared values and interests by informed and responsible politicians, it probably would have collapsed long ago. Absent trust, egoistic self-interest by and of itself has great difficulty explaining social cooperation, even in the stylized two-person games of rational choice theory (Ostrom, 1998; Putnam, 1993). Yet it is all too true that self-interest alone provides a very fragile basis for trust, and that thinking that democratic politics is nothing but self-interest can transform it into a harsh and self-destructive form of politics that undermines rather than enhances the very benefits of social cooperation it is designed to provide (Uslaner, 1993).

It was not for accidental or idle purposes that Madison's standard was the public interest—not the mere management of conflict between interests—and that he saw legislative deliberation and the quality of legislators as keys to the success of republican government. Placing conflict and compromise in proper perspective for the public, educators, and journalists thus requires more than making the point that a system of government that seeks to base action on consent necessarily involves controversy and the reconciliation of conflicting views. If nothing more than self-interest is assumed, then the only standard for legitimacy is equal access and power for all interests. Yet, given the highly disproportionate distributions of social and economic power that a free society involves, this standard is more difficult to specify and satisfy than a more substantive one. More important, even to the degree that it is satisfied, results that serve only particular interests at the expense of other interests will not be legitimizable or, in cases of serious conflict, capable of settling anything. To return to our robber-band analogy, there can be no trust if the processes of democratic politics are seen simply as processes in which might makes right. With all its difficulties and frailties, the importance of shared concerns and values as a basis for politics has to be recognized. Otherwise, the public can increase its sophistication about conflict without any reduction in its distrust for the workings of the political system.

In arguing that current approaches to value neutrality in civic education are counterproductive, we do not wish to imply that change will come easily. Hepburn and Bullock present a detailed analysis of the substantial barriers that exist as well as the areas of opportunity. Nor, as in the case of the media, do we mean to recommend that teachers and textbooks simply become cheerleaders for governmental processes and politicians in America. Indeed, it was revulsion against the simplicity, if not the hypocrisy, of a simple cheerleading approach in the troubled times of the 1960s that led to its utter rejection, except with regard to democratic values in their most abstract and general form. In part, this reaction was quite correct. Core democratic values are properly very demanding, and politicians should be held accountable for policy outcomes and behavior in terms of those values. However, if serving as mere apologists for whatever happens is a betrayal of the basic purpose of civic education, teaching democratic politics with little or no sense of its normative purposes and the tensions these purposes involve is equally unacceptable.

It is true, of course, that a purposive approach has dangers as well as advantages. Still, what is true of the media is also true of schools and colleges. The quest for objectivity is not one that should be pursued in some absolute manner, but it is also not one that should be totally abandoned. If neutrality entirely independent of value premises is a delusion, neutrality conditioned by value premises is not. Civic education thus should largely be confined to exploring the tensions in democratic values and beliefs and their impacts on practice. It is an enterprise that requires a foundation in factual knowledge and shared values, but it best proceeds by emphasizing the framing of questions and their treatment as items for rational discussion. How should a member of Congress balance his or her duties as delegate and trustee? What is the difference between compromise and demagoguery? To what degree do the reasons for inaction lie in the ambivalence and divisions of public views on policy as channeled through a highly representative set of institutions, and to what degree are particular interests overly advantaged? All this does not mean that teachers and scholars should not take positions—indeed, the enterprise requires exposition and argument to be effective. It only means that no one should assume that their positions are definitive and that the thrust of civic education should be to enlighten students on the necessities and issues of democratic practice.

In sum, if we ask the media to do a better job of serving as a reliable guide to the ambiguities and contradictions of democratic values, it is even more important that textbook writers and teachers do so as well. What we require are not pat answers to shallow questions, but rather greater awareness of the tensions implicit in democratic beliefs and the ability to raise difficult issues in ways that neither overly justify failure nor render cynicism a victor by default. In proposing to re-institute a more purposive Madisonian approach to teaching democratic politics, we do not pretend that it would be a panacea. In the end, democratic systems must perform in a manner that proves satisfactory to their citizens. However, as I have argued, such judgments are ultimately a seamless web of brute aspects of performance and evaluative expectations. Citizen satisfaction over time is thus dependent on the emergence of public philosophies and policy paradigms whose results can be transformed into matters of consensus. Trust is a critical ingredient in this process, and civic education a critical ingredient in maintaining necessary levels of trust.

Conclusion

The discontinuities that exist between different levels of trust help to explain the fact that, despite deep public cynicism, the American political system is not in any sense close to imminent demise. Nonetheless, we should take care not to allow ourselves to be falsely reassured. What is noteworthy is that since the mid-1960s trust in the representativeness and integrity of governmental processes and officials has remained low, whether job approval scores were low, as has often been the case with respect to Congress, or high, as they now are in the spring of 1998 (Gallup, 1998; Pew, 1998). Either of these situations is cause for concern. When distrust at the policy level and distrust at the governmental level reinforce each other, a heavy burden is placed on trust at the system level. When satisfaction at the policy level is not translated into trust at the governmental level, one suspects that general conditions of peace and prosperity are the primary reasons for heightened job approval. But "good times" inevitably alternate with "bad times," and they thus provide a fragile reed on which to nourish and sustain trust at any of its various levels.

In this chapter, I have argued that in recent decades low levels of trust, especially at the pivotal governmental level, have served as both cause and effect of a pattern of politics that has disrupted the historic, cyclic rhythms of American democracy. It follows from my analysis that to reactivate the traditional processes of redefinition and renewal in American politics, the inclination and ability of politicians to lead must be strengthened. This, in turn, requires mitigating the conditions that produce timid and fearful politicians by bolstering trust at the governmental level. The best approach to attaining this goal is to focus on the cognitive dimensions of public life and seek to identify forms of action that can contribute to redefining public expectations. Expectations are the key to trust, and their ability to sustain trust can be strengthened both by disciplining expectations in terms of the needs of democratic practice and disciplining practice in terms of the needs of democratic ideals.

It is true, of course, that there are harsh constraints on our ability to implement this or any other strategy for bolstering trust. The conditions and character of modern politics are causally determined by factors and forces that cannot simply be wished away. Nonetheless, passivity is neither necessary nor desirable. The existence of determinants does not mean determinism. Rather, patterns of interaction are complex and conditioned, with the result that relationships are contingent, not rigidly determined. Moreover, in human affairs far more than in the natural world, our beliefs and assessments can and do affect the character and constraints of empirical reality. In the end, human beings are not stones or gases, but reflexive actors who can and do modify their beliefs and behavior to achieve their goals. If we prize our political system, it behooves us to understand it and guard it, lest we lose what the Framers so wisely regarded as its great blessings.

References

Aldrich, John H., and Richard G. Niemi. 1996. "The Sixth American Party System: Electoral Change, 1952–1992." In *Broken Contract? Changing Relationships Between Americans and Their Government,* ed. Stephen C. Craig (pp. 87–109). Boulder, CO: Westview Press.

Arnold, R. Douglas. 1993. "Can Inattentive Citizens Control Their Elected Representatives?" In *Congress Reconsidered,* ed. Lawrence C. Dodd and Bruce I. Oppenheimer (pp. 401–416). Washington, DC: Congressional Quarterly Press.

Beer, Samuel H. 1978. "In Search of a New Public Philosophy." In *The New American Political System,* ed. Anthony King (pp. 5–44). Washington, DC: American Enterprise Institute.

Bennett, Linda L. M., and Stephen E. Bennett. 1996. "Looking at Leviathan: Dimensions of Opinion About Big Government." In *Broken Contract? Changing Relationships Between Americans and Their Government,* ed. Stephen C. Craig (pp. 23–45). Boulder, CO: Westview Press.

Bessette, Joseph H. 1994. *The Mild Voice of Reason: Deliberative Democracy and American National Government.* Chicago: University of Chicago Press.

Blendon, Robert J., et al. 1997. "Changing Attitudes in America." In *Why People Don't Trust Government,* ed. Joseph S. Nye, Philip D. Zelikow, and David C. King (pp. 205–216). Cambridge, MA: Harvard University Press.

Bowman, Karlyn, and Everett C. Ladd. 1994. "Public Opinion Toward Congress: A Historical Look." In *Congress, the Press, and the Public,* ed. Thomas E. Mann and Norman J. Ornstein (pp. 45–58). Washington, DC: American Enterprise Institute/Brookings Institution.

Brady, David W. 1988. *Critical Elections and Congressional Policy Making.* Stanford, CA: Stanford University Press.

Brady, David W., and Craig Volden. 1998. *Resolving Gridlock: Politics and Policy from Carter to Clinton.* Boulder, CO: Westview Press.

Citrin, Jack. 1996. "Who's the Boss? Direct Democracy and Popular Control of Government." In *Broken Contract? Changing Relationships Between Americans and Their Government,* ed. Stephen C. Craig (pp. 268–293). Boulder, CO: Westview Press.

Cooper, Joseph. 1975. "Strengthening the Congress: An Organizational Analysis." *Harvard Journal on Legislation* 12: 307–368.

_____. 1981. "Organization and Innovation in the House of Representatives." In *The House at Work*, ed. Joseph Cooper and G. Calvin Mackenzie (pp. 319–355). Austin: University of Texas Press.

Craig, Stephen C. 1993. *The Malevolent Leaders: Popular Discontent in America.* Boulder, CO: Westview Press.

_____. 1996. "Change in the American Electorate" and "The Angry Voter and Popular Discontent in the 1990s." In *Broken Contract? Changing Relationships Between Americans and Their Government*, ed. Stephen C. Craig (pp. 1–20 and 46–66). Boulder, CO: Westview Press.

Davidson, Roger H., David Kovenock, and Michael O'Leary. 1966. *Congress in Crisis: Politics and Congressional Reform.* Belmont, CA: Wadsworth.

Dionne, E. J. 1991. *Why Americans Hate Politics.* New York: Simon & Schuster.

Dodd, Lawrence C. 1993. "Congress and the Politics of Renewal: Redressing the Crisis of Legitimation." In *Congress Reconsidered*, ed. Lawrence C. Dodd and Bruce I. Oppenheimer (pp. 417–446). Washington, DC: Congressional Quarterly Press.

_____. 1994. "Political Learning and Political Change: Understanding Development Across Time." In *The Dynamics of American Politics: Approaches and Interpretations*, ed. Lawrence C. Dodd and Calvin Jillson (pp. 331–364). Boulder, CO: Westview Press.

_____. 1997. "Re-Envisioning Congress: Theoretical Perspectives on Congressional Change." Paper delivered at the annual meeting of the American Political Science Association, Washington, DC (August 28–31).

Durr, Robert H., John B. Gilmour, and Christina Wolbrecht. 1997. "Explaining Congressional Approval." *American Journal of Political Science* 41: 175–208.

Easton, David. 1965. *A Systems Analysis of Political Life.* New York: Wiley.

Fenno, Richard F. 1978. *Home Style: House Members in Their Districts.* Boston: Little, Brown.

Fishkin, James S. 1991. *Democracy and Deliberation: New Directions for Democratic Reform.* New Haven, CT: Yale University Press.

Flanagan, William H., and Nancy H. Zingale. 1998. *Political Behavior of the American Electorate.* Washington, DC: Congressional Quarterly Press.

Gallup Organization. 1998. Gallup Poll. Available at www.gallup.com/poll/index.

Graber, Doris A. 1993. *Mass Media and American Politics.* Washington, DC: Congressional Quarterly Press.

Greenberg, Stanley B. 1995. *Middle-Class Dreams: The Politics and Power of the New American Majority.* New York: Times Books.

Gross, Martin L. 1996. *The Political Racket: Deceit, Self-Interest, and Corruption in American Politics.* New York: Ballantine Books.

Hibbing, John R., and Elizabeth Theiss-Morse. 1995. *Congress as Public Enemy: Public Attitudes Toward American Political Institutions.* Cambridge: Cambridge University Press.

Hunter, James D., and Carl Bowman. 1996. "Summary Report and Summary Tables." In *The State of Disunion: 1996 Survey of American Political Culture* (vols. 1 and 2). Charlottesville, VA: Post-Modernity Project.

Huntington, Samuel P. 1981. *American Politics and the Promise of Democracy.* Cambridge, MA: Harvard University Press.

Jones, Charles O. 1995. *Separate but Equal Branches: Congress and the Presidency.* Chatham, NJ: Chatham House Publishers.

Kimball, David C., and Samuel C. Patterson. 1997. "Living Up to Expectations: Public Attitudes Toward Congress." *Journal of Politics* 59: 701–729.

King, Anthony. 1997. "Running Scared." *Atlantic Monthly* 279 (January): 41–61.

Ladd, Everett C. 1990. "Public Opinion and the 'Congress Problem.'" *The Public Interest* 100: 57–68.

Lee, Emory G. 1997. "Representation, Virtue, and Jealousy in the Brutus-Publius Dialogue." *Journal of Politics* 59: 1073–1096.

Lindblom, Charles E. 1965. *The Intelligence of Democracy.* New York: Free Press.

Lipset, Seymour M., and William Schneider. 1987. *The Confidence Gap: Business, Labor, and Government in the Public Mind.* Baltimore: Johns Hopkins University Press.

Lowi, Theodore. 1967. "The Public Philosophy: Interest Group Liberalism." *American Political Science Review* 61: 5–24.

Maass, Arthur A. 1970. "Public Investment Planning in the United States: Analysis and Critique." *Public Policy* 18: 211–243.

_____. 1983. *Congress and the Common Good.* New York: Basic Books.

McCubbins, Mathew D. 1992. *Under the Watchful Eye: Managing Presidential Campaigns in the Television Era.* Washington, DC: Congressional Quarterly Press.

Macmahon, Arthur. 1948. "Conflict, Consensus, Confirmed Trends, and Open Choices." *American Political Science Review* 42: 1–15.

Mann, Sheilah, et al. 1996. "Symposium: Political Scientists Examine Civics Standards." *PS: Political Science and Politics* 29: 47–63.

Mayhew, David R. 1974. *Congress: The Electoral Connection.* New Haven, CT: Yale University Press.

Mayer, William G. 1992. *The Changing American Mind: How and Why American Public Opinion Changed Between 1960 and 1988.* Ann Arbor: University of Michigan Press.

Morone, James A. 1990. *The Democratic Wish: Popular Participation and the Limits of American Government.* New York: Basic Books.

Neustadt, Richard E. 1997. "The Politics of Mistrust." In *Why People Don't Trust Government,* ed. Joseph S. Nye, Philip B. Zelikow, and David C. King (pp. 179–201). Cambridge, MA: Harvard University Press.

Orren, Gary. 1997. "Fall from Grace: The Public's Loss of Faith in Government." In *Why People Don't Trust Government,* ed. Joseph S. Nye, Philip B. Zelikow, and David C. King (pp. 77–107). Cambridge, MA: Harvard University Press.

Ostrom, Elinor. 1990. *Governing the Commons: The Evolution of Institutions for Collective Action.* New York: Cambridge University Press.

_____. 1998. "A Behavioral Approach to the Rational Choice Theory of Collective Action." *American Political Science Review* 92: 1–22.

Parker, Glenn R., and Charles J. Barrilleaux. 1996. "The Electoral Connection: Images of U.S. Senators and Representatives." In *Broken Contract? Changing Relationships Between Americans and Their Government,* ed. Stephen C. Craig (pp. 229–250). Boulder, CO: Westview Press.

Patterson, Thomas E. 1994. *Out of Order.* New York: Vintage Books.

Perrow, Charles. 1986. *Complex Organizations: A Critical Essay.* New York: Random House.

Pew Research Center for the People and the Press. 1998. "Overview, Survey, and Selected Tables." In *Deconstructing Distrust: How Americans View Government* (March 10). Available at www.people-press.org.

Price, David E. 1992. *The Congressional Experience.* Boulder, CO: Westview Press.

Putnam, Robert D. 1993. *Making Democracy Work: Civic Traditions in Modern Italy.* Princeton, NJ: Princeton University Press.

Sorauf, Frank J. 1992. *Inside Campaign Finance: Myths and Realities.* New Haven, CT: Yale University Press.

Sniderman, Paul M. 1993. "The New Look in Public Opinion Research." In *Political Science: The State of the Discipline II,* ed. Ada W. Finifter (pp. 219–245). Washington, DC: American Political Science Association.

Thompson, Dennis F. 1995. *Ethics in Congress: From Individual to Institutional Corruption.* Washington, DC: Brookings Institution.

Uslaner, Eric M. 1993. *The Decline of Comity in Congress.* Ann Arbor: University of Michigan Press.

Will, George F. 1992. *Restoration: Congress, Term Limits, and the Recovery of Deliberative Democracy.* New York: Free Press.

Epilogue

The Clinton Impeachment Controversy and Public Trust

JOSEPH COOPER

Since the completion of this volume in the spring of 1998, a series of historic events has occurred that bear significantly on the problem of public trust. These events include the appearance of President Clinton in August 1998 before a federal grand jury, impaneled by Independent Counsel Kenneth Starr, to rebut allegations of perjury and the obstruction of justice. They also include the referral of the independent counsel's report on these charges to the House of Representatives and its release to the public in September; the approval by the House of an impeachment inquiry in October; and the passage by the House Republican majority of two articles of impeachment against President Clinton in December as the 105th Congress (1997–1999) came to an end. Last, but certainly not least, they include the initiation of an impeachment trial by the Senate in January at the start of the new 106th Congress (1999–2001) and its termination six weeks later when the Senate acquitted the president of both the charge of perjury before a federal grand jury and the charge of obstruction of justice. In addition, a midterm congressional election was held in November in which the House Republican Party lost seats and soon after the election deposed its speaker. These events require a brief, further exploration of three primary themes in this volume: the determinants of and relationships between the various levels of trust, the impact of the current character of politics on trust, and the need and possibilities for augmenting trust. It should be clear, however, that the argument and analysis that follow represent the views of the author of this Epilogue and are not necessarily shared in whole or in part by other authors in this volume.

Analyzing Public Trust

Survey data on the state of trust at both the policy and governmental levels during the last half of 1998 both support the analysis in this volume and highlight several key issues in analyzing public trust. One continuing issue concerns the determinants and interpretation of frequently used measures of trust at the policy level—presidential job approval scores, congressional job approval scores, and more general measures of policy satisfaction and confidence in the ability of government to respond effectively to the needs of the nation. As noted in Chapter 1, in the first four months of 1998 presidential job approval climbed from the high 50s to the high 60s soon after the Lewinsky scandal broke and declined only to the mid-60s in March and April. In these same four months congressional job approval, which had averaged in the mid-30s in 1997, climbed well into the 50s before declining to the high 40s. In the months that followed, presidential job approval ranged from the low to mid-60s, fell in early September into the high 50s, climbed with some variation until it again reached the high 60s in December, and remained at this level through the end of the impeachment trial in February. Congressional job approval ranged from the mid-40s to high 40s through August, climbed into the mid-50s in the early fall before retreating again to the mid-40s in October, and remained at this level with some variation through the end of the impeachment trial in February. As for the more general measures of trust at the policy level that we have relied upon in this volume, they reveal their own distinctive inconsistencies. Satisfaction with "the way things are going in the United States" ranged only between the high 50s and low 60s through the summer of 1998 (Gallup, 1998). In contrast, belief that the "nation is headed in the right direction" rose from the mid-40s to the low 60s in January 1998, declined in an irregular fashion to the low 50s by September, climbed again into the mid-50s by November, and remained at this level through the end of the impeachment trial in February (*Washington Post*, 1998 and 1999).

These results provide further testimony to the persistent lag in congressional approval scores versus presidential approval scores, but under conditions very different from those that normally prevail. The past year has been a time when both approval scores have been unusually high, despite substantial evidence of presidential misconduct, on the one hand, and widespread public opposition to congressional efforts to impeach the president, on the other (*Washington Post*, 1998). The trends in 1998 and early 1999 thus raise as many questions as they answer regarding the determinants and meaning of the approval scores.

The existing literature agrees that congressional job approval is typically low and lags behind that of the president because the Congress is viewed as overly self-interested and partisan, because of public intolerance for controversy, and because of the public perception of its role and responsibility (Hibbing and Theiss-Morse, 1995; Patterson and Kimball, 1998). But there is no clear consensus on the relationship between the presidential and congressional scores or its determinants (Durr, Gilmour, and Wolbrecht, 1997; Patterson and Caldeira, 1990). Many claim that both scores respond to economic conditions. They undoubtedly do, but what is also clear is that they respond to a host of other factors as well. Hence, while the congressional score almost always lags behind the presidential score, both scores respond to events, even when general indicators of satisfaction, such as "satisfaction with the way things are going," remain stable. Moreover, job approval scores can change in ways that contradict general indicators of satisfaction when those indicators are more sensitive to noneconomic forces, as is true of the "right direction" measure. Finally, total or primary reliance on economic conditions as the determinant of these scores undermines claims that the presidential score drags the congressional score and conflicts with the evidence on the importance of political determinants, especially in analyses of congressional job approval.

In truth, none of these factors in isolation adequately explains the determinants of and relationships between presidential and congressional job approval scores over the past fifteen months. The variations in these scores appear to have been highly sensitive to particular events in the struggle between President Clinton and his accusers, whereas the height of the scores seems attributable to more basic contextual factors. What we continue to lack is an explanation that more successfully integrates contextual and situational factors and gives adequate weight to prior opinion, political as well as economic factors, and events (Ostrom and Simon, 1988). Until these defects are corrected, conclusions drawn from these scores regarding the degree and significance of public confidence in the policy performance and capabilities of the president and Congress will remain far less than conclusive.

A second and even more important issue concerns the relationship between trust at the policy level and trust at the governmental level. Judging purely by the absolute values of the scores, it would appear that the discontinuities between the policy level and the governmental level have been stretched even further by the events that preceded the House impeachment vote. If presidential job approval has been high, feelings of trust in the character of the president have declined. Whereas in June 1997, 41 percent of the electorate affirmed that President Clinton had "high personal moral and ethical standards," only 21 percent agreed in December 1998 (*Washington Post*, 1998). Since the personal component is an important facet of trust in the processes of decisionmaking at the governmental level, one might expect that trust at the governmental level would decline. Similar expectations derive from events with respect to Congress. Although congressional job approval was relatively high going into the election, the majority party lost seats in the House and overthrew its speaker, in large part because he was regarded as a detriment to public confidence in the Republican Party and the House. Again, one might therefore expect that trust in government would, if anything, decline over the course of 1998 and be accompanied by loss of confidence in the Congress and the president as decisionmaking entities.

Whether this has actually occurred in any permanent way is not clear. One senses that public disgust with and cynicism toward politics have deepened. Surely the victory of Jesse Ventura, a professional wrestler, in the Minnesota gubernatorial race points in that direction. Similarly, the poll evidence indicates that the decline in trust in the honesty and integrity of the president has persisted (*Washington Post*, 1998 and 1999; Gallup, 1998 and 1999). Finally, disapproval of the Republican leadership in Congress and its handling of the Clinton impeachment increased substantially over the course of the dispute (Morin and Deane, 1999). In contrast, the general trust in government score appears to be buttressed by trust at the policy level and has recovered most of the ground lost in 1998. Thus, whereas a CBS News–*New York Times* survey in October 1998 indicated that those who trust the government all or most of the time had fallen to 26 percent, a *Washington Post* survey in mid-February 1999 found that the number had increased to 32 percent, only two points below its level in early 1998 (*Washington Post*, 1999).

Despite such mixed results, the issues highlighted in this volume remain of concern. To the degree that trust at the government level declines, one may continue to ask two critical questions. How far can the discontinuities between the policy level and the governmental level proceed without igniting powerful third parties and a major challenge to the American party system? Moreover, how far can they proceed without beginning to affect levels of trust in the legitimacy of the system itself? Nor is the relevance of these questions undermined by a recovery in the general trust in government score. The reversal in this score has only restored trust in governmental decisionmaking to the low state that prevailed in mid-January 1998, when the president's relationship with Monica Lewinsky first became headline news. The buttressing effects of trust at the policy level are thus limited. Equally important, they are quite fragile. Given the persistence of large amounts of distrust at the governmental level, any sizeable increase in distrust at the policy level, due to economic hard times or foreign policy failures, is likely to depress trust at the governmental level severely. In short, current patterns of party politics and belief in legitimacy can be undermined whether trust at the governmental level falls independently of trust at the policy level or in response to a decline in trust at this level. The point is that the problem is not one of simply maintaining current levels of trust at the governmental level. If trust at this level is not augmented, the continuities between levels pose as much of a threat as the discontinuities once "good times" become "bad times."

Three conclusions follow. First, the argument often heard in the midst of the controversy over the Clinton presidency, that only results that directly and immediately affect the lives of citizens matter, is specious. Indeed, if it is not, this book has little rationale or purpose. As many authors in this volume argue, the success of policy initiatives is not unrelated to trust in processes and leaders but rather influenced and advanced by them. Equally important, policy initiatives, even when implemented, may not control actual outcomes, and thus trust in political leaders apart from immediate results is critical if severe turbulence in the forms and practice of government is to be avoided.

Second, what the travails of President Clinton do validly raise as a concern is the importance of the presidency as a component of trust at the governmental level.

Although this volume, for good and substantial reasons, has focused on trust in Congress, the conflict over whether to remove President Clinton highlights the importance of trust in the presidency in a manner that requires notice and acknowledgment. Given the variety and strength of the factors that promote distrust in Congress and congressional leaders as the nation prepares to enter a new century, trust in the president may now constitute a critical threshold for maintaining a minimally adequate degree of trust at the governmental level. If so, while we may continue to argue that trust in the Congress needs to be enhanced, we may also conclude that trust in the presidency needs to be guarded, not dismissed as inconsequential, and that this need relates to belief in the personal trustworthiness of the president as well as to his political skills and his policy commitments.

Third, and last, the election of 2000 looms as one of unusual importance. Although many advocates of a speedy end to the impeachment process assumed that returning to the regular processes of policy discussion and dispute would put the impeachment controversy behind us, this assumption is far too optimistic. The impeachment fight has left a residue of bitterness and suspicion that endures, even as the details of the dramatic events that unfolded in various federal courts and in Congress fade from memory.

It thus will be no easy matter to escape the negative effects of the controversy over President Clinton's impeachment at either the policy or the governmental levels of trust. Although it is true that a large majority of the country opposed removing the president from office, it is also true that a sizeable minority felt that he should be removed and that many Americans strongly disapproved of both the president's conduct and the partisan divisions and maneuvering that marked House proceedings (*Washington Post*, 1998 and 1999). Moreover, though the Senate failed to convict on either count of impeachment, there was no consensus in the country or in the Senate on the appropriate punishment for Clinton's behavior. In the electorate, Republican voters favored removal and opposed censure, whereas Democratic voters and independents split between censure and simple acquittal (Morin, 1998). In the Senate, the great majority of Republicans voted to convict the president of perjury and obstruction of justice, and a large number of leading Democrats and some Republicans sought to censure the president but were frustrated by the difficulties of imposing cloture and public pressure to end the whole sorry affair (Baker and Dewar, 1999).

The Senate did successfully end the impeachment process without further deepening partisan division in the country. In so doing, it succeeded in not exacerbating the situation with respect to public trust—but it did little to improve it. The Senate's accomplishment therefore stands as only a first and very limited test of our ability to put the issues of the Clinton impeachment behind us. A second and more important test is the degree to which the new 106th Congress (1999–2001), by its actions and tone, can significantly reduce the bitterness and suspicion generated by the impeachment fight. Unfortunately, expectations in this regard are more likely to be disappointed than realized.

When divided government prevails in a highly partisan age, legislative politics becomes a volatile mix, and especially so in Congresses preceding presidential elections. Strong incentives to pass programs the public wants clash with strong incentives to maneuver in ways that will gain political advantage in the upcoming election and to defer to the core base of partisan support. The result is to make policy outcomes and the conduct of politics even more captive to chance and circumstance, both at home and abroad, than is usually the case. Moreover, given deep divisions between Democratic and Republican voters on the seriousness of President Clinton's offenses and a further and substantial decline in trust among lawmakers in Congress and between Congress and the president, prospects for returning to even the mediocre levels of trust and comity that prevailed in Washington before the Clinton scandal are not favorable (*Washington Post*, 1998; Uslaner, 1993). Ironically enough, the potential for the kind of deliberate and constructive action by Congress that is needed to bolster public trust at both the policy and governmental levels will itself be undercut by weaknesses in the underlying levels of trust and comity among elected officials in Washington that the events of the Clinton impeachment have reinforced and extended (Harwood, 1998).

We can conclude that what is most likely is that the 106th Congress will be largely prologue to the presidential election of 2000. The bitterness and suspicion that are the legacy of the impeachment fight are likely to constrain major policy achievements and render the outcomes of divided government in a partisan age even more problematic than usual. If so, our ability to restore and renew our politics must await the next presidential election. It will be the effects of this election, in terms of the leaders who are chosen to assume responsibility for governing and their success in reuniting the nation, that will shape the future course of public trust in the twenty-first century. It is these outcomes, not those of a Senate trial, no matter how historic, that will determine whether the rigid and divisive politics of the Clinton impeachment were a bleak harbinger of the future of American politics or merely a passing storm.

The Current State of Politics

Another primary theme of this volume concerns the current state of politics and the manner in which it has obstructed the processes that have traditionally served to build and renew trust at the governmental level. What the conflict between President Clinton and his defenders and the independent counsel and his supporters reveals is how much the practice of plebiscitary democracy in the United States has advanced and how detrimental such practice is to relieving the high degree of cynicism and suspicion about politics and politicians that now prevails (Lowi, 1985).

In the past quarter-century the rise of the electronic media and the nationalization of American politics have brought us far closer to the immediacy, intimacy, and commonality of ancient city-state democracy than at any prior point in our history. Moreover, they have done so in a manner that has been aided and abetted by new technologies of polling and communication that substantially extend the possibilities for both enriching and prostituting the dialogue between politicians and citizens. At the same time, the emergence of a rhetorical presidency, spawned by the rise of active and energetic presidential policy leadership in the first half of the century, has increased the incentives for and importance of symbolic action, whether as a component of or substitute for substantive policy (Cohen, 1997). This same momentum for "going public" and giving enhanced attention to the symbolic aspects of politics has in the second half of the century become as characteristic of Congress as of the presidency (Harris, 1998). Although the causal forces differ in some critical respects, members of Congress in recent decades have also become far more concerned with defining a collective partisan image that will "sell" to the public, whether it mutes policy differences and realities or not, and with employing all the mechanisms of modern communications to promote it.

In recent decades party leaders in Congress have thus been actively engaged in seeking to package and present their policy commitments to the public in new and appealing ways. The "Contract with America" represented an advanced extension of this trend and testifies far more to the inclination of contemporary party leaders to adopt the techniques of modern public relations than to any sudden desire to adopt the practices of parliamentary government. It is no accident, but rather quite revealing, that members of Congress now speak far more often and vehemently about the need for their leaders to articulate a clear and appealing message to the public than was true even in the early 1970s, or that the Republican setbacks in the November 1998 congressional election were quickly and commonly attributed to the lack of a clear message. Indeed, when a majority party deposes its speaker for the first time since the Civil War, and for reasons relating to dissatisfaction about his ability to craft a favorable image of himself and his party, the evidence is strong that there must be something very different about American politics in the 1990s as compared even to the recent past.

What the fight over impeachment has also vividly demonstrated is the high degree to which the emergence of cable TV and the new economics of broadcast news have undermined traditional standards of professionalism in reporting the news and led the media to put a higher premium on profit and entertainment and a lower premium on substantive and accurate reporting (Kalb, 1998; Shribman, 1998). These developments have made the media not only less careful about getting a story but also more dependent on and manipulable by their sources as well as less trusted by the public (Pew, 1998b). In national politics a far more extensive and sophisticated emphasis on "spin" has emerged, conducted by a new class of professionals adept at polling, message framing, and media strategies (Kurtz, 1998). Nor are these developments simply a product of technology. The new professionals of polling and spin stand on the shoulders of the inventors of modern advertising and market research and benefit as well from late-twentieth-century intellectual trends. They can and do feel quite at home in a cultural climate in which belief in objectivity and truth has diminished and regard for the use of language to construct reality has increased.

All these elements played an important role in the fight over the impeachment of the president and the related struggle to win the congressional election. The controversy over the guilt and fate of the president involved an intense media competition for audience, in which the primary consideration was not missing a story rather than accurate reporting. Given the appetite and power of the electronic media, the result was to transform the conflict over President Clinton into public spectacle, if not soap opera, to a degree that is rivaled by few, if any, disputes in our history. Concomitantly, there was a nonstop daily struggle between the White House and its opponents over winning the battle to frame events for public perception and continuing polling and use of polls not only to determine opinion but also to influence results. Equally important, negative and personal attacks on the prime actors in the impeachment controversy, as well as on candidates in the midterm election, increased as the fight over impeachment grew more intense. Readily prompted by the effectiveness of negative politics in an era in which suspicion and cynicism reign, and easily justified in an era of heightened value disagreement by assumptions of the baseness of the opposition's motives and goals, personal attacks of a variety of hues became the modal approach to persuading the public to see the issues as the participants in the dispute wanted them seen.

The underlying premise of all these techniques and strategies has been that impeachment should and would be decided by public opinion in a direct and immediate fashion. Although this premise is based on crude caricature of the complexities and subtleties of popular rule, it has been widely accepted as an integral requirement of representative government, and thus in many eyes it has legitimized, or at least condoned, the spinning, polling, media circus, and negative attacks that became commonplace. It is utterly understandable, when plebiscitary politics defines the rules of the game, that the Starr report, as well as additional supporting grand jury evidence gathered by the special counsel, were released prior to any committee hearings, and that even the majority of Democrats felt that they could not resist giving the public this information before the inquiry began. It is just as easy to understand why the Republicans, in releasing the information, would see no conflict between seeking to gain political advantage in both the impeachment process and the midterm election and properly performing their constitutional duties, whereas the Democrats would focus their defense of the president on poll evidence regarding the opposition of the public to impeachment and charges that the special counsel had acted in an unfair and arbitrary manner. Finally, given the degree to which plebiscitary politics has been strengthened in the United States, it is also not surprising that after the setbacks the Republicans suffered in the election, they not only threw their own speaker out of office because he was judged not capable of crafting the message they wish to convey to the American people, but also lost their speaker-designate in an ongoing campaign of attack politics that was prompted and inspired both by bitter partisanship and by current patterns of reliance on shaping and mobilizing public opinion through deft use of the media to win political battles.

All this is not to deny that the new technologies of polling and communication have made the conflicts in the representative responsibilities of members even more difficult to reconcile, or that the fight over impeachment has brought the forces and factors involved in plebiscitary politics into sharper relief than disputes over policy normally do. The point I wish to make is that the increased inclination toward plebiscitary politics, manifest in the impeachment struggle, will not serve the cause of preserving the viability of representative government any better than it served Republican desires to gain bipartisan support for impeachment or to win the election. The relation between elected officials and constituents must involve a delicate balance between responsiveness and leadership in which officials are neither the puppets nor the puppeteers of constituent opinion. Mere responsiveness cannot bring about accommodation, nor can accountability in and of itself produce positive results. Viable representative government requires reason, fairness, and deliberation, as well as responsiveness and accountability, if it is to produce policy results that successfully balance the needs of consent and action and maintain the kind of trust in basic processes and procedures that is indispensable to preserving them as more than a facade.

In plebiscitary politics the appearance of responsiveness is heightened, but the reality is one of increased manipulation (Cohen, 1997). In the end, trust is vitiated, not enhanced, because leaders are induced either to pander to the public and avoid facing difficult issues or to manipulate the public when difficult issues must be faced. It is this element of American politics, as exemplified in the impeachment fight, that underscores the concerns over plebiscitary democracy expressed in this volume. What remains at issue is how far plebiscitary politics in the United States has progressed. Do the events of the impeachment controversy testify to the strength of blind partisanship in the service of political ends or to the continuing ability of members to act deliberately in a Burkean manner? Do they testify to the fact that the balance between responsiveness and deliberation remains strong or to the power of plebiscitary politics, in a context marked by heightened value disagreement, more intense and rigid partisan division, and low levels of trust, to replicate the conditions of a classic prisoner's dilemma game and thereby produce an outcome that intensifies rather than relieves distrust?

The verdict is unclear at this time, despite the more bipartisan tenor of the Senate trial. Indeed, the story is not yet complete. The aftermath of the impeachment fight, both in terms of the performance of the government during the remainder of the Clinton administration and in terms of the emergence of new information that bears on matters disputed during the impeachment controversy, will affect the ultimate judgment of the experience. Still, even in the highly unlikely event that additional evidence provides support only for the defenders of the president, it is doubtful that in the end there will be agreement, as there was after Watergate, that the process was appropriate and fair and the result wise and just. The deep divisions on values that separate the opposing sides, the intensity of partisan warfare, and the manipulative forms of media politics that have marked the impeachment fight make anything better than a mixed verdict on the character and implications of this historic episode unlikely.

What is clear, however, is that to the degree that American democracy becomes more plebiscitary in ideal and in fact, the greater the danger that politics will be spectacle, not deliberation; that leadership will be judged in terms of image and celebrity, not substance and achievement; that attack politics will flourish; and that distrust will increase, not abate. It is no accident that when plebiscitary politics dominates, it is the Alcibiadeses and Antonys of the world who win, not the Niciases and Ciceros, and that hallowed constitutional processes and procedures soon erode or disappear. There is thus one lesson that can be drawn from the events of the past year, even in the absence of any consensus on how the political system should have responded to President Clinton's misdeeds. It is that the current tendencies toward plebiscitary politics in American politics must be constrained. Though some would dispute this, their confidence that the benefits of enhancing electoral power at the expense of institutional power would outweigh the costs is misplaced (Citrin, 1996). The "unfreezing" of the system they anticipate is far more likely to further subordinate reason and deliberation to passion and interests and to impair the delicate balances between consent and action and responsiveness and leadership on which the viability of free government ultimately depends. Madison wrote in Federalist #55 that if every Athenian had been as wise as Socrates, the Athenian Assembly would still have been a mob. He was right. Polities that succumb to plebiscitary politics are very likely to end in despotism, either by tearing themselves apart in factious partisanship, as many of the Greek city-states did, or by rotting from the inside out, as in the case of the Roman Republic, so that only the facade of republican government remained.

Reform

Our analysis of the implications of the controversy over the impeachment of President Clinton leads directly to issues of reform. Indeed, the arguments we have made strongly reinforce the case for reform in the three prime areas of reform identified in this volume—the performance of the media, campaign finance, and civic education.

Whatever its sins, the media's performance in reporting the events that led to impeachment has had the beneficial effect of shattering media self-satisfaction and resistance to criticism (Kalb, 1998). It has dramatically highlighted the fact that a new age of media technology and economics has defined new and serious challenges for the role of the media in a democratic order, challenges that the media thus far have not responded to in a manner that meets their critical public responsibilities. As previously argued, the media must find its way to a new set of reporting standards that are sensitive to the constraints that bar "objectivity" in any pure and simple sense but are equally cognizant of the lure and dangers of indulging either personal policy biases or cynical preconceptions. What emerges as a lesson from the Clinton scandal is a complementary facet of the problem of professional standards and discipline. That is, that the media must also confront and overcome the inducements the power of electronic technology and the pressure of competition for a national audience have created to subordinate information to entertainment and transform finding the facts into being "spun" by sources.

There are no pat or simple answers to these problems. The media's character as both a private and public entity poses a dilemma that can be resolved only at the peril of their unique and indispensable role in a democratic order. The media's role conflicts thus must be accepted and accommodated, not eliminated. The media are necessarily constrained by the fact that they are organized and operate as businesses. At the same time, they have critical public responsibilities and are properly subject to governmental regulation and subsidies that serve the public interest by fostering competition, encouraging public service, and limiting the costs of campaigns (Cook, 1998). Nonetheless, the role of government vis-à-vis the media must be highly circumspect. It must not impair or distort the media's role as information provider but rather must be highly deferential to the freedom-of-speech requirements of representative government. The nation, as a result, is highly dependent on the media's own sense of professionalism and responsibility. If the media are to avoid both destructive politicization and crass commercialization in reporting the news, they themselves must chart this course. The stakes are high both for the media and for representative government in the United States. But the process of critical self-examination must be serious and must begin to evolve a new set of standards and strategies attuned to the America of the new millennium, not the America of the 1950s.

Similarly, recent events testify eloquently to the need for campaign finance reform. If it is true, as is often said, that money is "the mother's milk" of politics, it is even more true in the case of plebiscitary politics. The primary reason campaign costs have risen so dramatically in recent years is television, and the explosion of PACs and advocacy groups that also mark the politics of the 1990s is tied to their ability to raise and deploy financial resources (Herrnson, 1998). Moreover, although charges of campaign finance abuse in the 1996 election did not become a significant aspect of the case to impeach the president, they have been widely discussed, investigated by both House and Senate committees, and put forward by major national newspapers as appropriate topics for independent counsel investigations. What is clear more than ever, whatever the legal status of the practices engaged in by President Clinton and Senator Dole, is that soft money has made a mockery of present legal restrictions and that practice with respect to soft money, PACs, and independent campaigns follows a form of Gresham's Law in which bad practice feeds on itself and drives out less pernicious behavior. Equally important, present campaign finance practice affects and intrudes into all aspects of American politics in detrimental ways. One illustration is the impact that the power of money, combined with the role of the media, has had in transforming the role of interest groups in campaigns so as to enhance their leverage over both political parties and individual candidates (Cigler and Loomis, 1998). A more immediate illustration is the manner in which the front-loading of presidential primaries in 2000 will combine with the costs of campaigns to limit competition to those few candidates who can build a kitty of $20 million before a single primary is even conducted.

Here again, there are no simple or pat answers to this problem, but the congressional majority that now supports campaign finance reform should be allowed to express its will and test whether something short of public financing will suffice. Otherwise, the public can correctly conclude that it is primarily the career and partisan interests of members that block reform in the public interest, and one can easily anticipate that the practices that will be engaged in during the election of 2000 will be at least as unsavory and destructive of trust as those in the last presidential election, and possibly more. Congress needs to act, and it would be best for both deliberate policymaking and the preservation of public trust if it did so before some major scandal forces action upon it.

The final area of reform is civic education, and once again the events surrounding the Clinton impeachment provide strong evidence of the need for improvement. Judging by the polls, the public lacks a sense that the liberties and material benefits it enjoys are tied far more to our system of government than to any single politician. If, as many believe, the impeachment controversy would have had a different tone and outcome if the nation had been experiencing troubled economic times rather than enjoying a prosperous economy marked by a low unemployment rate, a rising stock market, and a low inflation rate, that is a sign of weakness, not strength, in representative government in the United States. Whatever the merits of the case to impeach the president, the decision needed to be made on institutional grounds, not the halo effects of a good economy.

It is equally true that the degree of partisan divisiveness that has surrounded this issue does little to bolster confidence in the future of representative government in the United States. Policy positions, no matter how dear to the hearts of their adherents, rarely are important enough that they properly outweigh the needs of the system of government. To sacrifice institutional processes or the basic norms that sustain them to what are perceived to be the political exigencies of "good policy" in a particular instance is to undermine the conditions that make it possible to produce and benefit from "good policy" in all instances. Once again, then, although narrow and rigid action to defend or attack the president is easy to understand in human terms when members of the two parties begin to see themselves as hostile armies, such behavior remains only another way of subordinating enduring institutional needs to changing policy desires and conflicting political interests. Impeachment is properly a matter of the high politics of state-craft, not the ordinary politics of policy conflict and maneuvering to gain parti-san advantage. The fact that it was reduced to ordinary politics so readily by the public, the press, the White House, and many members of Congress speaks to more than the imperfections of human nature, current levels of cynicism and partisan division, or the difficulties of the case against President Clinton. It speaks as well to the quality of understanding about and dedication to the essentials of representative government.

None of this is new, to be sure. The removal of President Johnson was avoided by only one vote and, if it had been left to the people and the press, may well have resulted in conviction. But what this example illustrates is not simply the power and ubiquitousness of human passion—which were of so much concern to Madison and his fellow Framers—but also the importance of margins. Along with its institutional arrangements, civic education provides a vital ingredient in supplying representative government with the margins it needs to survive. The case for improving civic education thus does not rest on its ability to serve as a "magic bullet" for solving all the maladies of democratic orders. Both our ability to improve it and its effects are matters of degree, not absolutes, and progress will take time, ingenuity, and experiential learning. The case for civic education is rather comparable to finding ways to strengthen the immune system that the body politic can rely on to ward off and temper serious illness.

In all eras the fate of representative government is critically affected by citizen expectations and commitments. The challenges of contemporary politics make it more imperative than ever that the American people have a surer sense of what properly can be expected of representative government and what they should properly demand of it. Whatever the effects of the new technologies of commu-nication and polling thus far in promoting plebiscitary politics, we are still in the early stages of the information revolution. As the TV set, the computer, and the phone are transformed into one all-purpose instrument, and as the Internet in-creasingly becomes an alternative to the movies, the newspaper, and the shopping mall, can we doubt that political discourse and decisionmaking will continue to be powerfully affected? As suggested earlier, these new technologies will augment both the opportunities and the difficulties politicians confront in fulfilling their representative responsibilities. The danger is that current levels of distrust, untu-tored by an appreciation of the virtues of representative government and the de-fects of direct democracy, will provide elected officials with far more powerful in-ducements for demagoguery than for constructively balancing their dual role as both delegate and trustee. The impact of the information revolution could thus well be to provide a powerful engine for substantially enhancing government by polls and severely reducing the role and importance of discussion and accom-modation in the legislature. The result would be more spin, more spectacle, more importance for money, more divisiveness, and more distrust, and it is a result that can occur through the marriage of the Internet and the media without any formal provisions for referenda.

The American republic is founded on a deep sense of the complexity of human nature (White, 1987). Skepticism regarding the capacity of human beings to restrain their passions is combined with belief in the need and capacity for popular rule. The result is to produce a system of government that relies on institutional design to control self-interest but also recognizes that virtue and wisdom in the body of citizens is an essential ingredient in the ability of any republic to preserve liberty and promote the public interest (Rahe, 1994; Lee, 1997). Recent scholarship has rediscovered the vital importance of "social capital" in democratic orders and has been engaged in exploring the relationships between civic engagement, interpersonal trust, and trust in government (Brehm and Rahn, 1997). The framework of analysis is empirical, in line with the strictures of modern social science regarding value bias, and the findings indicate a high degree of reciprocity between the variables. Nonetheless, given the power of self-interest, it is doubtful that this approach can provide an adequate framework for understanding or action if it does not integrate the analysis of public trust with the traditional concern of proponents of republican government for a wise and responsible citizenry, committed to values and principles regarding the conduct of politics that transcend self-interest. Whatever the benefits that the perception of long-run as opposed to short-run self-interest confers in solving the problems of collective action, the evaluative and affective commitments that define the character of citizens, what Tocqueville called the "habits of the heart," provide an indispensable basis for generating the kind of trust that can successfully check the power of self-interest to make politics into an unrelieved and continuing prisoner's dilemma (Bellah, 1985).

The link between civic education and civic virtue thus becomes a factor in generating public trust that needs to be emphasized quite as much as civic engagement or interpersonal trust. Indeed, under modern conditions Tocqueville's analysis of the character of civic engagement and virtue in the United States has become far more problematic than Madison's analysis of the effects of representative institutions and divided power (Gamm and Putnam, 1998). As a result, if the forces of plebiscitary politics in the United States are to be constrained, we can no longer limit our attention to the kind of structural engineering of formal political decisionmaking arrangements that has characterized reform activities in the past century. Improving civic education, reducing the pernicious effects of the present system of campaign finance, and increasing the degree to which the media fulfill their public responsibilities are now more critical than traditional structural engineering, and civic education is perhaps the most critical of all.

The advent of the twenty-first century has thus brought us to a point where the problem of maintaining public trust and sustaining representative government requires far greater attention to basic aspects of political community, ranging from how we understand our political system to how we communicate in politics, to how we engage with one another socially and politically, to how we assess our responsibilities as citizens and the responsibilities of those we elect to govern us. The cognitive and evaluative dimensions of politics have, in short, become far more fluid and contested, and therefore far more determinative of results. This is a truth that neither current levels of prosperity nor current levels of cynicism should be allowed to obscure. If we wish to preserve representative government in the United States, the task is up to us. We must find ways of building trust, limiting divisiveness, and improving governmental performance. Our generation of Americans can no more escape the task of sustaining and renewing representative government than any of the generations that have preceded us. In the end, we, like they, will get just the kind of government we deserve.

References

Baker, Peter, and Helen Dewar. 1999. "Clinton Acquitted: Two Senate Impeachment Articles Fail to Win Senate Majority." *Washington Post*, February 13, p. A1.

Bellah, Robert N., et al. 1985. *Habits of the Heart: Individualism and Commitment in American Life.* Berkeley: University of California Press.

Brehm, John, and Wendy Rahn. 1997. "Individual-Level Evidence for the Causes and Consequences of Social Capital." *American Journal of Political Science* 41: 999–1024.

Cigler, Allan J., and Burdett A. Loomis. 1998. "From Big Bird to Bill Gates: Organized Interests and the Emergence of Hyperpolitics." In *Interest Group Politics,* ed. Allan Cigler and Burdett Loomis (5th ed., pp. 389–403). Washington, DC: Congressional Quarterly Press.

Citrin, Jack. 1996. "Who's the Boss? Direct Democracy and Popular Control of Government." In *Broken Contract? Changing Relationships Between Americans and Their Government,* ed. Stephen C. Craig (pp. 268–293). Boulder, CO: Westview Press.

Cohen, Jeffrey E. 1997. *Presidential Responsiveness and Public Policy-Making.* Ann Arbor: University of Michigan Press.

Cook, Timothy E. 1998. *Governing with the News: The News Media as a Political Institution.* Chicago: University of Chicago Press.

Durr, Robert H., John B. Gilmour, and Christina Wolbrecht. 1997. "Explaining Congressional Approval." *American Journal of Political Science* 41: 175–208.

Gamm, Gerald H., and Robert D. Putnam. 1998. "The Growth of Voluntary Associations in the United States, 1840–1940." *Journal of Interdisciplinary History* 29: 511–557.

Harris, Douglas B. 1998. "The Rise of the Public Speakership." *Political Science Quarterly* 113: 193–212.

Harwood, John. 1998. "Breakdown of Trust Threatens Orderly Government." *Wall Street Journal,* December 18, p. A16.

Herrnson, Paul S. 1998. *Congressional Elections: Campaigning at Home and in Washington.* Washington, DC: Congressional Quarterly Press.

Hibbing John R., and Elizabeth Theiss-Morse. 1995. *Congress as Public Enemy: Public Attitudes Toward American Political Institutions.* Cambridge: Cambridge University Press.

Kalb, Marvin. 1998. "The Rise of the 'New News': A Case Study of Two Root Causes of the Modern Scandal Coverage." Discussion Paper D-34. Joan Shorenstein Center on the Press and Politics, JFK School of Government, Harvard University.

Kurtz, Howard. 1998. *Spin Cycle: Inside the Clinton Propaganda Machine.* New York: Free Press.

Lee, Emery G. 1997. "Representation, Virtue, and Public Jealousy in the Brutus-Publius Dialogue." *Journal of Politics* 59: 1073–1096.

Lowi, Theodore J. 1985. *The Personal President: Power Invested, Promise Unfulfilled.* Ithaca, NY: Cornell University Press.

Morin, Richard. 1998. "Poll: Punish Clinton, Don't Remove Him." *Washington Post,* December 21, p. A17.

Morin, Richard, and Claudia Deane. 1999. "Public Gives Clinton Blame, Record Support." *Washington Post,* February 15, p. A1.

Ostrom, Charles W., and Dennis M. Simon. 1988. "The President's Public." *American Journal of Political Science* 32: 1096–1120.

Patterson, Samuel C., and Gregory A. Caldeira. 1990. "Standing Up for Congress: Variations in Public Esteem Since the 1960s." *Legislative Studies Quarterly* 15: 25–49.

Patterson, Samuel C., and David C. Kimball. 1998. "Unsympathetic Audience: Citizens' Evaluations of Congress." In *Great Theatre: The American Congress in the 1990s,* ed. Herbert Weisberg and Samuel Patterson (pp. 52–82). Cambridge: Cambridge University Press.

Pew Research Center for the People and the Press. 1998a. "Overview, Survey, and Selected Tables." In *Deconstructing Distrust: How Americans View Government,* March 10, available at: www.people-press.org.

_____. 1998b. "Overview, Questionnaire, and Overall Breakdowns." In *Election Pleases Voters Despite Mudslinging,* November 6, available at: www.people-press.org.

Rahe, Paul A. 1994. "Inventions of Prudence: Constituting the American Regime." In *Republics Ancient and Modern,* vol. 3. Chapel Hill: University of North Carolina Press.

Shribman, David. 1998. "Hollywood, D.C." *Boston Globe Magazine,* August 9, pp. 12, 24–30.

Uslaner, Eric M. 1993. *The Decline of Comity in Congress.* Ann Arbor: University of Michigan Press.

Washington Post. 1998. "Beyond Impeachment." In Richard Morin, "Punish Clinton, Don't Remove Him," December 21, p. A17.

White, Morton. 1987. *Philosophy, The Federalist, and the Constitution.* New York: Oxford University Press.

ADDRESSES FOR POLL DATA AND REPORTS

American National Election Studies: www.umich.edu:80/~nes/nesguide

Gallup Organization: www.gallup.com/poll/index

National Journal's Cloakroom: www.cloakroom.com

Washington Post Polls: www.washingtonpost.com/wp-srv/politics/polls/polls.htm

Appendix

Trends in Public Trust: 1952–1998

The tables in this Appendix have been chosen to provide the reader with detailed information on trends with respect to public trust in the federal government and in Congress in recent decades.* Their purpose is to provide background information that supplements and reinforces the data and arguments presented in the individual chapters of this volume.

The emergence of survey research in the 1930s and its professionalization and institutionalization in a variety of academic, media, and commercial settings since the 1930s have provided a wealth of data on public attitudes toward a variety of questions regarding the character and conduct of democratic politics in the United States, including the question of trust in government. As a result, in contrast to the situation that prevailed before the late 1950s, we now possess a large body of longitudinal data that provide measures or indicators of trends in public trust over the past four decades. The tables in this Appendix represent a selective sample of the available data and are designed to highlight general, but highly salient, aspects of the trends in public trust since the 1950s.

The choice and presentation of tables has been guided by the assumption that public trust is a complex and layered entity, not a simple and uniform one. The sections that follow are therefore based on the notion that trust in government involves three interrelated but distinguishable levels or dimensions. As noted in the first and final chapters, these are the system level, the governmental level, and the policy level. Trust or confidence at the system level pertains to the degree of faith or belief in the legitimacy of the political system generally and abstractly considered. Trust or confidence at the governmental level pertains to faith or belief that the actual operations of governmental decisionmaking conform to and serve basic democratic decisionmaking values and goals. Trust or confidence at the policy level pertains to faith or belief in the ability of the political system to produce policy outputs that satisfy citizen needs.

---

*The Appendix tables were prepared with the assistance of J. Todd Segal.

In the current literature on public trust, distinctions between these levels are often implicit or only partially identified. Nonetheless, they are rarely absent, even if incompletely specified. Trust at the system level is usually an underlying concern of students of public trust, even when they center their attention on lower levels of trust. In addition, students of public trust typically focus on trust at the governmental level and often treat this level as pivotal or as mediating among the three, even though they can and do vary greatly in the explicitness and breadth of their analyses. Finally, students of public trust clearly understand that belief or faith in successful performance is distinguishable from belief or faith in the legitimacy of democratic processes, even though they may treat this distinction simply as an unstated premise when they concentrate their efforts on other levels of trust or differ widely in their conclusions when they do focus on the impacts of performance on trust at other levels. In sum, whether by acts of commission and omission, all these levels of trust figure significantly in framing the analysis of public trust.

What is true of the general literature on trust is also true of this volume. These three levels of trust and their relationships have been explored in a variety of ways and with varying degrees of explicitness in the individual chapters of this book. Moreover, the critical role of trust at the governmental level has been recognized and emphasized, especially in the Hibbing and Cooper chapters. In presenting the tables in this Appendix, I begin with the governmental process level because of its pivotal or mediating role in determining patterns of autonomy and dependence among the three levels.

Two final caveats with respect to the data should be mentioned. First, the questions commonly used in surveys designed to measure trust have not been guided by any developed or sophisticated concern for the differences between the three levels or dimensions of trust or their interrelationships. Rather, they are based on a broad and generic sense of the character of public trust and the individual attitudes that may be presumed to be components and indicators of it. Nonetheless, what is true qualitatively is also true quantitatively. The levels I have identified inevitably figure in the definition of the questions used in the surveys because the generic sense that is relied upon to frame the questions is informed by and necessarily reflects the three basic levels of trust I have identified. As a result, the questions commonly asked can be roughly distinguished and organized in terms of their pertinence for different levels of trust, and I can present a selection of the most salient of these in this Appendix. Though overlaps between levels are unavoidable in questions that have been framed generically rather than analytically, they vary in their seriousness and the data in all cases become more informative and instructive when seen in relation to the levels of trust I have identified.

Second, many of the most suggestive questions in surveys of trust do not distinguish between federal, state, and local governments or between the branches of government. Our primary concerns are with the federal government generally and Congress in particular. I assume that questions framed in an unqualified manner in terms of trust in government capture attitudes about the federal government generally and are also indicative of attitudes regarding Congress. Given the character of responses to questions framed with specific reference to the federal government or Congress, this appears to be a fair assumption, and it is one that has guided our selection of tables.

Trust at the Governmental Level

As has been noted, the analysis of public trust is typically focused at what I have called the governmental level. It is not surprising, then, that the majority of questions asked in surveys for the purpose of measuring trust pertain wholly or largely to faith or confidence in the actual operations of representative government. These questions vary in their character and can be divided into three categories. Some are very general and seek to capture trust in the representativeness, integrity, and effectiveness of governmental decisionmaking in a broad and comprehensive manner. I include the two most commonly asked questions of this type in our first category. Both of these questions are often relied upon in the scholarly literature and the press to delineate the contours or character of trust in the federal government and Congress generally. This is understandable because they also have clear implications for trust at the policy level. Nonetheless, I have chosen to treat these questions primarily as indicators of trust in representative government. In the first case, I do so because of its concern with the worth or normative quality of governmental decisionmaking, and in the second case because of the breadth of its assessment of the Congress and the presidency as working institutions.

Others questions commonly asked in surveys to measure the state of trust at the governmental level are more focused and quite variable in their substance. The span of the subject matter reflects the varied components of trust at the governmental level. Trust in the workings or operations of American government is necessarily both procedural and substantive in its determinants. Representative government assumes not only that decisionmaking processes will be responsive to all citizens in a fair and equitable manner, but also that these processes will operate so as to serve the general welfare or public interest. Given this assumption, trust at the governmental level also necessarily involves personal considerations as well as matters of process. As the authors of the Federalist Papers well recognized, the needs of representative government make the honesty, dedication, and ability of officials, as well as the character of the processes, an important determinant of success in satisfying basic values and goals. Our second category in this section therefore includes a number of commonly asked questions that tap public attitudes on substantive, procedural, and personal components of representative government. I also include a summary measure or index of trust across these components, devised by the National Election Studies unit of the Institute of Social Research at the University of Michigan.

Finally, though questions specifically concerned with the processes and integrity of congressional decisionmaking are far fewer in number in surveys of public trust, our final category is devoted to such questions. I present two commonly asked questions with respect to the role of leaders and the integrity of members. Results on these questions provide some interesting differences from results on similar questions that are more broadly defined either in terms of government generally or Congress as an institution, but the reasons for and significance of these differences are arguable.

General Measures of Trust in Governmental and Congressional Decisionmaking

TABLE A.1   Trust in Goverment

How much of the time do you think you can trust the government in Washington to do what is right?

Year	Just About Always [a]	Most of the Time	Some of the Time	None of the Time	Don't Know, Depends
1958	16%	57%	23%	0%	4%
1960	–	–	–	–	–
1962	–	–	–	–	–
1964	14	62	22	0	1
1966	17	48	28	2	4
1968	7	54	36	0	2
1970	6	47	44	0	2
1972	5	48	44	1	2
1974	2	34	61	1	2
1976	3	30	62	1	3
1978	2	27	64	4	3
1980	2	23	69	4	2
1982	2	31	62	3	3
1984	4	40	53	1	2
1986	3	35	57	2	2
1988	4	36	56	2	1
1990	3	25	69	2	1
1992	3	26	68	2	1
1994	2	19	75	3	1
1996	3	26	69	2	1
1997	2	36	60	2	–
1998	5	29	61	4	–

[a] Because of rounding, rows may not add to 100.

SOURCE: American National Election Studies; source of 1997 and 1998 data: Pew Research Center for the People and the Press.

More Focused Measures of Trust in Governmental Decisionmaking

TABLE A.2   Confidence in Congress and Other Institutions

How much confidence do you have in the following institutions—a great deal, quite a lot, some, or very little? (Percent saying "a great deal" and "quite a lot" combined.)

Year	Congress	Presidency	Supreme Court	Military	Public Schools	Newspapers
1973	42	–	45	–	58	39
1974	–	–	–	–	–	–
1975	40	–	49	58	62	–
1976	–	–	–	–	–	–
1977	40	–	45	57	53	–
1978	–	–	–	–	–	–
1979	34	–	45	54	53	51
1980	–	–	–	–	–	–
1981	29	–	46	50	42	35
1982	–	–	–	–	–	–
1983	28	–	42	53	39	38
1984	29	–	56	61	48	35
1985	39	–	56	61	48	35
1986	41	–	54	63	49	37
1987	–	–	52	61	50	31
1988	35	–	46	58	49	36
1989	32	–	46	63	43	–
1990	24	–	47	68	45	39
March 1991	30	72	48	85	44	32
October 1991	18	50	39	69	35	32
1993	18	43	44	68	39	31
1994	18	38	42	64	34	29
1995	21	45	44	64	40	30
1996	20	39	45	66	38	32
1997	22	49	50	60	40	35

SOURCE: Gallup.

TABLE A.3   Is Government Run for Special Interests?

Would you say the government is pretty much run by a few big interests looking out for themselves or that it is run for the benefit of all people?

Year	Benefit of All[a]	Few Big Interests	Don't Know, Depends
1964	64%	29%	7%
1966	53	33	13
1968	51	40	9
1970	41	50	9
1972	38	53	9
1974	25	66	9
1976	24	66	10
1978	24	67	9
1980	21	70	9
1982	29	61	10
1984	39	55	6
1986	–	–	–
1988	31	64	5
1990	24	71	5
1992	20	75	4
1994	19	76	5
1996	27	70	3

[a] Because of rounding, rows may not add to 100.

SOURCE: American National Election Studies.

TABLE A.4   Does Government Waste Money?

Do you think that people in the government waste a lot of the money we pay in taxes, waste some of it, or don't waste very much of it?

Year	Not Very Much[a]	Some	A Lot	Don't Know
1958	10%	42%	43%	4%
1960	–	–	–	–
1962	–	–	–	–
1964	7	44	47	2
1966	–	–	–	–
1968	4	34	59	3
1970	4	26	69	1
1972	2	30	66	2
1974	1	22	74	2
1976	3	20	74	3
1978	2	19	77	2
1980	2	18	78	2
1982	2	29	66	3
1984	4	29	65	2
1986	–	–	–	–
1988	2	33	63	2
1990	2	30	67	1
1992	2	30	67	1
1994	2	27	70	1
1996	1	38	60	1

[a] Because of rounding, rows may not add to 100.

SOURCE: American National Election Studies.

TABLE A.5   Are Government Officials Crooked?

Do you think that quite a few of the people running the government are crooked, not very many are, or hardly any of them are?

Year	Hardly Any [a]	Not Many	Quite a Few	Don't Know
1958	26%	44%	24%	6%
1960	–	–	–	–
1962	–	–	–	–
1964	18	49	29	4
1966	–	–	–	–
1968	19	52	25	4
1970	16	49	32	3
1972	14	45	36	4
1974	10	42	45	3
1976	13	40	42	5
1978	13	42	39	6
1980	9	41	47	4
1982	–	–	–	–
1984	14	50	32	4
1986	–	–	–	–
1988	11	45	40	4
1990	9	40	48	3
1992	9	44	46	2
1994	8	39	51	1
1996	9	48	43	1

[a] Because of rounding, rows may not add to 100.

SOURCE: American National Election Studies.

TABLE A.6   Do Public Officials Care?

"I don't think public officials care much what people like me think."

Year	Agree[a]	Disagree	Neither	Don't Know, Depends
1952	35%	63%	–	2%
1954	–	–	–	–
1956	26	71	–	2
1958	–	–	–	–
1960	25	73	–	2
1962	–	–	–	–
1964	36	62	–	2
1966	34	57	–	9
1968	43	55	–	2
1970	47	50	–	3
1972	49	49	–	2
1974	50	46	–	4
1976	51	44	–	4
1978	51	45	–	4
1980	52	43	–	4
1982	47	50	–	4
1984	42	57	–	1
1986	52	43	–	5
1988	51	37	11%	0
1990	63	23	13	1
1992	52	37	10	1
1994	66	23	11	1
1996	61	25	15	0

[a] Because of rounding, rows may not add to 100.

SOURCE: American National Election Studies.

TABLE A.7   Do Elections Count?

How much do you feel that having elections makes the government pay attention to what the people think—a good deal, some, or not much?

Year	A Good Deal[a]	Some	Not Much
1964	68%	26%	7%
1966	65	26	9
1968	62	30	9
1970	58	32	10
1972	56	37	8
1974	52	36	11
1976	53	36	10
1978	57	33	10
1980	52	35	13
1982	–	–	–
1984	43	37	20
1986	–	–	–
1988	38	45	18
1990	–	–	–
1992	47	41	12
1994	–	–	–
1996	43	42	15

[a] Because of rounding, rows may not add to 100.

SOURCE: American National Election Studies.

TABLE A.8   Trust-in-Government Index

Year	Most Trusting		Most Cynical
1964	64.9%	12.7%	22.4%
1966	–	–	–
1968	54.6	13.6	31.8
1970	44.0	13.8	42.2
1972	41.2	13.2	45.7
1974	26.5	12.0	61.5
1976	25.7	11.8	62.5
1978	23.0	12.4	64.6
1980	19.2	10.5	70.4
1982	–	–	–
1984	37.5	14.3	48.2
1986	–	–	–
1988	30.3	17.1	52.6
1990	22.9	13.7	63.4
1992	21.3	17.0	61.7
1994	16.8	15.2	68.0

NOTE: This index was created based on responses to four questions: (1) "How often does the respondent trust the government to do what's right?" (2) "Does the respondent believe government is run for the benefit of all or for a few big interests?" (3) "Does the respondent believe government wastes a lot of tax money?" and (4) "Does the respondent believe government officials are crooked?" Respondents who give "trusting" responses to three or four questions (i.e., they trust government to do what is right, believe government is run for the benefit of all, etc.) are "most trusting." Respondents who give "trusting" responses to two questions are in the middle category. Respondents who give "trusting" responses to only one or none of the questions are "most cynical."

SOURCE: American National Election Studies.

More Focused Measures of Trust in Congressional Decisionmaking

TABLE A.9   Confidence in the Leadership of Congress, the White House, and the Supreme Court

As far as people in charge of running (READ EACH ITEM) are concerned, would you have a great deal of confidence, only some confidence, or hardly any confidence at all in them? (percent saying "a great deal")

Year	Congress	White House	Supreme Court
1966	42	–	50
–	–	–	–
1971	19	–	23
1972	21	–	28
1973	–	18	33
1974	18	28	40
1975	13	–	28
1976	9	11	22
1977	17	31	29
1978	10	14	29
1979	18	15	28
1980	18	18	27
1981	16	28	29
1982	13	20	25
1983	20	23	33
1984	28	42	35
1985	16	30	28
1986	21	19	32
1987	20	23	30
1988	15	17	32
1989	16	20	28
1990	12	21	32
1991	9	21	23
1992	10	16	30
1993	12	23	26
1994	8	18	31
1995	10	13	32
1996	10	15	31
1997	11	15	28
1998	12	20	37

SOURCE: Louis Harris and Associates.

TABLE A.10   Confidence in the Integrity of Congressional Representatives and Other Professionals

Please tell me how you would rate the honesty and ethical standards of people in these different fields—very high, high, average, low, or very low. (percent saying "very high" and "high" combined)

Year	Congressmen	Senators	State Officeholders	Bankers	Druggists, Pharmacists
1976	14	19	–	–	–
1977	16	19	11	39	–
1981	15	20	12	39	59
1983	14	16	13	38	61
1985	20	23	15	38	65
1988	16	19	11	26	66
1990	20	24	17	32	62
1991	19	19	14	30	60
1992	11	13	11	27	66
1993	14	18	14	28	65
1994	9	12	12	27	62
1995	10	12	15	27	66
1996	14	15	13	26	64
1997	12	14	17	34	69

SOURCE: Gallup.

Trust at the System Level

Questions that tap trust at the system level have been less frequently asked than questions that tap trust at other levels. Given the importance of the concept of legitimacy in the scholarly literature, this is somewhat surprising. Most scholars see politics as involving values and ideas as well as interests. They therefore accept the argument that political systems rest in part on sets of normative ideals that shape the character of the political institutions within them. It follows as a necessary corollary that the strength of citizen belief in the worth and realism of these ideals critically affects the ability of the political system and its component institutions to operate successfully and to survive.

The explanation for the relative lack of attention given to measuring the degree of legitimacy accorded to the American political institutions lies in two factors that conflict in their logical implications but nonetheless reinforce each other in practice. On the one hand, most scholars believe that American politics is distinguished by a high degree of consensus on the legitimacy of the system, and thus they have not been motivated to investigate the complexities of a truth they take for granted. On the other hand, understanding of the different levels or dimensions of trust and their relationships has not been perceived as an important problem, with the result that the theoretical payoffs of seeking better and more extensive measures of legitimacy are masked and not adequately appreciated. Nonetheless, from time to time various surveys have included questions that directly or indirectly pertain to the strength of belief in the legitimacy of the American political system. I present most of these measures and divide them into two categories.

The first simply groups various measures of system support, taken from more general surveys of political attitudes and organized by time period. The second presents attitudes toward patriotism over time and correlates attitudes toward patriotism and violence with trust in government in 1997. The data in the correlations are especially interesting. They demonstrate that distrust at the governmental level does not significantly undermine the strength of either highly positive attitudes toward patriotism or highly negative attitudes toward violence among the American people. These results testify eloquently to both the independence and the strength of trust at the system level in the United States.

Measures of System Support

TABLE A.11   1976 System Support

Are problems such as Watergate, sex scandals, and corruption in government the fault of "individual politicians" or because "there's something more seriously wrong with government in general and the way it operates"?

Individual politicians	56.9%
Government in general	34.5
Other	8.6

Is "a change in our whole system of government" needed to solve the problems facing our country, or should government "be kept pretty much as it is"?

Need big change	23.7%
Need some change	26.2
Keep as is	43.6
Other	6.6

Choose one: "I am proud of many things about our form of government," or, "I can't find much in our government to be proud of."

Proud of government	74.4%
Not much to be proud of	18.4
Other	7.2

Have people lost faith and confidence "because of the individuals in office," or is there "something more seriously wrong with government in general and the way it operates"?

Individuals in office	61.1%
Government in general	28.7
Other	10.1

SOURCE: American National Election Studies. Cited in Stephen C. Craig (1993). *The Malevolent Leaders: Popular Discontent in America.* Boulder: Westview Press.

TABLE A.12   1988 System Support

When you see the American flag flying, does it make you feel . . .

Extremely good	51.2%
Very good	33.1
Somewhat good	13.5
Not very good	1.5
Other	0.8

How strong is your love for your country?

Extremely strong	55.8%
Very strong	35.4
Somewhat strong	7.4
Not very strong	0.6
Other	0.8

When you hear the national anthem, does it make you feel . . .

Extremely emotional	32.9%
Very emotional	34.3
Somewhat emotional	24.6
Not very emotional	7.6
Other	0.6

How proud are you to be an American?

Extremely proud	66.5%
Very proud	26.3
Somewhat proud	5.8
Not very proud	0.6
Other	0.8

SOURCE: American National Election Studies. Cited in Stephen C. Craig (1993). *The Malevolent Leaders: Popular Discontent in America.* Boulder: Westview Press.

TABLE A.13   1996 System Support

Do you have respect for political institutions in America? (1 = none at all; 7 = a great deal)	
6–7	33%
4–5	43
2–3	19
1	6

Are you proud to live under our political system? (1 = none at all; 7 = a great deal)	
6–7	60%
4–5	28
2–3	10
1	3

Do you feel our system of government is the best possible system? (1 = none at all; 7 = a great deal)	
6–7	52%
4–5	31
2–3	13
1	4

Do you feel you should support our system of government? (1 = none at all ; 7 = a great deal)	
6–7	64%
4–5	27
2–3	7
1	2

Do you think the best years for America are in the future? (1 = none at all; 7 = a great deal)	
6–7	37%
4–5	36
2–3	21
1	6

SOURCE: Institute for Advanced Studies in Culture, 1996 Survey.

Measures of Patriotism, Violence, and Trust

TABLE A.14   Patriotism in the United States

"I am very patriotic."

Year	Completely Agree	Mostly Agree	Mostly Disagree	Completely Disagree	Don't Know, Refused
1987	43%	46%	7%	1%	3%
1988	51	38	6	2	3
1989	51	40	6	1	2
1990	48	40	8	2	2
1991	58	33	5	2	2
1992	52	39	5	2	2
1993	–	–	–	–	–
1994	51	40	6	2	1
1995	–	–	–	–	–
1996	–	–	–	–	–
1997	48	42	6	2	2

SOURCE: Pew Research Center for the People and the Press.

TABLE A.15   Patriotism and Trust in Government, 1997

	Trust Government	Do Not Trust Government
Very patriotic	91%	86%
Not very patriotic	8	12
Don't know/refused	1	2

NOTE: Trust is based on the ANES question from Table A1. Those who say they trust the government to do what's right "just about always" or "most of the time" are considered to trust the government. Those who respond "some of the time" or "none of the time" are considered to not trust government.

SOURCE: Pew Research Center for the People and the Press.

TABLE A.16   Violence and Trust in Government, 1997

	Trust Government	Do Not Trust Government	Total
Violence against the U.S. government may be justified in some cases	21%	30%	27%
Violence against the U.S. government is never justified	77	67	71
Other/don't know	2	3	2

NOTE: Trust is based on the ANES question from Table A1. Those who say they trust the government to do what's right "just about always" or "most of the time" are considered to trust the government. Those who respond "some of the time" or "none of the time" are considered to not trust government.

SOURCE: Pew Research Center for the People and the Press.

Trust at the Policy Level

Trust at the policy level derives from satisfaction with patterns of governmental policymaking. It consists of belief that the government has addressed and will continue to address citizen needs in a successful manner. Data of this type are the most ubiquitous of all and are frequently reported in the print and electronic media. However, the relationships between policy decisions or outputs, the actual outcomes of policy decisions, and systemic performance have remained ambiguous. Nor have the dynamics of the relationship between satisfaction with past performance and trust in current and future performance been probed, though a firm relationship may be presumed to exist. In short, there has been no rigorous attempt to distinguish between the determinants and effects of different variants of performance or to ascertain the size of the gap between satisfaction and trust. The measures available to us are thus quite broad and focus on institutional job approval, approval of the broad course of public policy, and approval of the power of government. Such measurement serves very practical interests and concerns and mirrors the inclination of the public to give governmental leaders credit for favorable conditions of life and blame for unfavorable ones, no matter what their actual degree of responsibility for either. But it ignores the complexities of the relationship between policy decisions and the substantive performance of the political system, as well as the fact that satisfaction is an imperfect measure of trust. Thus, while current tendencies to sidestep the difficulties of measuring the determinants and effects of satisfaction with the performance of government have some practical benefits, they come at the cost of limiting understanding of the relation between policy outputs and performance and between patterns of satisfaction with performance and patterns of trust. The result is impaired analysis, not only at the policy level but also at other levels because of the impacts of trust at the policy level on trust at the governmental and systemic levels.

With these problems noted, I confine myself here to existing measures of policy or performance satisfaction and focus on popular and familiar measures. These can be divided into direct measures and indirect measures. In the former case, measures seek to pin down the degree of citizen satisfaction with the state of the nation and/or the directions in which it is headed. High scores can be read as indicators of satisfaction with past governmental policy or performance accomplishments. In the latter case, I include three very familiar and commonly asked questions that focus on job approval of key actors or institutions, but I also supplement the job approval measures with a measure of citizen assessment of governmental power.

I regard the job approval measures as surrogate measures of general satisfaction with the adequacy or success of past governmental policy or performance in the United States. This is especially true of the question that relates to presidential job approval. The questions that relate to congressional job approval are less pure measures of policy satisfaction and reflect concerns and expectations that also pertain to the governmental level. Many of these aspects of congressional approval have been explored in the Hibbing, Davidson, Mutz and Flemming, and Cooper chapters. Nonetheless, measures of congressional job approval are best seen as measures of trust at the policy level. Not only do they correlate far more closely with measures of presidential job approval than with measures of trust at the governmental level, but they also share the far greater volatility of measures of trust at the policy level. Indeed, there is perhaps no better testimony to the status of measures of presidential and congressional job approval as surrogate measures of policy satisfaction than the rise of both presidential job approval and congressional job approval scores to unusually high levels in early 1998, in close correlation with a substantial increase in positive public feeling in late 1997 and early 1998 about the state of the nation and the directions in which it is headed.

The measure that focuses on citizen assessments of the power of government is framed with specific reference to the federal government. It testifies to the complexities and ambiguities currently present in the conceptualization and measurement of trust at the policy level. It is quite possible that this measure taps attitudes that shape the strength of trust at the governmental level. Nonetheless, what should be noted is the high degree of ambivalence toward the power of the federal government in both the 1960s and 1990s, despite the significant differences in trust at the governmental level in these two decades. Once again, the data provide evidence of discontinuities between the levels that we need to understand far better than we presently do.

Finally, some technical points about the data presented in the tables should be mentioned. In contrast to the data presented in tables in other sections, the data presented in this section of the Appendix often do not reflect all the data that are available. In most cases, these questions have been asked many times in one year, and I have limited our presentation to an early point and later point in each year, choosing exactly the same months whenever possible. We have done so to make the tables more readable and intelligible. In addition, in the case of presidential job approval we begin not with the year in which the question was first asked, 1938, but with 1961 because it better fits the time period of the Appendix.

Direct Measures of Policy Satisfaction

TABLE A.17   Approval of Policy Direction

Do you think things in this country are generally going in the right direction, or do you feel things have gotten seriously off on the wrong track?

Year	Month	Right Direction	Wrong Track	No Opinion
1973	October	16%	74%	10%
1974	October	15	75	11
1975	October	19	71	9
1976	–	–	–	–
1977	February	41	44	14
1978	February	34	53	13
1979	–	–	–	–
1980	February	20	70	10
1981	–	–	–	–
1982	January	39	56	5
	October	35	57	8
1983	March	43	53	3
	November	51	44	5
1984	May	47	48	5
1985	January	59	36	4
	July	52	43	6
1986	January	45	47	8
	September	50	48	2
1987	January	39	56	5
	September	43	54	4
1988	January	39	59	2
	September	48	44	8
1989	March	46	52	2
1990	January	48	49	3
	October	19	79	2
1991	January	49	48	4
	October	26	71	3
1992	January	19	78	3
	October[a]	18	78	4
1993	January	31	63	6
	November	25	69	6
1994	January	31	60	10
	October	27	69	4
1995	January	27	68	6
	April	23	73	3
1996	January	21	77	3
	October[a]	44	51	5
1997	March	34	62	4
	August	39	57	4
1998	January	44	50	6
	April	55	41	4

[a] Registered voters.

SOURCE: *Washington Post.*

TABLE A.18   Satisfaction with the State of the Nation

In general, are you satisfied or dissatisfied with the way things are going in the United States at this time?

Year	Month	Satisfied	Dissatisfied	No Opinion
1979	February	26%	69%	5%
	November	19	77	4
1980	–	–	–	–
1981	January	17	78	5
	December	27	67	6
1982	April	25	71	4
	November	24	72	4
1983	August	35	59	6
1984	February	50	46	4
	December	52	40	8
1985	November	51	46	3
1986	March	66	30	4
	September	58	38	4
1987	August	45	49	6
1988	May	41	54	5
	September	56	40	4
1989	February	45	50	5
1990	February	55	39	6
	October	29	67	4
1991	February	54	40	6
	October	39	57	4
1992	February	21	78	1
	November	26	68	6
1993	February	25	71	4
	November	27	70	3
1994	February	36	61	3
	November	30	66	4
1995	March	30	66	4
	August	33	64	3
1996	January	24	72	4
	October	39	56	5
1997	January	50	47	4
	December	50	46	4
1998	February	59	37	4
	April	58	38	4

NOTE: If more than one poll was conducted in a given month, results from the month's first poll are reported.

SOURCE: Gallup.

Indirect Measures of Policy Satisfaction

TABLE A.19   Presidential Job Approval

Do you approve or disapprove of the way the president is handling his job?

Year	Month	Approve	Disapprove	No Opinion	
1961	February	72%	6%	22%	Kennedy: January 1961
	October	77	12	10	
1962	February	78	11	10	
	October	62	25	14	
1963	February	70	18	12	
	October	58	29	13	
1964	February	74	9	18	Johnson: November 1963
	November	70	19	11	
1965	February	69	18	14	
	October	66	21	13	
1966	February	56	34	10	
	October	44	42	14	
1967	February	45	42	13	
	October	38	51	12	
1968	February	41	47	12	
	November	43	44	13	
1969	February	60	6	34	Nixon: January 1969
	October	58	24	18	
1970	February	56	27	18	
	October	58	28	15	
1971	February	50	37	14	
	October	52	38	10	
1972	February	52	37	11	
	November	62	28	10	
1973	February	65	25	10	
	October	30	57	14	
1974	February	28	59	13	
	October	52	29	19	Ford: August 1974
1975	February	39	45	16	
	October	47	37	16	
1976	February	48	38	14	
	December	53	32	15	
1977	February	66	8	26	Carter: January 1977
	October	55	29	16	
1978	February	47	34	19	
	October	49	36	15	
1979	February	42	42	16	
	October	29	58	13	

(continues)

TABLE A.19   *(continued)*

Year	Month	Approve	Disapprove	No Opinion	
1980	February	55%	36%	9%	
	December	34	55	11	
1981	February	55	18	27	Reagan: January 1981
	October	56	35	9	
1982	February	47	43	10	
	October	42	48	10	
1983	February	40	50	10	
	October	45	44	11	
1984	February	55	36	9	
	October	58	33	9	
1985	February	60	31	9	
	October	63	29	8	
1986	March	63	26	11	
	October	63	29	8	
1987	February	40	53	7	
	December	49	41	10	
1988	March	51	37	11	
	October	51	38	11	
1989	February	63	13	24	Bush: January 1989
	October	68	20	12	
1990	February	73	16	11	
	October	66	25	9	
1991	February	79	18	3	
	October	66	25	9	
1992	February	44	48	8	
	October	33	58	9	
1993	February	51	34	15	Clinton: January 1993
	October	50	42	8	
1994	February	53	41	6	
	October	42	52	6	
1995	February	49	44	7	
	October	46	42	12	
1996	February	53	40	7	
	October	58	34	8	
1997	February	57	33	10	
	October	55	36	9	
1998	February	66	30	4	
	April	67	28	5	

NOTE: If more than one poll was conducted in a given month, results from the month's first poll are reported.

SOURCE: Gallup.

TABLE A.20   Congressional Job Approval

Do you approve or disapprove of the way the U.S. Congress is handling its job?

Year	Month	Approve	Disapprove	No Opinion
1963		33%	60%	7%
1964		59	33	8
1965		64	26	10
1966		49	42	9
1967		38	55	7
1968		46	46	8
1969		34	54	12
1970		26	63	11
1971		–	–	–
1972		–	–	–
1973		38	45	17
1974	April	30	47	23
	August	48	35	17
1975	February	32	50	18
	November	28	54	18
1976	January	24	58	18
1977	March	36	42	22
	September	29	49	22
1978	September	29	49	22
1979	June	19	61	20
1980	June	25	56	19
1981	June	38	40	22
1982	June	29	54	17
1983	April	33	43	24
1984		–	–	–
1985	June	54	37	9
1986	April	42	37	21
1987	September	42	49	9
1988	September	42	42	16
1989		–	–	–
1990	October	28	65	7
1991	July	32	53	15
	October	40	54	6
1992	March	18	78	3
1993	February	27	54	19
	July	24	65	11
	November	24	69	8
1994	February	28	66	6
	July	27	65	8
	October	21	73	6

(continues)

TABLE A.20   *(continued)*

Year	Month	Approve	Disapprove	No Opinion
1995	February	38%	53%	9%
	July	35	55	10
	September	30	61	9
1996	April	35	57	8
	October	34	51	15
1997	February	37	48	15
	July	34	57	9
	October	36	53	11
1998	February	57	33	10
	April	49	40	11

NOTE: If more than one poll was conducted in a given month, results from the month's first poll are reported.

SOURCE: Gallup; source for 1963–1970 and 1973 data is Louis Harris and Associates. Harris's wording: "How would you rate the job Congress has been doing so far this year— excellent, pretty good, only fair, or poor?" Harris considers "excellent" and "pretty good" to be "positive" opinions of Congress's job performance, and "only fair" and "poor" to be "negative."

TABLE A.21   Member Job Approval

Do you approve or disapprove of the way the representative from your congressional district is handling his or her job?

Year	Month	Approve	Disapprove	No Opinion
1977	March	55%	17%	28%
1978	November	57	37	6
1979		–	–	–
1980	July	53	43	4
1981	October	53	40	7
1982	June	69	15	16
1983		–	–	–
1984		–	–	–
1985	July	59	36	5
1986		–	–	–
1987		–	–	–
1988		–	–	–
1989	June	63	34	3
	December	55	38	7
1990	August	66	19	16
	October	55	33	12
1991	October	64	27	9
1992	March	58	31	12

SOURCE: Gallup; source for 1978, 1980, 1981, 1985, and 1989 data is Louis Harris and Associates. Harris's wording: "How would you rate the job being done by your congressman right here in this district—excellent, pretty good, only fair, or poor?" Harris considers "excellent" and "pretty good" to be "positive" opinions of a representative's job performance, and "only fair" and "poor" to be "negative."

TABLE A.22   Governmental Power

Which one of the following statements comes closest to your views about government power today?

	1964	1997
The federal government today has too much power.	26%	33%
The federal government is now using about the right amount of power for meeting today's needs.	38	32
The federal government should use its power even more vigorously to promote the well-being of all segments of people.	29	33
Don't know/refused	7	2

SOURCE: 1964 data are from Gallup; 1997 data are from Pew Research Center for the People and the Press.

Internet Addresses for Data Sources

American National Election Studies: www.umich.edu:80/~nes/nesguide

Gallup Organization: www.gallup.com/poll/index

Institute for Advanced Studies in Culture: www.virginia.edu/iasc/research-survey

Louis Harris and Associates: www.louisharris.com

Pew Research Center for the People and the Press: www.people-press.org

Washington Post Polls: www.washingtonpost.com/wp-srv/politics/polls/polls.htm

NOTE: Not all data presented in these tables are available from these sites.

About the Editor and Contributors

Editor

Joseph Cooper is Professor of Political Science at Johns Hopkins University and a former provost of the university. He has served as Autrey Professor and Dean of Social Science at Rice University, staff director of the U.S. House Commission on Administrative Review, and president of the Southwestern Political Science Association and National Capital Area Political Science Association. He has authored and edited numerous books and articles on congressional topics that include the historical development of congressional structures and processes, the role of congressional parties and party leaders, the legislative veto, the application of organization theory to congressional analysis, the proper roles of the president and Congress in a separation-of-powers framework, and congressional reform.

Contributors

Senator Bill Bradley served as a U.S. senator from New Jersey from 1979 to 1997. In the Senate he made important contributions in many key areas of legislation, including tax reform, international trade, pension reform, community building, and improving race relations. Since leaving the Senate, he has been affiliated with Stanford University, the University of Maryland, and the University of Notre Dame. He has also served as chair of the National Civic League, chair of the Advertising Council's Advisory Committee on Public Issues, an essayist on *CBS Evening News,* and vice chair of the International Council at J. P. Morgan and Company. Bradley is a graduate of Princeton, a Rhodes Scholar, a basketball All-American, the winner of the Sullivan Award as the country's outstanding amateur athlete, an Olympic gold medalist, and a member of two NBA championship teams as a member of the New York Knicks. He has written four books that deal with his experiences with the Knicks and in the Senate: *Life on the Run* (1976), *The Fair Tax* (1982), *Time Present, Time Past* (1996), and *Values of the Game* (1998).

Charles S. Bullock III is the Richard B. Russell Professor of Political Science at the University of Georgia. His teaching and research interests are in legislative politics and southern politics. His most recent book, *The New Politics of the Old South,* coedited with Mark Rozell, was published in 1998 by Rowman and Littlefield. *Runoff Elections in the United States,* which he coauthored with Loch Johnson, won the V. O. Key Award in 1993.

Roger H. Davidson, Professor of Government and Politics at the University of Maryland, has been a congressional scholar for much of his professional career. He has taught at Dartmouth and the University of California and has lectured on U.S. politics both here and abroad. He is coeditor of *The Encyclopedia of the U.S. Congress* (1995) and coauthor of the leading textbook *Congress and Its Members,* 7th ed. (2000).

Gregory N. Flemming is survey director at the Pew Research Center for the People and the Press in Washington, D.C. His primary research interests are campaigns and elections, congressional politics, and survey research methods. He is author or coauthor of articles published in *Legislative Studies Quarterly, American Politics Quarterly,* and several books.

Mary A. Hepburn, Professor of Social Science Education, was head of the Citizen Education Division, Carl Vinson Institute of Government, University of Georgia, for fourteen years until her retirement in November 1998. She currently serves on the Task Force on Civic Education of the American Political Science Association and on the governing board of the Social Science Education Consortium. Her recent publications include "A Disquieting Outlook: Mass Media, News, and Citizenship" in *Citizenship Education in a Changing World* (1998); "The Power of the Electronic Media in the Socialization of Young Americans," *The Social Studies* (1998); "Community Service Learning in Civic Education," *Theory into Practice* (1997); "The Rebirth of Political Socialization," with Richard Niemi, in *Perspectives on Political Science* (1995); and "Collaborative Education in the Political Science Education of Teachers," *PS: Political Science and Politics* (1993).

John R. Hibbing is Professor of Political Science at the University of Nebraska. He has been chair of his department, editor of the *Legislative Studies Quarterly,* a NATO Fellow in Science in Great Britain, an adviser to the Hungarian National Assembly in Budapest, and a Senior Fulbright Fellow in Spain. His articles and books have focused on congressional elections, comparative legislatures, and congressional careers, but his current interests center on public attitudes toward Congress specifically and toward government more generally.

Diana C. Mutz is Associate Professor of Political Science at the University of Wisconsin at Madison. She has published her research on public opinion, political psychology, and the role of mass media in a variety of journals. Her most recent book, *Impersonal Influence: How Perceptions of Mass Collectives Affect Political Attitudes,* was published by Cambridge University Press in 1998. She also serves as the editor of *Political Behavior.*

David M. Shribman is Washington bureau chief of the *Boston Globe* and winner of the 1995 Pulitzer Prize for his writing on Washington and American political culture. He writes a nationally syndicated column, "National Perspective." He is a graduate of Dartmouth College and serves as a trustee of the college. He was a James Reynolds Scholar at Cambridge University and a Viginius Dabney Distinguished Fellow in Journalism at Virginia Commonwealth University in 1997. Shribman delivered the Dillon Lecture at the University of South Dakota in 1998.

Index